ALSO BY ANDREW HUDGINS

POETRY

American Rendering: New and Selected Poems

Shut Up, You're Fine!: Poems for Very, Very Bad Children

Ecstatic in the Poison

Babylon in a Jar

The Glass Hammer: A Southern Childhood

The Never-Ending

After the Lost War: A Narrative

Saints and Strangers

ESSAYS

Diary of a Poem

The Glass Anvil

The Joker

A memoir

Andrew Hudgins

Simon & Schuster

New York   London   Toronto   Sydney   New Delhi

Simon & Schuster
1230 Avenue of the Americas
New York, NY 10020

First Simon & Schuster hardcover edition June 2013

SIMON & SCHUSTER and colophon are registered trademarks of
Simon & Schuster, Inc.

For information about special discounts for bulk purchases,
please contact Simon & Schuster Special Sales at
1-866-506-1949 or business@simonandschuster.com.

The Simon & Schuster Speakers Bureau can bring authors to your live event.
For more information or to book an event contact the
Simon & Schuster Speakers Bureau at 1-866-248-3049 or
visit our website at www.simonspeakers.com.

Designed by Ruth Lee-Mui

Manufactured in the United States of America

1   3   5   7   9   10   8   6   4   2

Library of Congress Cataloging-in-Publication Data is available.

ISBN 978-1-4767-1271-0
ISBN 978-1-4767-1273-4 (ebook)

This book is for my longtime joke-swapping buddies—Chase Twichell, Tom Doherty, Dan Thrapp, Jim Cummins, and Rick Anderson—and to the memory of my father-in-law, Tom McGraw, a wonderful laugher.

Contents

The Joker

Introduction

Where the Naughty Boys and Girls Live

Though I've been a serious poet, a student of poetry, and a teacher of poetry for forty years, I can't recite from memory ten consecutive lines of William Butler Yeats, Shakespeare, Emily Dickinson, or even Robert Frost, about whom I'm writing a book. But I can tell you the knock-knock jokes I heard when I was ten, all of them, and every week I still read *Doodles*, the children's comic strip in the Sunday paper, just in case it runs a pun or knock-knock joke I don't know. ("Q: What do you call a cow with two legs? A: Lean beef.")

Since junior high, I've been a joker, a punster, a laugher—someone who will say almost anything for a laugh. I don't mean the chuckle that greets the mild obligatory jokes that ease the congregation into the sermon or punctuate an after-dinner speech—though I enjoy those too. What I love is raucous gut laughter—the kind that earns angry stares from the tables near you in a restaurant and makes strangers in the mall exchange knowing looks about the prevalence of drug use among nearsighted middle-aged bald men in polo shirts and chinos. Laughing until you are weak, gasping, holding your sides, barely able to stand is like a drug. I have laughed until I have fallen on the floor in public places. I couldn't have stopped myself if I wanted to, and I didn't want to.

I love how jokes either work or don't. You are either a funny man or a fool, and to my anguish I am often a fool. I live uneasily with the fact that my joking sometimes makes others uneasy: uneasiness is the spring of the jack-in-the-box. Jokes delight us by making us nervous and then relieving the nervous tension. Pleasure needs friction as well as lubrication: the friction comes from fear and pain; wordplay releases the tension. Jokers make us anxious because they want something from us. Or to be more precise: I make you nervous because I want something from you—laughter—and to make you laugh I have to juggle subjects that make you laugh.

Shortly before his death in 2009, Fritz Darges, a Waffen-SS officer, told a German newspaper that he still believed Hitler was a genius, "the greatest man who'd ever lived," and he'd gladly serve him again. I don't exactly take Darges as my hero, but there is one moment in his life I ponder with renewed delight as well as a frisson of incipient panic. Darges was awarded two Iron Crosses and a Knight's Cross, but the bravest thing he ever did—also the stupidest—took place in a 1944 strategy meeting in Hitler's famous Wolf's Lair when he was serving as army adjutant to the Führer. As Hitler and his staff officers consulted a large map stretched out on a table, a fly buzzed around the confined bunker, landing first on the map, then Hitler's shoulder, and then the map again. Annoyed, the Führer ordered Darges to kill it. Without a moment's hesitation, Darges informed Hitler that the fly was an airborne pest and therefore the responsibility of Nicolaus von Below, the nearby Luftwaffe adjutant.

I love the joke, but I love, fear, and identify with the impulse that drove Darges to tell it. By 1944, when he'd been Hitler's adjutant for fifteen months, he must have had an inkling that the Führer wasn't blessed with a wide and generous sense of humor. Didn't matter. Darges had his joke, it was a good one, and he had to tell it—and the joke is funnier now because it was dangerous then. In fact, Hitler turned to Darges and screamed, "You're for the Eastern Front!" Darges's cleverness wouldn't be a tenth as funny if he'd cracked wise to an indulgent and chuckling Uncle Adolf.

Darges's impulse is one I know well. I'm one of those compulsive jokers whose need to laugh can seem peculiar, immature, and even socially corrosive to those who do not share it. Our need to tell jokes trumps our sense of propriety and good sense. Here's an example. After a section of this book was published in The *Kenyon Review*, I received an e-mail from the poet Chard deNiord, who reminded me of a joke I told at the Sewanee Writers' Conference. Drinks in hand, Chard and I were talking to the poet Richard Wilbur. I was in awe, almost cripplingly so, that I was *having a drink with Dick*—he asked me to call him Dick—*Wilbur*, the man who had written some of the best poems of the last century, not to mention the libretto for Leonard Bernstein's *Candide*. Because the joke had been burning a hole in my mind for a couple of days, I asked Dick if he'd heard the latest O. J. Simpson joke. Only a month before, Nicole Simpson had been murdered along with her friend Ron Goldman, who had dropped by her house to return a pair of glasses left at the restaurant where he waited tables, and I was fascinated by the jokes the murder had inspired.

"No," Wilbur replied warily. I doubt many people in his circles luxuriate in jokes about tabloid murders, but my social discomfort made me stupidly stubborn. I'd already committed myself to telling the joke, hadn't I? Wasn't it better to be a boor than a coward or a tease?

"What's the first thing Ron Goldman said to Nicole Simpson in heaven?" I asked.

Even more warily than before, the poet who had translated Molière, Corneille, and Racine into English, asked, "What?"

"Here're your *fucking* glasses!"

Chard tells me that he laughed. Wilbur, the most gracious genius I have ever met, chuckled politely. And I let out a belly laugh at my own joke. "I'll never forget how unabashed you were and how much I admired you for that," Chard wrote. I was startled by his admiration, because I *was* abashed. At the time, I thought I'd made a fool of myself, and in retrospect I'm sure of it. My insecurities and obsessions had turned me into a clown. But I'm pleased Chard laughed and holds the memory fondly in mind. That's a pretty good payoff for telling a joke pinned to a crime rapidly passing into the vast chronicles of celebrity homicides. Still, a clown knows the cost of being a clown. For a laugh, I exploded any chance of becoming friends with Mr. Wilbur, a poet I admire immensely. But the clown also knows the joke was especially funny to Chard because he heard it against the background of Richard Wilbur's wariness.

Here's another story. Again it takes place during the Sewanee Writers' Conference, during my first summer teaching there. To my discomfort, I was a junior colleague to Anthony Hecht and John Hollander, poets whose poems and essays I'd read, admired, and studied for a quarter of a century. Hecht and Hollander's mandarin erudition was intimidating, and the one time I finagled a seat at Tony Hecht's lunch table, he offered only short, distracted answers to direct questions. I read his shyness as distaste for me and for my poems, which I assumed (and still assume) he found crude—the unrefined product of an unrefined mind. And by God, when people think I'm a vulgarian, I'll do my damnedest to prove them right. I can't stop myself. Freud would call this impulse a minor manifestation of the death wish. Edgar Allan Poe more resonantly termed it "the imp of the perverse," a phrase that captures the ornery humor of deliberately discharging a pistol into one's metatarsals to astound people with my talent for insouciantly crippling myself, and then limping off on bloody feet as if I had accomplished something—the limp of the perverse.

During their poetry readings both Hollander and Hecht paused to sip water. As they did, each remarked that the poet Randall Jarrell had once observed that sipping water during a poetry reading was the single most pretentious thing a poet can do. It did not occur to me that they, famous as they were, might feel self-conscious reading to a room full of writers. But I was. And in my insecurity I thought it might be funny to follow their lead and then go further. At the podium, I held up a glass of water, reminded the audience what Jarrell had said, and speculated that Jarrell might not have known there is a pretentious side of the glass and a non-pretentious side.

I placed my finger on the lip of the glass closest to me and said, "This is the pretentious side." Then, pointing to the far side of the glass, I pronounced, "And this is the unpretentious side. Do you know why?" Someone said no, and I tipped that side into my mouth. Water poured out the lower lip of the glass and down my shirt and pants. It's a junior high joke I'd often heard of but never seen, so I was surprised at how thoroughly I drenched myself with a small cup of water. The audience sat still for half a breath, before someone laughed and the laughter took off. But only half the audience joined in. The non-laughers obviously thought my clowning was a breach of the decorum of poetry readings—precisely the thing the laughers enjoyed. From what I gathered later, Hollander and Hecht perceived my buffoonery as a barely concealed way of calling them pretentious. That was not my conscious intention, though now, to my regret, I see that interpretation is inevitable. After the reading, a small group laughed with me about the reading and my stunt, among them the wonderful playwright Horton Foote. His pink face shining with amusement, Horton took my hand between his and said he'd love to direct me in a play. He'd seen the teasing and playfulness I'd intended, and appreciated my playing with the audience instead of ignoring their presence. Maybe he shared my discomfort with the near-religious solemnity that often accompanies literary readings. His kindness saved me from even more self-loathing than I later felt. But as I put the glass to my mouth, when I was already committed to the act and couldn't back down, I understood that I was as likely to annoy people as amuse them, though I only wanted to entertain, to jest.

Being a jester is, historically, a high-risk profession. In medieval and Renaissance courts, jesters softened with humor truths forbidden those without official license to amuse the monarch. But a successful jester needed tact and a discerning alertness to the king's mood. After assuring us that it was extremely rare for a jester to be punished, Beatrice Otto, in *Fools Are Everywhere*, goes on to recount enough beheadings, stranglings, disfigurements, banishments, and autos-da-fé to give even the most benign wit a reason to think twice before teasing a king.

Just in case you think, as I do, that it might be amusing to imply that a king's wife is promiscuous and his daughter a bastard, you should know that when his beloved jester Will Somers did just that, Henry VIII threatened to kill him with his bare hands. Somers, who amused Henry by eating and sleeping with the royal spaniels, was forgiven. Archibald Armstrong, jester to James VI and Charles I, was not. Archy disliked William Laud, the diminutive Archbishop of Canterbury, and at a royal supper, the jester offered grace before the meal with a pun: "Great praise be given to God and little laud to the devil." His joke was good enough for him to keep his head and his job despite his audacious effrontery. But after Laud's attempt to impose Anglican religious services on the Presbyterian Scots led to the Scottish rebellion of 1637, Archy, meeting Laud in the street, asked, "Who's fool now?" After Laud complained, "it was ordered he

[Armstrong] should be carried to the porter's lodge, his coat pulled over his ears, and kicked out of the court, never to enter within the gates." Being stripped of the king's scarlet livery seems fair punishment for a fool who, in anger and animosity, resorted to calling his victim the true fool, the oldest and bluntest arrow in any fool's quiver.

Though I'm not particularly worried about being beheaded or burned at the stake, I do worry about losing my job or offending friends and acquaintances. On recent teaching evaluations, one student complained that I made far too many references to bodily fluids "even for a graduate class," and another participant at a writers' conference expressed concern that my delight in a particular joke was detrimental to the good reputation of the conference. Am I sorry about that? Of course. Am I going to stop telling the joke? Of course not. The next time you see me, just ask me for "The Barbie Joke," and I'll perform it for you. But still, I wake up in the middle of the night after parties, thinking, *My god, I can't believe I made that joke about O. J. Simpson to Richard Wilbur.* Or I walk out of my classroom, stricken with nervous regret, praying nobody files a complaint because I told the joke about the Scotsman and the goat, which I will tell you in chapter 10.

I don't want to end up like John "Santa John" Toomey, who for twenty years in a San Franciso Macy's belted out rich baritone *ho-ho-hos* over Santaland. Children adored him and so did adults, for different reasons. When adults sat on his lap, Santa John asked if they'd been good that year. When they said yes, he replied, "Gee, that's too bad." Santa, he told them, was jolly because he "knows where all the naughty boys and girls live." It was a bit of shtick he'd been doing for twenty years, and never, he insisted, when children could hear. But in 2010, a middle-aged couple unacquainted with humor asked to sit in his lap, and the sixty-eight-year-old Santa soon found himself, like Archy Armstrong, stripped of his red coat. He died of a heart attack nine months later.

With all due respect to Bill Maher and Don Imus, both fired for jokes they told, the most famous joke-instigated firing in recent history was probably the 1976 canning of Earl Butz, President Gerald Ford's secretary of agriculture. Butz was apparently an inveterate joker. At the 1976 Republican National Convention, he amused himself by pitching pennies at the secretary of the treasury, a stunt that walks the line between gratingly juvenile and almost charming. Who better to pitch pennies at?

After Ford was nominated, Butz flew out of Kansas City, accompanied by John Dean, who was covering the convention for *Rolling Stone*. In "Rituals of the Herd," Dean recounts how he introduced Butz to Pat Boone, and then asked Butz about the tepid reaction to Bob Dole's vice presidential acceptance speech. Butz, with what John Dean called a "mischievous smile," said, "Oh, hell, John, everybody was worn out by then. You know, it's like the dog who screwed the skunk for a while until it finally shouted, 'I've had enough!'" Folksy and apt, it's a wonderful metaphor for a political convention grinding to an exhausted end, and it demonstrates Butz's humorous acuity at its most incisive.

But there was something else going on too. Butz was enjoying messing with Pat Boone's head. Boone, the 1950s pretty-boy alternative to Elvis, was so excruciatingly proper he once refused to kiss his movie costar because she was married in real life. In the presence of such a famous Goody Two-shoes, the earthy Butz couldn't resist telling a joke about a dog screwing a skunk to a standstill. Butz didn't stop there:

> Pat gulped, then grinned and I [Dean] laughed. To change the subject Pat posed a question: "John and I were just discussing the appeal of the Republican party. It seems to me that the party

of Abraham Lincoln could and should attract more black people. Why can't that be done?" This was a fair question for the secretary, who is also a very capable politician.

"I'll tell you why you can't attract coloreds," the secretary proclaimed as his mischievous smile returned. "Because coloreds only want three things. You know what they want?" he asked Pat.

Pat shook his head; so did I.

"I'll tell you what coloreds want. It's three things: first, a tight pussy; second, loose shoes; and third, a warm place to shit. That's all!"

Pat gulped twice.

We can easily understand why Pat gulped, but it's almost as easy to understand why Butz enjoyed messing with Pat Boone. Confronted by Boone's historically naïve question about why blacks don't vote for the Party of Lincoln—there was a long century between Ford's Theatre and the resignation of Richard Nixon—Butz must have found it irresistible to tell a racist joke that also requires he say "pussy" and "shit." Who wouldn't want to rattle such an earnest interlocutor? The joke jabs a cruelly precise needle into Boone's assumption that Republicans took the black vote seriously. It doesn't just explain why blacks don't vote Republican; it consciously demonstrates why. Blacks know that Republicans like Butz perceive them as little more than animals, and Butz knows they know. He is not only telling Boone all this, he's also deliberately flaunting his personal contempt as well as enacting his political calculation of how little chance Republicans have of attracting black voters.

For all the subtexts buried in it, the joke is still a nasty piece of work, its racism supercharged by the rhythm of the punch line but unadulterated with wit. It relies almost entirely on the shock value of cramming as much racism, misogyny, and scatology into as few words as possible. Interestingly, Butz avoided the charged word that's obviously missing; he substitutes "coloreds" for "niggers," slightly ameliorating the shock he's depending on.

I'm not the only reader curious about where the humor might be hiding in this painfully crude joke. According to Gareth Morgan in "Butz Triads: Towards a Grammar of Folk Poetry" published in *Folklore*, Butz's joke is actually a "fairly well-known" southwestern triad:

The three things that a nigger likes:

Tight pussy,
loose shoes,
and a warm place to shit.

It's the same pattern as "What are little girls made of? / Sugar, / and spice / and all things nice, / that's what little girls are made of" and "Pease porridge hot, / pease porridge cold, / pease porridge in the pot, nine days old"—with the third item in the list having twice as many beats as the first two. Morgan traces the pattern back to an epigrammatic masterpiece from ancient Sumer: *"Aba garra? Aba galla? Aba urma ganna aburu?"* ("Who is miserly? / Who is opulent? / For whom shall I reserve my vulva?") The rhythm of Butz's joke gives it some power, but these examples demonstrate just what's missing: rhyme, wordplay, or wit. The only surprise is the loose shoes—a mildly amusing image leavened with assonance—but that's hardly enough to make anyone laugh.

Or is the whole crudeness of the humor somehow the point? Does the joke simply hope to keep piling up ugliness till someone laughs in incredulity or agreement? Is it supposed to work like the joke I heard when Ricky Walker leaned over to me in tenth grade and asked, "Do you know what the American Dream is?"

"Yeah, it's some ideal about, uh . . ."

"No. It's all the niggers swimming back to Africa. With a Jew under each arm."

"How could they swim like that?" I said, sneering at the contradiction in his joke, only to be told, witheringly, "That's the point." Then he laughed at my dawning consternation.

Was Ricky's joke only a joke?

"It's only a joke" was more or less Butz's defense, and it's one every joker resorts to when a humor bomb blows up in his face: "You know, I don't know how many times I told that joke, and everywhere—political groups, church groups, nobody took offense, and nobody should. I like humor. I'm human." Butz was almost certainly lying. It's hard to imagine many pastors, even those few who didn't flinch from the racism, chortling at "pussy" and "shit" while mounding their Styrofoam plate with scalloped potatoes and Sea Foam Salad. But like Butz, I too have weakly mustered "It's only a joke," when my love of a joke's audacity enticed me into an amoral blindness to what's being said. Every time I think of Earl Butz, I wince and think, *There but for the grace of God—and the fact that reporters don't follow me around the country—go I.*

Religious bigotry, racism, sexual discomfort, and death provide the tension in jokes, the friction to wordplay's lubrication, and in this thematic memoir of my life as a joker, the story of my life shifts back and forth in time as I explore how I learned to think about religion, race, and sex through the complex and often unattractive medium of jokes. Even in their frequent ugliness I love jokes. They illuminate how we think and the often irresolvable contradictions our lives are built on. The laughter they draw from us both expresses our sorrow at our inconsistency and soothes it. I love the sound of laughter; my voice joining almost musically with yours in a fearful celebration of how the frailties of others are also our own.

One

Catch It and Paint It Green

I was slow to delight in disorder, in which words didn't mean what I'd understood them to mean and in which phrases had secret histories I couldn't know. I was an anxious child, one who sat at his desk and, sounding out words so he could spell them, felt them dissolve on his lips. Or I wrote them with such attention to each mark of the pencil that they disintegrated into their component lines and curves, hooks, and squiggles. Clutching a child's fat pencil, I painstakingly etched words, upstroke and downstroke, onto the lined paper of my Blue Horse Pencil Tablet, paper so near to pulp you could see brown flecks of bark and heartwood in it. I concentrated on the letters until they started to look queer, alien, wrong. I looked back and forth from the book to my handwriting, trying to see what I had copied incorrectly. When I found no mistake, I distrusted my eyesight. I often erased the word and wrote it again, spelling it the same correct way as the first time but trying to make it *look* right in my handwriting. I wrote and erased and wrote and erased till I rubbed holes through the paper.

The sounds of the words were even slipperier than their shapes. Certain small, obvious words were the most likely to crumble in my mouth. As I repeated them, the sounds shifted and the word warped. The word *word* was one of the worst. The *w* stretched out or shortened as I said it different ways. So did the *ur* sound following it. And the *duh* at the end could be the end of one syllable or break off and establish itself as a separate syllable if I over-enunciated, which I almost always did once I started to think about what I was saying. I was terrified by the porcelain delicacy of words. Language was so fragile I could break it just by trying to grasp it, and since it was the only tool I had to make sense of the world, if I destroyed it I also destroyed my own identity. Several times I was so terrified by a word's crumbling in my mouth that I stretched out on the floor between my brother's bed and my own—a place where no one could see me—and cried until I was panting.

Maybe I should have asked my mother for help, but I remembered working myself into a frenzy when, trying to write a sentence for a homework assignment, I had a word slip out of my mind—a basic word, one I should've known. I burst into the kitchen, gasping, "Wuz! Mama, wuz!" I was frantic, my face sticky with tears, but even in my agitation I saw excessive alarm spread across her face. I'd been born two and a half months premature and then placed for several weeks on a respirator that stunted some babies' development by over-oxygenating their brains. Mom had watched for it, braced for it, probed for it, and at long last brain damage had raced into her kitchen, clutched her leg, clamped its damp face to her belly, hysterically begging, "Wuz!"

"What? What are you saying?" she demanded as I clung to her, wailing, "Wuz, Mama, wuz?" Her body was stiff with fear.

Finally she grasped what I couldn't put into words. I could feel her muscles relax. Smiling with more amusement than I thought my stupidity called for, she spelled out, "W-A-S."

Wuz was restored to its essential was-ness, and I immediately calmed down. But words remained skittery. *The* was a persistent vexation, shifting between a short *e* sound and or a long *e* that knocked it up against *thee* from the Bible. Not much later, *mama* changed. One day she snapped, "Don't call me *Mama*, boy. I'm your *mom*." She didn't want to be a countrified mama, as her mother was to her and her sister back in Georgia was to her boys. The wife of an air force officer, she wanted to be that modern thing, a mom. My calling her *Mama*, especially in front of her friends, undermined how she wanted to see herself. It was hard for me to imagine words having the power to change who we are and still being able to fall apart when looked at too closely, but there was Mama's—Mom's— clear demonstration of it happening.

Words were, I thought, like eggs. Hold them loosely and they fall through your fingers and splatter on the linoleum; grasp them too tightly and they are crushed, messily, in your hands. Or maybe words were more like the photos in the newspaper. If I looked at them from across the room, they blurred into blotchy gray shadows, but if I hovered over the pictures, my nose grazing the page, all I could see were individual gray dots. The discomfort of trying to focus on the dots made me suspect that eyes weren't supposed to be used this way. To make sense of the photos, I had to hold them somewhere between too far and too close, just as I had to hold the egg firmly enough to control it but not so firmly that it cracked. Words worked the same way. Words, and maybe the whole world, had to be held gently and understood from the proper distance if they were to mean something.

The funniest thing about the first joke I ever heard is that my father told it to me. I was sitting on the living room floor in front of the couch, building a cage of Tinkertoys around a cabin made of Lincoln Logs. The long Tinkertoy spokes kept tapping the green roof slats of the log cabin out of place, which was infuriating to a seven-year-old. Frustrated, I was always on the verge of smashing the whole thing flat. I did not like the green slats. I was pretty sure, even then, that the roof of Lincoln's childhood cabin wasn't made of boards greener than lime Kool-Aid. The slats' bright dye made me want to suck them, which I did compulsively, especially once I was forbidden to do so. They turned my lips a morbid gray-green.

Dad stood over me in his air force uniform. He was a captain. He had just returned home from work to the tract house on North Carolina's Seymour Johnson Air Force Base. Craning my neck, I looked up the long expanse from his summer khakis to his pink face, pale blue eyes, and prematurely bald head, and in the tensing of his thin lips, I saw him hesitate. He seemed to be pondering— pondering me. Did the color of my lips give me away?

"What's black and white and red all over?" he asked.

What? Wait. Why was he asking? This question sounded a bit like the bullets he fired at me over supper: "What's four plus seven?" "What's our address?" "What's the capital of South Dakota?" "Why can't you just do what you're told without pouting and whining?"

But this question sounded different. There was something worrying and peculiar in the way he almost chanted, as if he both did and didn't expect me to answer. He seemed amused by my answer before I'd given it. And what a confusing question. If something was black and white, it couldn't be red at the same time. That was just basic to knowing what words meant, wasn't it? My father's lips were now pressed into a tight line. I was taking too long to answer.

The only thing I could think to say always meant trouble.

"I don't know."

"A newspaper," he said, grinning.

I closed my eyes, retreated into my mind to absorb the answer.

I couldn't do it. I opened them, looked at my father, my head cocked to the side—apprehensive, stupid, trying to think and failing. Nothing connected. This was not unusual in my relations with the adult world. I must have looked like a beagle instructed to determine pi.

"I don't understand."

"A newspaper is read," he said and nodded. He was encouraging me to keep working at it.

I conjured a picture of a newspaper painted red. I envisioned Dad painting the kitchen stool. He'd spread newspaper on the carport floor and then placed the unfinished wooden stool upside down in the middle of it. The paint often over-sprayed onto the *Goldsboro News-Argus*, covering much of the paper with a glossy coat of royal-blue enamel. In my mind I turned the blue paint to red. But that didn't help. Where the newsprint was red, it was no longer black and white.

"A newspaper is read after you read it," Dad said.

"But it's not *red*. It's still black and white."

"Listen to me! It's R-E-A-D, not R-E-D. The same word means different things."

"That's not fair! It's cheating!"

"It's not cheating. It's a joke."

"It doesn't make sense!" I wailed.

"It's not supposed to make sense. It's a *joke*, you stupid idiot!" he snapped, and marched out of the room.

After he was gone, I remember sitting on the carpet, tapping one Lincoln Log with another. *Read* sounds the same as *red*. Now that my father's expectant eyes were no longer locked on me, I got it. The joke had faked me out by leading me to think the sound meant one thing when it really meant another. If that wasn't cheating, I didn't know what was. But the margins in a newspaper, I thought, weren't "read," so it wasn't actually read *all* over, was it?

And what about the pictures? Did looking at them count as reading? I didn't think so.

A few minutes later, Dad came back in the living room—to make amends, I now realize—and asked me why the chicken crossed the road.

"I don't know," I said. That seemed to be a safe answer to these joke things.

"To get to the other side."

I nodded as if I understood, tried to smile, and he left the room again, appeased if not happy. In a way I did understand. The joke was a parable about simplicity. The chicken's crossing the road was broken down to its simplest possible motivation, but one so fundamental as to be completely dull and unsatisfying. I'd come dangerously close to asking Dad what chicken we were talking about. The chickens in my grandmother's grassless backyard waddled in circles, scratching the Georgia red clay for bugs and overlooked feed corn, and not a single hen had ever shown the least interest in crossing Vineyard Road. I had, though, seen plenty of others flopped dead by drainage ditches, their red and brown feathers erect in the backwash of air as our station wagon shot past, and I vividly remembered seeing a dead chicken humped at the base of a mailbox, a dog jabbing his muzzle into the carcass. Crossing the road was a skill in which many chickens were fatally deficient but maybe they possessed desires I was unaware of.

I was a single-minded little literalist and these jokes seemed like annoyances made of words, not life, the way math problems at school were annoyances made of numbers. If you had two apples and Mr. Smith gave you three, Mrs. Johnson gave you four, and Miss Ingle gave you three, how many apples would you have? I understood the mathematics behind the silly question, but I couldn't imagine a world where grown-ups I didn't know stopped me one after the other and gave me more than I could eat of a fruit I didn't like.

Later, when I encountered more complex word problems in arithmetic, I believed them to be especially lame versions of jokes, dubious contraptions made of words that led to an answer that had nothing to do with life as I knew it. I couldn't conceive of caring what time the train leaving Santa Fe at noon at forty miles an hour would pass the train leaving from Denver an hour later at fifty miles an hour. Maybe I'd care if I was on one train, my mother was on the other, and I could remember to look up at the exactly calculated minute and wave to her as we passed each other, but I doubted that would be possible. I'd get engrossed in reading a comic book, forget the time, forget to look for her, and then, later, I'd get fussed at for not paying attention.

At school, I met my father's first joke again, and once more it flummoxed me. "What's black and white and red all over?" asked the joke page of *My Weekly Reader*. *Well, I know that one*, I thought with jaded triumph. *It's a newspaper. Everybody knows that.*

Wrong! said *My Weekly Reader*. It's a blushing zebra. *That's just dumb*, I thought, enraged. Zebras don't blush. What could make a zebra blush? And even if it did, it wouldn't blush all over its body, just as people didn't blush all over theirs. *My Weekly Reader* helpfully printed a black-and-white picture of a zebra, its head radiating squiggly heat-lines of embarrassment as it looked back over its shoulder with an abashed grin. Its white stripes were shaded gray, to suggest it was blushing. But the picture made me crazier than the joke. Even in the picture, the black stripes of the zebra remained black, which was—*aha!*—a clear refutation of the joke's logic.

What was this *joking*? It was challenging my grasp of reality. Was joking like what my mother often said as she flipped off the bedroom light after tucking me and my brother into bed? Hand hovering over the switch, she sang, "Where was Moses when the light went out?" *Click* went the light, and framed in the doorway by the hall light behind her, my mother, chuckling, answered her own question, "In the dark!" Other times the question had a different answer, one that made her laugh out loud: "Down in the cellar with his shirttail out!"

"In the dark" was an obvious non-answer answer, like "to get to the other side," and "down in the cellar with his shirttail out" was nonsense with a hint of naughtiness. Other than that, all I understood about these moments was Mom's pleasure in the words. "Where was Moses when the light went out?" was, I discovered many years later, the refrain of a novelty song from her youth. In the song, Moses is courting Becky Cohen, and when the lights go out, old man Cohen is relieved to hear Becky keep playing the "pianer" in the dark while he leaves the room to find money to feed the gas meter. He is, he tells Becky, sure her Moses was courting her respectably—"loving in a Yiddisher manner," but Cohen still wants reassurance: "Tell me, darling daughter, while I went to get the quarter / Where was Moses when the light went out?"

The refrain broke free of its source, became a catchphrase, and people simply invented answers for it, including one I never heard at home: "Down in the cellar eating sauerkraut." We Southern Baptists weren't notable consumers of fermented cabbage, and the only Moses I'd heard of was the one who led the children of Israel out of Egypt. In my mind, he was the Moses in the dark with his shirttail flapping free. I wondered why he was not wearing the long heavy robe he wore in my illustrated Bible. My lack of understanding did not, however, keep me from absorbing (if not entirely appreciating) how my mother, after she had turned out the lights on another day that ended with me safely in bed, allowed herself a moment of carefree nonsensical pleasure imported from a time before I was born.

•   •   •

I slowly eased my grip on my natural literalism, and began to enjoy the unrealities that language made possible. Chickens yearn to cross roads, zebras blush, and newspapers are red all over while remaining black and white. You could play with words, just as you played with marbles, yo-yos, kites, and Matchbox cars.

Jokes were toys made of words. They were like the jack-in-the-box whose handle I spent hour after hour cranking, listening to the rink-a-tink tune of "Pop! Goes the Weasel" and then crowing with laughter when the clown shot out of his box, flung his folded arms wide, and bobbed at the end of his spring, idiotic and yet sinister with his huge hooked nose, bright red cheeks, and derisive grin. Frightening as he was, Jack was mine to control. I determined when he lunged out of his box, and once he did, I folded his hands across his chest and shoved him back down into his dark enclosure. I could spin the crank rapidly, frantic notes pelting from the box till the clown popped out. More often I turned the handle with obsessive patience, feeling the bumps on the roller inside the music mechanism flick over the tines, making "Pop! Goes the Weasel" unwind as a tinny dirge, until Jack's spring overpowered the loosening latch and the clown once more launched to the end of his hidden spring. I loved the absurdity of the clown with his arms flying apart wider than the box that held him and his long black gown that, stretched over his uncompressed spring, made him look much taller than the box from which he'd leapt.

The tune tinked out of the box, and I screeched along with it, reveling in the song as I conjured the unsurprising surprise of Jack's appearance:

> *All around the mulberry bush*
> *The monkey chased the weasel;*
> *The monkey thought 'twas all in fun,*
> *Pop! goes the weasel.*

A penny for a spool of thread
A penny for a needle—
That's the way the money goes,
Pop! goes the weasel.

Half a pound of tuppenny rice,
Half a pound of treacle.
Mix it up and make it nice,
Pop! goes the weasel.

Up and down the London road,
In and out of the Eagle,
That's the way the money goes,
Pop! goes the weasel.

I've no time to plead and pine,
I've no time to wheedle,
Kiss me quick and then I'm gone
Pop! goes the weasel.

To my ears the words were joyously cockeyed. I knew that weasels and monkeys didn't belong together, and the two of them had no natural connection to mulberry bushes, which I had at least seen with my own eyes and not in picture books. The appearing and disappearing clown simply increased the mental anarchy that baffled, tickled, and intrigued me.

I loved the slight, giddy menace in how "needle," "treacle," "eagle," and "weasel" inexactly rhymed. There was something eerie in the way the tune forced me to pronounce the last syllables of the words with unnatural weight: Wee-ZUL, knee-DUL, ee-GUL, whee-DUL.

The song changed a bit from songbook to songbook, class to

class, and even singer to singer. Did it begin "All around the mulberry bush" or "Around and around" or "Round and round"? Once, in a new class, I launched into the song, and when all the other kids, who had belted out "Round and round the cobbler's bench," turned to look at me, I felt stupid and flatfooted, betrayed by my full-throated devotion to the mulberry bush. Though I was perturbed by the unfixed lyrics and the unmoored world they implied, the exuberance of the song and the sheer pleasure it gave me made it easy to understand that all our versions were basically the same— and I learned that what I knew was not the only way something could be known. More crucially, I learned that pleasure can lead us to want to understand something and that understanding is not entirely necessary for pleasure.

I had no idea that "Pop! Goes the Weasel" was a drinking song, the Eagle a pub, and that the beer mugs were raised and drained at *pop!*—as a teacher once told the class. Or, depending on whom you read, the weasel is a weaver's shuttle, a tailor's iron, a coat, or a stolen bit of silver—all of which could be "popped" at the pawn shop to pay for drink and food or a tumble in the hay. No one knows for sure what the monkey was. Perhaps, one writer speculates not very confidently, a Frenchman. And I loved the cavalier shrug of "That's the way the money goes." Money was never talked about so dismissively in our house, or in any house I'd ever entered. A world where money was splashed out casually with a laugh and without a second thought—I enjoyed a frisson of illicit extravagance just mouthing the words.

For years, I tried to understand the song and couldn't, which was a huge part of its continuing appeal. Did "pop" mean the weasel exploded? That didn't seem right. Did it mean the weasel had leapt on the monkey, caught it, and killed it? Might have been right. Had the monkey caught the weasel and squeezed it till it popped? That explanation made more sense than anything else and I was guiltily fond of the image it formed in my mind, though I still wouldn't have bet my lunch money on it.

Looking back, I'm surprised all over again that it was my father who told me my first two jokes. He was a melancholy man, one who, as the ancient Greeks said of the unlaughing, had consulted the oracle of Trophonius. According to Pausanias, the seeker who consulted the oracle to learn what the future held was taken into a cave at night and placed, feet first, in a small hole, which then seemed to pull him in: "Then the rest of his body is immediately dragged along and follows quickly after his knees, just as if the greatest and swiftest of rivers were about to engulf one caught in its current. . . . The way back for those who have gone down is through the same mouth, with their feet running before them." After enacting his symbolic death and rebirth, the seeker is brought to the priests, who sat him upon "the chair of Memory" and asked him what he learned in this quest. Then he is turned over to his relatives who "lift him, paralyzed with terror and unconscious both of himself and of his surroundings." Sources other than Pausanias say that in the underworld the melancholy leave behind their capacity to enjoy life and never laugh again. In a significant way, they are already dead.

When I first read about the oracle of Trophonius, I thought of how my father would occasionally pull my brothers and me up onto the bed with him and lay still while we crawled over his body, sat on his chest, or stared up his nose. At first he laughed a little at our tickling, but then he fell silent. Slowly we realized that he wasn't moving or speaking. Had he gone to sleep? How could he have fallen asleep with three boys clambering back and forth across his belly?

"Daddy, are you asleep?" we asked.

We poked his shoulder, but he didn't rouse. We traced the bottoms of his feet lightly with our fingertips, tickling him and his sides. He was ticklish in those places, we knew, but now he didn't flinch or jerk away.

"Daddy, are you okay? Are you okay?"

We peeled his eyelids back and peered into the motionless blurred circles. We pinched his nose shut to see if he was breathing.

"Daddy, are you alive?"

Dear God, what would we do if he were dead? Would we have to go live with our grandmother? What would we eat? Who would take care of us?

In desperation, sitting on his belly, I reared back my head and slammed my forehead into his face. Yelling, he sat up and swept us off the bed and onto the floor. Standing over us, he shouted, "We were having fun and you stupid idiots had to go and ruin everything."

Huddled at his feet, we sobbed in relief and terror. We were thrilled that he had returned from the dead and terrified at what he'd do next. *So it was a joke!* I thought. *Why aren't we laughing? Why does every joke end with someone crying and someone yelling?*

"Get out of my sight! Go to your rooms! Go to your rooms and stay there till I tell you you can come out."

I grew up in a sour family, with both my parents secretly grieving and depressed. They had visited the oracle of Trophonius and lost the ability to laugh. I didn't learn why until I was thirteen and my grandmother told me the family secret: I had a sister Andrea who died before I was born. According to my grandmother, my father believed God had taken Andrea back from him because in loving her so much he had committed idolatry before the Lord. My parents could not talk about her. Her life was too holy to mention. Her death in a car accident, my mother at the wheel, was a wound too raw for words to touch. By their silence my parents tried to protect me and my brothers from knowing about death. Instead, we learned sorrow and fear. The sorrow that pervaded our lives was the only world I'd known, and so it seemed natural, as did the rage that stalked in sorrow's footprints. Human existence was a joyless conscription to be marched through dutifully till death released us. I assumed our melancholy and anger grew from our Baptist belief in original sin, the depravity of man, and our knowledge that this world was a valley of temptation and suffering we warily pass through on our way to judgment. I was right, but not entirely right. My sister's death gave my parents' beliefs a terrible emotional force, the force of lived experience.

Because of that bleakness, I remember clearly the times I heard my father chuckle; they were aberrations, so marvelous and strange that I studied him out of the corner of my eye, suspicious that he was playing a trick on me. If there were a word that means at the same time fascination, skepticism, affection, sorrow, recurring surprise, and something just shy of wonder, that's the word that would describe how I felt when I heard him chuckle at *The Andy Griffith Show*, *Gomer Pyle—USMC*, and *The Beverly Hillbillies*—all shows about Southerners who, through naïve goodwill and innocence, triumphed in the world. Was that how he saw himself? It was certainly the way he wanted the world to work.

His harshness grew not just from unspoken grief over his daughter's death but also from an ongoing grief that the world did not conform to his faith. Church was his respite. Other than at worship services, the only times Dad relaxed were when his brothers came to visit, and those visits were rare. One uncle lived in Florida, the other in Ohio, and we, as a military family, were often in hard-to-drive-to military bases in Texas, New Mexico, England, North Carolina, California, or France—to list them in chronological order. When my uncles, both Methodist ministers, sat at our table after a long trip, my father didn't talk much, but he smiled readily at their stories. He trusted them, as his brothers and as ministers, to act appropriately. I was always intrigued by these two men who looked like my father but had laugh lines around their eyes and banter on their lips. When he was around them, my father became a little like them, at ease and agreeable, even happy—a man foreign to me.

Their visits were odd oases in our unhappiness. When I was young, my mother occasionally spent afternoons locked in her bedroom. I could hear her full-body sobbing through the closed door. Sometimes I'd kneel in the hall outside her door, trying to figure out what my father or I might have done to devastate her so utterly. Slowly, careful not to make the bolt tap against the strike plate, I pressed my ear against the hollow-core door and listened. All I could hear were sobs—gasping sobs as she fought for breath, then moments of calm, then moans that almost became words, then stabs at prayer that turned back to moans. Her crying spells lasted for hours, and after a while, bored and helpless, I'd slink off to lie on my bed and read, while listening for her door to open. Returning to my own inconsequential amusements while her comfortless sorrow wept itself toward a stopping place, I felt cruel and crudely separate from my mother, a feeling I understood was crass, necessary, and salubrious. When she came out to fix supper, her face was swollen and she walked as if she had been beaten over her back and legs. I had no idea what was wrong, and after the first time or two, I learned not to ask. "Crying? I don't know what you're talking about. Maybe you were hearing the neighbor's radio. I was asleep. You must've heard me dreaming."

Because she was so volatile, her pleasures, more full than my father's, were all the more my pleasures. She enjoyed listening to Arthur Godfrey on the radio while she ironed. His on-air folksiness and even his gravelly crankiness delighted her. He's down-to-earth, just like us, she said, with a satisfaction I adopted as my own. *The Breakfast Club* with Don McNeill, broadcast from "the Cloud Room of the Allerton Hotel, high above Chicago's famous magnificent mile," was another of our delights. Settling in for a morning's work, she arranged the ironing board so she could park her ashtray, Pall Malls, coffee mug, and water-sprinkling bottle on the kitchen table within easy reach. They often migrated back and forth from table to ironing board to table over and over each morning. In midmorning, the coffee was replaced by a Coke or Dr. Pepper. Mom dashed the wrinkled laundry with water from a Coke bottle with a cork-bottomed sprinkler cap jammed in it. When the sprinkler head went missing during one of our moves, she simply dipped her fingers into a bowl of water and flicked the laundry to moisten it. She loathed ironing, as she often told me, but she made the drudgery tolerable by balancing it with the workaday rewards of caffeine, tobacco, and radio.

I paid only fitful attention to Arthur Godfrey or Don McNeill. It was my mother I wanted to hear. I sat under the ironing board, and listened to her listening, attending to her chuckles, snorts, and muttered comments. "Well, that's just ridiculous!" she'd say to the radio, and I could hear enjoyment even in her judgment and disgust. More than once, when she laughed too hard at a joke or huffed too fiercely at a story in the news, there were wild moments when the ironing board tipped, and iron, water, ashtray, lit cigarette, and parts of my father's uniform flew past my head as she flailed at them to keep them from hitting me.

I happily sat at her feet and listened when she talked on the phone to her friends, trying to understand the whole conversation from the half of it I heard. What did it mean that Mrs. Wilcox had sat in the same pew as Jenny Carlow at church Sunday morning? That Mom's sister Joyce was looking for a job at the towel mill? That Jack Somebody from Dad's class at West Point had made colonel already? I couldn't puzzle it out, and wasn't supposed to. "Little pitchers have big ears," she said into the receiver before skirting around a story she was telling, filling it in for her friend with verbal nudges and auditory winks. In a few years, I would find myself mostly relegated to third base or banished to right field in Little League, but I always dreamed of being a pitcher, so I was mildly stung by Mom's derogatory assessment of my ears. For a couple of months, as I was getting ready for bed at night, she taped them to the sides of my head with white first-aid tape. She was training them not to stick out. Why, a big wind would blow me away. I didn't want to look like Dumbo, did I?

Even when I didn't know what she was talking about on the phone, I knew not to ask. If I did, I'd be sent from the room, away from her occasional laughter. When my parents laughed, they became, for a moment, younger and lighter. I sensed, though I could not have said so, a time when they had not been unhappy, and I blamed their unhappiness on the trials of raising children, the burden of responsibility. The burden of me. I was wrong. Or partly wrong. I was misinterpreting the burden: My parents were terrified that I would die, as my sister had, and they hovered over me, watched me with fearful vigilance, and corrected me vehemently so I would be careful, stay alive, not die. My father's rage grew, I imagine, out of fear. My rage grew out of my fear of him.

When I was small, he clenched my wrists in his hands and smacked my face with my own hands as he laughed and said, "Don't hit yourself." I fought to control my hands, to keep from hitting myself, but again and again my own hands slapped my face. In the struggle, he sometimes hit me—or I hit myself—sharply. My cheeks stinging, my own hands hurting me, and I could not stop them. Soon I was sobbing with frustration, and I was a bad sport, a sissy who couldn't take a joke. But when I clutched my brothers' wrists and popped their palms against their cheeks, crowing, "Don't hit yourself! Why are you hitting yourself?" my parents screamed that I was mean. I was hurting my baby brothers. Well, sure—and the joke was finally, for the first time, funny.

We seldom agreed on what was funny. On the last day of fourth grade, I raced home on my bike after a half day of class, and met my father getting out of the car in the carport, home for lunch.

"How'd school go today?"

"Fine," I said. I was elated. Last day of school!

"Did you find out who your teacher's going to be next year?"

"Yes, sir. It's Old Lady Porter." That's what I'd heard the other boys at school call her. *Old Lady Porter*. I relished the tough-guy knowingness of the phrase—one cowboy talking to another about the lady who owned the saloon. I thought it was funny because I knew I was a kid trying to sound like a cowboy, a hood, a detective, a Bowery boy.

I was still straddling my bicycle, toes touching the concrete, when Dad grabbed my arm, jerked me off the seat, and shook me by my shoulders, his face jammed up nose-to-nose with mine.

"Her name is Mrs. Porter to you, young man! Mrs. Porter! And that's what you'll call her. Do you hear me?"

"Yes, sir."

"Then say it!

"*Yes, sir!*" I shouted. I'd read this was how recruits addressed officers.

"Not that! Her name, you stupid idiot."

"Mrs. P—P—Porter."

The ensuing and scathing lecture on respect for adults in general, women in particular, and teachers especially, left me trembling with shock and, secretly, indignation. I could have understood the gravity of my transgression with a more temperate reprimand. But even as he yelled and I trembled, I saw that, though the yelling was probably unnecessary for me, for him, it was essential. Because of my thoughtless joking, he *had* to yell at me; he was morally compelled to correct a mockery I hadn't intended. And jokes, I also saw, were not something to share willy-nilly. I'd have to be cagier about whom I joked with.

•   •   •

My childish sense of humor was a weapon I honed on my brothers, who were younger than I and, for a while, weaker. My brother Roger and I were eating fried egg sandwiches for lunch when he eagerly announced that he'd read Edgar Allan Poe's "The Tell-Tale Heart" the night before. It had unnerved him so deeply that he'd spent the night awake, with the covers pulled up over his head. I must have been in the fifth grade then and he must have been in the third. I nibbled the bread and the egg white of my sandwich until one end of the naked yolk was visible. Holding it in front of Roger's face, I intoned, "The beating of his hideous heart!" and squeezed the bread. The still-liquid yolk bulged toward him. Over and over again, I chanted, "The beating of his hideous heart!" squeezing the yolk till it almost burst and jabbing it toward his face as he cringed. When he broke down blubbering, I popped the yolk, let the yellow run like blood down the toasted bread, and ate the imaginary heart with exaggerated appetite.

But the real and impossible target of all the anger I channeled into crude wit was my father. Since I was terrified of him, I practiced my sarcasm in silence, fashioning put-downs so cutting he would fall at my feet and beg forgiveness, I imagined, if I'd been stupid enough to say them. I knew that the wit of a ten-year-old boy would be no match for my father's intelligence, and even if it were, I'd simply be whipped for my success. I lived in my head, holding high-strung conversations with myself, forming witticisms and replying to them, topping myself, and then topping that top with even more cutting rejoinders. At the same time that I thought I was pretty darn clever, the Oscar Wilde of long division and the Oscar Levant of sentence diagramming, I knew to keep my mouth shut. My unspoken bon mots must have shown on my face as a smirk because both my parents snarled at me repeatedly, "If you don't wipe that look off your face, boy, I'll knock it off for you!" Sometimes, not often, they did. Usually, as soon as Mom's or Dad's right hand drew back, I assumed an expression of exaggerated neutrality and they were content not to have to slap me.

My father would sometimes hit us. But swear, never. Not so much as a "damn" or "hell" passed his lips in my hearing. "Fart" was verboten. Even "durn" and "darn"—my mother's curse words— were dodgy. But in his rage Dad hissed "stupid idiot" so venomously that it devastated me. A couple of times in my early teens I worked up the courage to tell people, in his presence, that I'd just recently learned that my name was Andrew, not Stupid Idiot. He responded that I'd only recently earned the promotion—a joke. Kind of. The few times my father assayed verbal humor, it was the dry, wounding type. When I was in high school, one of my aunts gave me a used watch, and my father, seeing me sit in the living room, winding it and admiring the faux-marbled red dial, asked if the watch were any good.

"It says it has a ten-jewel movement."

"Well, why don't you pry them out and sell them? Then we'll all be rich."

I reacted to his comment like the character in Edith Wharton's story "The Mission of Jane": "It occurred to him that perhaps she was trying to be funny: he knew there is nothing more cryptic than the humor of the unhumorous." Even at fifteen, I knew this was an inappropriate barb for a father to direct at a boy thrilled to flash around a watch with a red face, stiletto hands, and a snazzy silver-gray leather strap. I couldn't tell him his wit was unsuitable. But I reflexively analyzed the opening he'd left unguarded. All the nasty things I could've snapped back at him raced through my mind: "Well, it'd be more than you've ever done." "I've come to like being poor." "What do you mean *we*, *kemo sabe*?" I was tempted by the last option, but I was pretty sure he'd respond violently to the tone of it even if he didn't recognize it as a punch line. The Lone Ranger and Tonto are surrounded by hundreds of hostile Apaches, who are ready to sweep down on them. The Lone Ranger turns to Tonto, his faithful Indian companion, and says, "It looks like we're in trouble this time, Tonto."

"What do you mean *we, kemo sabe*?" Would the joke itself have amused Dad? Who knows? The joke is potentially racist and delights in disloyalty, choosing practicality over principle. I wasn't going to risk it.

Jokes are often—some would say *always*—intricately wound up with power. Unable to reply with a cutting remark of my own, I was tempted to smile at my father's joke, maybe chuckle subserviently to ease the tension of not laughing. Instead, I did something that many people have done to me in the years since: I stared at him, my head cocked with blank bewilderment—some of which was real—until he turned back to the TV.

How do you respond to the nearly humorless? Back in North Carolina, in the same house in which Dad told me my first joke, we were eating dinner at the kitchen table when I farted. Without a word, Dad, who was sitting next to me at the head of the table, lashed out and backhanded me across the face. I jolted backward with the blow, my chair tipped, and, falling, I smacked the back of my head against the washing machine.

Slumped on the linoleum in front of the washer, I blubbered, "I didn't do anything. What did I do? You didn't have to hit me." The front panel of the washer had some flex in it, so I wasn't hurt so much as shocked at suddenly being on the floor. By feigning more pain than I felt, I was trying to keep him from coming at me again.

"Quit making a show of yourself. You know what you did. You pooted at the table. Sit down, eat your supper, and if you need to go to the bathroom, go to the stinking bathroom."

"But I didn't know I was going to do it. It just came out."

"Don't lie to me. I saw you lean over to let it out."

He had me dead to rights. I *had* shifted my weight from my right buttock to my left and leaned over slightly to ease the gas out. I couldn't *believe* he'd seen me do it.

Forty years later, detached from the shame and ill usage I felt then, the moment seems irresistibly comic. I don't know why Dad didn't see the humor and couldn't laugh, and I wish I could have. If he had read Augustine's *City of God*, he would have known that flatulence has a long history as a public entertainment that the saint himself enjoyed: "Some have such command of their bowels, that they can break wind continuously at pleasure, so as to produce the effect of singing." And if he were a joker, he could've said what the third man said to the devil. Three men who had sold their souls were given a last chance to redeem themselves. All they had to do was name one request the devil couldn't fulfill. The first asked for a roomful of gold and the devil immediately conjured it up. The second asked for the most beautiful woman in the world to be his slave, and the devil, with a wave of his hand, produced her. The third man farted, and said to the devil, "Catch it and paint it green."

In fifth grade, every time one of the boys farted, the rest of us shouted, "Catch it and paint it green!" It was our tribute to the embarrassment of the body and the vividly impossible. We did not know the joke goes back to at least 1560, when, in a German version, the devil was ordered to catch a fart and sew a button on it. The joke is so common that folklorists have given it a number and a name inside the larger category of "Tasks contrary to the law of nature": "H1023.13, Task: catching a man's broken wind. Type: 1176."

When I was twelve or thirteen, I finally let one of my supposed witticisms escape my lips.

As we drove out of San Bernardino, California, to Lake Isabella, where the government rented old air force blue trailers for military families on vacation, my two brothers and I squirmed, whined, and elbowed each other in the backseat of a Volkswagen Beetle. In the un-air-conditioned car, our thighs sticking to the hot vinyl, we were practically pasted to each other from knees to shoulders. We were furious with Dad because, instead of taking the Chevy wagon, he'd opted for the VW to save on gas. We were miserable—ceaselessly, vocally miserable—and our jostling, quarreling, and carping must have been maddening to listen to. It was supposed to be.

As we approached a billboard advertisement for Volkswagens that announced, "It'll grow on you," my father read it to us and, with a triumphant snort, told us to settle down back there. "It'll grow on you."

"Yeah, it'll grow on us. Like mold," I said.

"Yeah, like fungus," Roger added, and laughed. The giddiness of our own incessant bitching had made us bold, and reversing the needle that Dad had jabbed at us improved my mood briefly.

He jerked the car to the side of the road and sat for a moment, his hands clenched on the steering wheel, before, his face red with rage, he turned and glared at us over the front seat.

"Get out," he snarled. "Both of you. You don't like what I provide for you, so you can just get out! I don't want you to ride in a car that's not good enough for you."

I froze. He was joking, wasn't he? He had to be joking. He got out of the car, tilted down his seatback, and snarled, "Go on! Get out!"

Roger shrugged, and slipped out of his spot behind the driver's seat, and stood beside Dad.

I sat where I was, waiting for Dad to say he'd made his point and we should just sit still and shut up till we got to the lake.

"You too," he said, and jerked his head in the direction he wanted me to move. "Get out."

I scrambled over Mike, who sat in the middle of the bench seat, his legs straddling the transmission hump, and stumbled out of the car. Blinking in the harsh California sunlight on the edge of Central Valley and near the desert, I looked through the window at Mike. He was safe because he was four, and he was studiously looking innocent.

Roger and I stood by the side of the road, nothing but sand and scrub brush as far as we could see. Dad slammed the car in gear and drove off. Roger and I watched till the car slipped around a curve and was gone. I kept staring at the last spot it had occupied before it had disappeared in the distance. Surely Dad was coming back. He couldn't just leave us by the road in the middle of nowhere, could he? It was against the law to abandon children, I knew that, but I knew it because I'd read newspaper reports of people who had done it. And I was thirteen. I wasn't sure I completely qualified as a child anymore.

After a couple of minutes, Roger said, "Let's go."

"Where?" I looked back where we'd come from and ahead to where the car had vanished.

"Let's just go," he said, and started marching down the shoulder in the direction the car had taken. After he'd gone about ten yards, I hurried to follow, my feet clumsy on the loose gravel and the steep rake of the shoulder. Before we'd walked a mile, my father puttered up on the other side of the road and braked to a stop across from us.

"Want a ride?" he called out the window. Beside him, my mother laughed. It was close enough to a joke for me. Almost whimpering with gratitude, I squeezed behind my father's seat, while he bent forward against the steering wheel to make room for me. On the road, Roger kept walking, his back rigid, his eyes fixed on the distance, acknowledging neither my father's presence nor my capitulation. Dad cut a three-point turn in the middle of the road, and crept along beside him in the car. Roger never turned his head. Finally, Dad yelled at him to stop being silly and get in the car.

Roger ignored him. Finally, Dad got out and wrestled him into the car by the neck. He looked like a cowboy bulldogging a steer.

For weeks, my mother teased me about my craven gratitude and Roger's stubborn refusal to be cowed, even though he was the younger brother. She laughed with a pleasure I resented, though I had to acknowledge the truth behind the laughter, and the justice of her repeatedly slamming it into my face like a cream pie. Roger was her favorite, as she told me, always adding that she loved me just as much. I was my father's, as she also told me, and all my life I've felt a little like Israel. Being the Lord's favorite is a difficult blessing. I wish I had been confident enough to laugh at the comedy of it all. But, like the devil, I couldn't catch it and paint it green.

Two

Hide in the Grass and Make a Noise like a Peanut

Away from home, at school, I learned I could make people laugh by being outrageous. Not witty, not clever, not smart—just obnoxious. I did things there I was terrified to do at home.

As soon as my father arrived home from work, my mother would scream out a litany of my transgressions during the day: mouthing off, ignoring her when she called, whining for a Hershey bar. Usually he tried to soothe her—who wants to be the wrath of God coming home with an empty, grease-spotted, brown lunch bag in his hand, one he'd reuse the next day? But sometimes my trespasses were grave enough that, as he was hearing her out, he looked at me and snarled, "Go to your room, pull down your pants, lean over the bed, and wait for me." I still remember the sound of his belt snaking out backward through his belt loops, the end of it snapping against each loop. I began screaming as soon as his hand went back.

"Shut up, I haven't even hit you yet," he'd yell in exasperation, a half second before he hit me.

Screaming had its pleasures, but it was safer to do it at school than at home. Though I was usually quiet at school and polite, about once a year, when the teacher was out of the room, I shrieked. My high-pitched yelp split the near silence of pencils scritch, scritch, scritching over notebook paper. Boys jerked in their seats, and a girl or two always squealed, ripped from reveries of Brazil. In my memory, we were always in Brazil on our tour of "South America: Land of Contrast." The boys laughed at me for screaming and at the girls for squealing. But someone always told the teacher, and the laughter guttered to an uneasy silence when I was flung into the hall and ordered to the principal's office. My rough exit usually provoked smothered laughs as parting gifts.

Other times, as the teacher walked down the classroom aisle, I would slip from my desk, stretch out on the floor behind her, and lay there until she noticed my classmates tittering. The longer I sprawled on the linoleum, letting the giggles build, the funnier my breach of second-, third-, or fourth-grade decorum became. But if I drew the joke out too long, the teacher jerked her head around and saw me scrambling back into my seat, and I was once more slung into the hall and shoved in the direction of the principal's office. If I got away with my stunt, I sat at my desk and picked at my shirt and pants, now gritty, smudged, and damp from the floor that thirty kids regularly tromped across. I could feel the eyes of the other students looking at me expectantly, as if waiting for me to do something else.

I hated the dead moments after the laughter was over. I felt stupid, exposed, unfinished, and lonelier than I had been before. My shenanigans, I saw, didn't change the tedium of the classroom; they depended on it. If there's no decorum, there's no shocked laughter in violating it. What disturbed me was how little a point my pointless stunts turned out to have and how lost I felt afterward, as if what I had done, the act I'd performed, had abandoned me.

Outside the principal's office, I slumped forlornly on a folding chair stationed there for miscreants. The first few times the principal called me in, he gave me a long heart-to-heart about "disruptive behavior." The yellow North Carolina sun streamed over his shoulder, and the playground spread behind him, the monkey bars and teeter-totters filled with kids from other grades, kids who were strangers to me. Though he tried to keep his expression vexed and his voice stern, he didn't seem to care much. Soon he took to letting me stew out in the hall for most of the hour, before leaning out the door of his office and telling me he was disappointed in me and that I should go back to class and behave myself. Everyone was disappointed in me, including me.

And I kept on disappointing us all. One prank, my masterpiece, I performed annually between fourth and seventh grade. With the teacher away on a coffee break and the other students answering the end-of-the-chapter questions about the plight of the Arcadians, the melancholy fate of Evangeline, the triumph of Athenian democracy, or the contrasts of "South America: Land of Contrast," I surveyed the classroom. All the other heads were bent into the work, engrossed in the corrosive tedium of copying each question and answering it in full sentences. I was so bored I thought I might be going insane.

I hefted the fat history book and weighed it on the flat of my palm, playing with my indecision, and then I reared back and threw the book as hard as I could toward the blackboard. As it arced above the heads of my classmates, the heavy book rotated in air, its pages riffling. I stared at it, hoping it wouldn't fly open and that I'd timed the rotation so the cover smacked flat against the board. When it did, it boomed into the silence, then slid down the wall, clipped the chalk tray, and toppled to the floor. Girls screamed, the boys laughed uneasily. What a blasphemous charge there was in throwing a book, which is why I always threw a history book. I *cared* about history. And history books were always thick enough to make a loud dusty *whap* against the chalkboard.

I only stopped throwing books because, in seventh grade, after someone ratted me out, I was invited back to the history classroom that afternoon for a couple of swats. The teacher was a gym coach, muscular and unamused. Though I wore my gym shorts over my underwear and under my pants for padding, he hit me hard enough, three times, to force tears to my eyes. Still I was grateful that he didn't call my parents, who promised that if they ever heard of my getting swatted at school, I could count on getting a double dose at home, and twice as hard, a prospect that kept me awake at night, meditating terror, throughout elementary school and junior high. From the coach's anger and my classmates' failure to laugh, I could see I'd gone too far this time.

Why was I doing these stupid things? The obvious answer is that I wanted attention, which I suppose I did, and I didn't have a better way to get it. I was average at math, better than average at social studies, and pretty good at spelling because my mother drilled me on each week's spelling list. But I was so socially maladroit that I was completely unable to talk to other kids. The one thing I excelled in, reading, no one could see I was good at, not even me; I assumed that what I was doing everyone else was doing just as well or better. And what did it matter anyway? I was a kid reading kids' books and I knew it.

Boredom alone didn't seem to be enough to explain my behavior. An earnestly churched boy, I also seriously pondered the possibility of demonic possession. I sometimes felt spurred to these occasional antics by a force outside myself. Was I possessed, like the Gadarene demoniac in the Bible? The naked wild man in the land of the Gadarenes was so powerfully infested with a legion of demons that, wailing and cutting himself with stones, he wandered day and night among the tombs. Jesus cast the demons into a herd of two thousand swine that immediately ran off a cliff into the Sea of Galilee and drowned, the porcine mass suicide making short work of the mercy Jesus had wasted on the disoriented devils. Two thousand demonically possessed pigs stampeding over a precipice—that's an image I long pondered. Like the demoniac, I heard voices competing to form me—the voices of parents, teachers, other kids, preachers, books, movies, and radio shows. And along with those voices, I felt an assertiveness that felt self-destructive, a force that might be more at home cast into the body of a suicidal hog. But while my yelping, sprawling on a dirty classroom floor, and throwing books was clearly naughty, could anyone call these outbursts evil? Whatever my motives were, they weren't malicious.

Lonely and isolated from the other kids at school, I yearned for a world where people laughed regularly and happily. Was I imagining their happiness? Desperation drove my laughter, not delight. When I finally encountered Percy Shelley's assertion that "Our sincerest laughter / With some pain is fraught," I knew what he meant because I had lived it. If my stunts ended with visiting the principal, being paddled, writing a hundred times that I would not talk in class, or standing at the blackboard on tiptoe for an hour with my nose pressed against a wad of gum I'd been chewing—though I've never liked gum and chewed it only because it was forbidden—the punishments didn't bother me much. They were just the cost of doing business. I stopped my stunts because, as we got a little older, the other kids stopped laughing. What used to be funny no longer was. I was moving in their minds from "odd guy" to something approaching "jerk." I wanted to stop before I got there.

At least one teacher thought I had already gone to "jerk" and beyond. In the fifth grade, playing kickball at recess, I caught a pop-up and hurled the big rubber ball toward a tall girl named Michelle, who had edged off first base. My throw caught her flush on the side of her head, knocking her glasses off. Her face looked naked without her glasses, and she seemed nearly featureless.

Double play! Game over! I was thrilled. It was just like the miracle endings I'd read about in sports novels, where the no-talent kid suddenly leads the Hogansville Cougars to the state championship of an unspecified state. So I was dumbstruck when Mrs. Thompkins dashed across the asphalt, grabbed me by my upper arm, and shouted into my face that I was a vicious little brat and she was going to keep me after school and call my mother. I was in more trouble than I'd ever dreamed of. She'd see to that.

It was against the rules, she said, to aim the kickball at someone's head. I'd done it deliberately. I was just *mean*.

That rule was news to me (and to everyone else, I believe). I was astonished at the accusation and flattered that she thought I was athletic enough to drill the ball from third base and hit a moving human head on purpose. I wished I were that good. I'd been aiming vaguely at a spot between her and first base, and had simply thrown the ball as hard and high as I could to get it there. I was so flabbergasted that I didn't even think to defend myself, and it took me another moment or two to understand that her accusation wasn't even the main point. This mishap was her excuse to punish me for screaming in class, rolling on the floor, throwing my book.

I was shocked to realize she didn't like me. I was a *kid*. Adults weren't *allowed* to dislike kids. None of the stupid stunts I'd pulled in class had anything to do with her. She was just there—an authority figure, a role not a person, a face I could throw myself at as if I were a cream pie in a Three Stooges movie. It never crossed my mind that what I did in class could ruffle her. We were both diminished by this new understanding. I was distressed to realize that the next time I did something stupid for a laugh that I wouldn't just be exploiting the role she played but also hurting a fellow human being. I saw myself as at worst mischievous but still innocent. My teacher, and maybe others—the principal, my classmates—saw me as a brat, a creep: someone who enjoyed being aggravating. For many days afterward, I lay on my bed after school and studied the overhead light, troubled by the difference between how I saw myself and how others perceived me.

Some military brats react to perpetual dislocation by becoming socially adept, at ease with new situations and new people. I was not of their company. I was one of the ones who withdrew into themselves as my family moved from Fort Hood, Texas, where I was born, to New Mexico, England, Ohio, North Carolina, California, France, and Alabama. Always being the new guy, the person learning the new rules and the new pecking order, wore me out.

After my father was transferred from North Carolina to San Bernardino, California, my family lived off base, "on the economy," as the military said, and I was suddenly attending Del Rosa Elementary with kids who mocked my southern accent, especially the over-enunciated way I'd been taught to say "the" with a biblical long *e* sound, like *thee*, while they used the casual and, I thought, rudely dismissive, short *e*: *thuh*. The most searing expression of contempt in my sixth-grade class was "farmer," and every time I opened my mouth, I revealed myself as a farmer, which I had up to that year thought a noble profession. "How could we eat without farmers?" my teachers in North Carolina had asked, though North Carolina's most famous and lucrative agricultural product was tobacco and the only field trips we took, other than to the Coca-Cola bottler, were to tobacco auctions and curing barns.

At Del Rosa Elementary when baseball teams were selected, the captains usually walked off with their players and left me standing alone on the playground, unselected. I was astoundingly uncoordinated, perhaps as the result of being born prematurely—that's what my mother thought. I was useless at sports. I retreated to the green bench beside our classroom and to my books with despair and relief.

One morning, over the top of my book, I saw a teacher walking across the asphalt toward the green bench. Sensing the purpose in her stride, I pretended to concentrate on my book while glancing at the ground, looking for her feet to come into view. Boys were not allowed *not* to play games. I'd been breaking the rules and now I'd been caught.

"Get your nose out of that book and go play with the other kids," she said. It was meant as gruff kindness, but what did she expect me to do?

I wandered down to the swing sets, because no one was there, sat on a swing and swung back and forth desultorily. She was watching me. I swung, cried a little, and sniffled until recess was over, then lined up with the rest of the kids and filed back into the classroom. The next day I took my book back to my spot. The teacher who had rousted me the day before glanced in my direction once or twice, but I could see she'd given up.

Like most adults, including my parents, she was probably reluctant to stop a boy from reading, a reverence I counted on to get out of things I didn't want to do. I let them think reading was work, learning, ambition—though it was always pleasure and only incidentally edifying. As soon as I could read, I retreated into books for the comfort of worlds that were comprehensible. I might not understand everything in the book I was reading, but I could understand the arc of the story. This was not true in life, which had no arc I could see. Books told me why people did what they did. In life, my parents' and my teachers' thoughts were a mystery, and most of what they did, kind or callous, a surprise. Books gave me an illusion of order, and step by slow step they taught me how to interpret what I saw: to see that the coach's crispness didn't mean he disliked me but considered me irrelevant; that the tightness of the lunch lady's lips meant she didn't like smacking food onto plastic trays for a living; that Mrs. Porter's constant anger, though often triggered by a student whispering in class, really came from somewhere else; that Mr. Alvin's long stories about serving in Korea meant he was bored to stupefaction after twenty years of teaching fractions and he really didn't much care anymore if we learned them or not. Books helped me understand that Mrs. Thompkins, who thought I was mean, was an easily frazzled woman and that only some of her rage against me was caused by what I'd done.

Soon after we moved to California, I discovered books in the library by the great comedians of my parents' generation: Fred Allen, Sam Levenson, Steve Allen, Bob Hope, Jack Benny, and Jack Paar. I was astounded that men my father's age could tell jokes one after the other, mock themselves, and treat their dignity as something to cast away and then pull back like a yo-yo. They turned their sense of self into a toy and played with it. These comedians didn't see their self-respect as a bulwark against the world. They used humor to clear some ground in the world for them to stand on, a trick I wanted to learn—and of course they made me laugh.

I practically memorized two books that came as part of a six-books-for-only-ninety-nine-cents enticement to join the Book of the Month Club: *Bennett Cerf's Bumper Crop* ("His 5 biggest best-sellers, complete and unabridged in 2 volumes") and a collection of hillbilly anecdotes called *Tall Tales from the High Hills*. I assume the books were my mother's choice. Cerf's omnibus was packed with anecdotes from a literary milieu so foreign I thought of it as Oz—skyscrapers, subways, cocktails, celebrities, and anecdotes about Ernest Hemingway's chest hair—while the other rollicked with the thumb-in-your-eye humor of my Georgia relatives: one world was sophisticated and beckoning while the other rejected and mocked that world. Both seemed right to me. To laugh, you have to stand outside yourself and look at what is happening now as transient, passing so quickly as to be already past—and I was scrambling toward that vantage point. In my scramble, I was assisted by elephants.

Q: What's gray and dangerous?
A: An elephant with a machine gun.

Q: Why'd the elephant paint his toenails red?
A: So he could hide in a cherry tree.

Elephant jokes became a national craze the year I entered Del Vallejo Junior High in San Bernardino, and I was enraptured.

The first elephant joke I ever heard was almost like the first chicken joke I'd heard, the one about the chicken and its fixation on roads: How do you stop an elephant from charging? Take away his credit card. The answer is probably figure-out-able if you are alert to the double meaning of "charge." But what about "How do you catch an elephant?" "Hide in the grass and make a noise like a peanut." Or even sillier: "How's an elephant different from peanut butter?" "An elephant doesn't stick to the roof of your mouth." The jokes are so far beyond logic—and then so far beyond rudimentary illogic!—that you have to be given the answers to know them. You have to be instructed.

When I heard kids telling these jokes, fascination got the best of my self-consciousness, and I edged into the circle to listen. I didn't mind saying "I don't know" to riddles even if I already knew the answers because, as the social inferior of the group, it cost me nothing to play the straight man. Another voice to swell the laughter is always welcome. The cool guy or the pretty girl may eye you for a moment, but they almost always decide that a larger audience beats a smaller one. If you laugh appreciatively, as I did, you are welcome to join and welcome to come back. Sooner or later, you get a chance to tell your own joke. The jokers want to laugh too.

Hide in the Grass and Make a Noise like a Peanut

In a long pause after a joke, making sure I was not jumping in front of someone else with a riddle to tell, I leaned over the outdoor lunch table and asked, "Why don't elephants like to wear black lace panties?"

I was so nervous I could taste the fish sticks from lunch ascend to the back of my tongue before someone said, "I don't know."

With what I thought a raffish arching of my right eyebrow, I said, "Who says they don't like black lace panties?" I do not remember where I had first heard the joke, but the self-mocking lasciviousness of the delivery was stolen from Johnny Carson, who had taken over as host of *The Tonight Show* a year or two earlier.

They laughed rich, unfeigned, unforced, give-yourself-over-to-it laughter, and though I didn't trust the acceptance to last past the fifteen or twenty seconds of laughter, it did. I didn't become a popular kid, but I noticed that a couple of the girls' eyes, as they passed over me, no longer narrowed at the corners. Now, when I joined the jokers, I no longer had to work my way into the circle. The other kids scooted over and made room for me.

Joke telling was a perfect way to learn how to talk to other kids. With a joke, you get everyone's attention without being the center of attention yourself. The joke is the focus. If people laugh, they are sharing your pleasure at the thing itself, and some of the credit washes over you too. Even if the joke tanks, people's razzing is usually good-natured joshing, not real animosity, and it's aimed at the joke more than the teller. I watched the listeners intently and tailored the jokes to what I saw, speeding up if they looked bored, slowing down at complicated and crucial parts of the joke, and pausing to build suspense.

Though I'd rather have been one of the boys who could smack a baseball solidly with a bat, my talent, it seemed, was telling jokes. I was fascinated with them as mechanisms—machines made of words, to use William Carlos Williams's definition of poetry. I tinkered with them as obsessively as other boys enjoyed taking apart radios, jack-in-the-boxes, and frogs to see what was inside. In bed at night, walking home from school, sitting in church, I sharpened the details of jokes, changing the settings, naming the characters after kids in my classes, and altering elements that had flopped the last time. I didn't even have to try to memorize jokes. After I heard a joke, I, like an elephant, never forgot.

Other kids knew a few elephant jokes, but I knew them all. I even persuaded my mother to buy me a book of elephant jokes. I had to cash in my birthday wish to do it, and still it took some lobbying, arguing, and whining because Mom did not—emphatically *did not*—see the point in spending good money on books. That's what the library is for.

"But, Mom, it isn't in the library yet. I checked."

"They'll get it sooner or later." She always said that. "Now, hush. You've got a birthday coming up and maybe we'll see about it then."

I still remember the cheesy black-and-white drawings of elephants with machine guns and elephants hiding in the cherry trees. I was embarrassed by the drawings. They took the jokes I was enthralled with and treated them as if they were just something dumb for kids, even though I was a kid and I loved the jokes and I knew they were stupid. But that was the point, wasn't it? I remember asking other kids, "How do you kill a blue elephant?" They hesitated, and before they could even say, "I don't know," I said, "Shoot it with a blue elephant gun." Then, quickly, "How do you kill a red elephant?" When they said, "Shoot it with a red elephant gun?" with real glee and false scorn, I screamed, "No! You squeeze its trunk till it turns blue and then shoot it with a *blue* elephant gun"—and we all cackled together.

Elephant jokes mock logic, deliberately deranging the senses of sense. They are an adolescent intellectual's version of spinning around till you fall down. The jokes partake of surrealism, which was famously defined by the Comte de Lautreamont as "the chance meeting on a dissecting table of a sewing machine and an umbrella." What's gray, stands in a river when it rains, and doesn't get wet? An elephant with an umbrella. Determinedly capricious, elephant jokes are an inside game—much funnier if only one person doesn't know the joke and everyone else yells the answer in his face. If you ask someone why elephants can't be policemen, the punch line is not really funny, but it's funny to inflict your private knowledge on a listener: because they can't hide behind billboards! I was interested in seeing who'd go along with the absurdity of the initiation into false knowledge and who twisted his lips, sneered, "That's just stupid," and stalked off. The rejection stings briefly, sure; but the sneerers were declaring themselves serious people, non-laughers. It's useful to know who those people are.

Traditional riddles are difficult, but fair. But the echt elephant jokes deconstruct riddles. They are so arbitrary that you couldn't possibly work out the answer. Their whole purpose seems to be to display your ignorance. Answering the unanswerable question for his listener, the joke teller is a teacher correcting a dim-witted student.

In school, I learned that many countries counted bauxite as their chief export without ever being told what bauxite was. Ditto milo. Flying buttresses? Doric, Ionic, and the other kind of column? "The mitochondria are the powerhouses of the cell," I wrote on test after test, wondering what it meant. Though I knew iambic pentameter was what Shakespeare wrote, I had no idea what it was, how it worked, or why I should give a flip—and I doubted the teachers knew either. Just what did Paul Revere, Molly Pitcher, Betsy Ross, Patrick Henry, Sojourner Truth, Buffalo Bill, Annie Oakley, Walter Winchell, and Abner Ducking Fubbleday actually *accomplish* that was so damn great? John Hancock had a cool signature that I tried to imitate for a couple of weeks in sixth grade, but Hancock's John

Hancock seemed to be the only reason he was included on posterity's pop quiz. Virginia Dare, Crispus Attucks, George Armstrong Custer, Davy Crockett, Jim Bowie, and what's-his-name Travis's renown derived from obstructing the paths of armed men who outnumbered them. I was unimpressed with George Washington Carver's wizardry with peanuts, whatever it was, and though I thought it was just fine that Helen Keller could spell *water*, I couldn't for the life of me figure out why that made her important.

I knew that the trivium and quadrivium—the two stages of the seven liberal arts in medieval education—were very, very important, but if I'd ever been asked what they were, I'd have had as much chance answering as I did when I was first asked how an elephant is like a banana. They are both yellow. Except for the elephant. I did love to say *twivium* and *quadwivium*, over and over again in an Elmer Fudd voice, much to the annoyance of my teachers, and long past the time when even my most easily amused friends had hardened their hearts against these particular bon mots. But it was the comic changeability of their sound that makes them stick in my head to this day, long after they've lost any association with grammar, logic, and rhetoric—let alone arithmetic, geometry, music, and astronomy.

The elephant riddles spoofed not just the questions the teachers asked and the whole experience of education, but thinking itself. At first, I was impressed with logic, this "thinking clearly," which teachers and my parents made such a big honking deal about. Logic was, I first thought, like a train. Get on it and the rails would carry everyone to the same destination, and when they got there they'd see it was the only place to be. But I soon understood that, outside arithmetic class, logic was more like a taxi. You told it where to take you, and it took you there. If you were in favor of the death penalty, it found a street that led to the electric chair and nailed the accelerator to the floorboard. If you hated the death penalty, it took the same street just as fast, but in the opposite direction. Sure, I could see that logic was useful, but it never did anything surprising. But messing with logic—thinking things that were anti-rational—now *that* lightened the leaden step of dialectics, put swan's wings on reason's nine-pound hammer, and made causality turn off the interstate and career down a dark dirt road with the speedo's needle pegged into the triple digits. Why do ducks have flat feet? From stomping out forest fires. Why do elephants have flat feet? Stomping out burning ducks. A joke gets you a roller-coaster-with-a-Mobius-strip-twist thrill ride of anti-logic, ending in a laugh, because you return to where you started, but upside down. What does logic get you? A disquisition on how ducks have, over many millennia, evolved flat feet to help them swim.

At school, you learn to be a member of the group of people who know certain stuff—science, history, literature, and who Abner Doubleday was. Elephant riddles were a reductio ad absurdum of that process. You subject yourself to the joke teller's arbitrary knowledge so others will then come to you for answers. To be superior, you first have to be subordinate. To be active, you must first be passive. The pure caprice of elephant jokes gave me the sense that we jokers were enrolled in a free-floating and oddly democratic club, and yet exclusive, too, because the jocks, hoods, and class officers, who didn't care for the silliness we valued, excluded themselves.

If jokes were my first step out of social isolation, they were also my way out of books. My language, even by the time I was eleven, had grown bookish and artificial. The vocabularies of Robert Louis Stevenson, Walter Scott, or Sir Thomas Malory rocketed around my head and occasionally burst from my mouth. I noticed the startled look on my fifth-grade teacher's face when I asked permission to go to the restroom because I needed to "make water," but I didn't know why she was startled. I suffered awkward moments before I learned that *zounds, nay, nary, grand,* and *bloody* were best left on the pages where I had met them. "I had nary an inkling that such a grand idea could go so bloody cockeyed" may be a sentence I never uttered, though I did make, separately, every single gaffe in it.

A year or two later, when I was deep in the hard-boiled thrillers of Hammett, Chandler, and Ross Macdonald, it seemed natural to tell my friend that going trick-or-treating was jake with me, to inform my mother that I couldn't go to the matinee if she didn't give me some scratch, and to warn a Dumb Dora in my seventh-grade class I was going to smack her in the puss if she didn't stop ragging me and vamoose—natural, that is, until I actually said them. These slips drew looks of strained forbearance, like the overly patient expressions on adults' faces when five-year-olds explained the plot of a cartoon or when the retarded boy in my Sunday school class took off his shoes and socks and started counting to ten on his toes while the rest of us were singing. But as soon as I started telling jokes, I began paying more attention to how the kids around me talked. People drew back from you if you pitched your vocabulary too high, wound your sentences too tight, or recited a joke rotely.

I also paid attention to what the jokes were about. A joke can be told well or poorly, but it has to be *about* something. The more nervous-making the subject matter, the tighter the jack-in-the-box spring is compressed—and the more forcefully jack leaps out. So of course I liked the edgy jokes best, the ones that sidled up against the taboos that I was just becoming conscious of.

The elephant joke I thought funniest is "What's that black stuff between an elephant's toes?" "Slow natives." I see now that the joke built part of its hilarity on racism, and I indistinctly sensed then that the smug superiority of an American schoolboy toward the squashed natives drove some of my laughter. The joke affirmed the naïve racism I absorbed through Tarzan and Jungle Jim movies, which I'd watched intently as a young kid. Natives run in wild panic ahead of stampeding elephants, saved only by their speed, despite having lived around elephants all their lives. At the time, though, I focused on the black stuff between the elephants' toes. I was a boy. Gross stuff enchanted me. At the end of almost every day with my feet bound into dark, damp shoes, I wrenched off my sneakers, peeled off my socks, and found black lines of sloughed skin between my toes.

It was filth, filth made from my body. It represented the corruption of the flesh that preachers sorrowed over in church, but it was also farcical. Toe jam fell below the solemnity of Saint Paul's animadversions of the "works of the flesh": "fornication, uncleanness, immodesty, luxury, witchcrafts, enmities, contentions, emulations, wraths, quarrels, dissensions, sects, envies, murders, drunkenness, revelings, and such like." But it symbolized all those uncleannesses, and if the apostle had continued "and such like, including toe jam, snot, spit, mucus, eye buggers, gnawed fingernails, peeled blisters, dingleberries, and both number one and number two," he would have resolved some theological implications that had vexed me as a boy.

Toe jam was oddly sinister then, but also gross, comic, and mysterious. The joke about the poky Africans reduced human life to sloughed skin, and I feared that, in life, I was a slow native, one who'd be trampled by the ambitions and talents of other people. And of course I was afraid of death itself, the elephant that tramples and smashes us all to black stuff between its toes. My mind careened through these possibilities, never settling on any one for long, and the unsteady equation of myself with natives, toe jam, failure, and death, along with the image of a ridiculously outsized elephant who didn't even notice people smushed between its toes, made me laugh. In the shifty joke, I glimpsed fears that I didn't want to think about nakedly because they were too frightening without some clothes thrown over them. I was becoming a teenager, a time when taboos are as fascinating as they are frightening, and they're a potent force in jokes.

Death, religion, race, and sex make jokes funny because fear, tripped as it stalks toward us, makes the reversal of expectation more powerful. It's funny when a clown trips over his big shoes, funnier when a banker in a bowler slips on a banana peel, and funniest of all when a boogeyman jumps out of the bushes, skids on wet leaves, and falls on his face as he's shouting "Boo." Our relief at not being harmed makes us laugh even harder because we know we might not be laughing at all the next time the boogeyman jumps out at us.

Death is a fine taboo, but sex is finer. My joke about elephants and their dislike for black lace panties went over so well at the junior-high lunch table because it nudged up against the naughtiness of sex, though I was myself as sexually uninformed as it was possible to be. I affected a jaunty knowingness that in retrospect is funnier than the joke, which worked despite the fact that the boy telling it didn't really understand it. But I knew enough to evoke the taboo subject of sex and twist it for a laugh. The joke, though small, lived larger than its medium.

Neither did I, as a teenager, entirely understand this joke: "What does an elephant use for a tampon?" Answer: A sheep. I told the joke a time or two, uneasily, and laughed at it; when I laughed, it was uncomfortably and self-consciously. Until I was married, menstruation was a mystery. I understood the physiology, but not what it meant in practical terms. So, though I seldom repeated the joke, I thought about it a lot. I was tickled by the image I concocted of an elephant grabbing a sheep with its trunk and jamming it up under its tail, and the white sheep turning red. But when the mysterious sexual opening was enlarged to the point that it took a sheep to cover it, I squirmed, nervous both about what the joke implied about the largeness and bestial nature of sex, and afraid that someone more honest than I would say, "I don't get it" and ask me to explain. I could have babbled something like, "See, elephants and sheep don't go together naturally, and so it's funny that an elephant would have to use a sheep for something an elephant doesn't need, and take it and jam it into her private parts." True enough, as far as it goes. But isn't the point of the joke that human fastidiousness about sexual taboos, like the "uncleanness" of menstruation, is unknown to animals, and our ideas of civilization are mocked when we see an elephant try to find a natural equivalent to a tampon? That was a possible truth I was not ready to entertain or be entertained by.

Despite my queasiness with the sheep, most elephant jokes were becoming a bit tame for my changing taste. Before long, elephant jokes were on TV and in magazines. They were printed in the newspapers. What was the fun of knowing something that everybody else already knew? By then I'd moved on to the dead-baby jokes, mutilation jokes, and Helen Keller jokes that boys began telling when I was in junior high and high school. I laughed at them hysterically, in both senses of the word, with a sense of pleasurable fear that approached panic. I was thrilled as what could be said slid toward the unspeakable, the unthinkable, and the forbidden. These subversive jokes were thoroughly disapproved of by adults and squeamish kids, unlike the Little Moron, Polack, and elephant jokes—and having to keep them secret from adults sharpened the edge of laughter.

Dead-baby jokes, quadriplegic jokes, and Helen Keller jokes were over the line. They could get you yelled at, smacked, wept over, prayed for, and sent to bed hungry. At least in my house. I loved having the power, even if I knew better than to use it, to provoke such a passionate response. I loved being wicked without doing anything mean. The jokes were so far beyond common decency that they always startled me, no matter how often I told them, and the more graphic they were the better I liked them. My favorite was "How is a truckload of dead babies different from a truckload of bowling balls?" "You can't unload the bowling balls with a pitchfork." Because I was familiar with both bowling balls and pitchforks, I reveled in the tactile uneasiness that shuddered along my nerve endings every time I told the joke. I imagined, without intending to, what the difference would be between the tines of a pitchfork clinking against a bowling ball and sliding into baby flesh. It was unthinkable, but I thought it. Nobody else, not even the hardened thirteen-year-old joke tellers I hung out with, thought the joke was as funny as I did. I suspected they had never held a pitchfork, much less tossed hay with one, and so the visceral disgust the joke evokes was lost on them. I was thinking of myself on both sides of the pitchfork, pushing the pitchfork into the body and being the body the pitchfork slid into. I was at the age when I was beginning to see in myself the power to harm awfully and the power to be harmed awfully.

For some of the same reasons, I adored the pun in "How do you make a dead baby float?" "Two scoops dead baby. Fill with root beer." The gross—or is it sentimental?—image of a dead baby suddenly becomes grosser—cannibalism played for laughs. Sure, the idea was revolting. But by disgusting ourselves, we boys were assuring ourselves we'd never do something just because we could imagine it. Basic as it seems, the point was important to me because in church I sat through many sermons that, paraphrasing Jesus, assured me that to think something was the same as doing it. All that stood between thinking and doing was volition—as if volition was nothing! To be pure, I had to make myself an unblemished vessel, untainted in thought and deed. But my thoughts, I knew, moved in their own ways. Logic clumped along on its ordained path while imagination buzzed erratically from lilac to honeysuckle to rosebud, as well as violet, dandelion, red clover, morning glory, and all the other weeds I spent long afternoons prying out of the yard with a forked cultivator. I saw no harm in seeing where logic went—or imagination either, as long as I didn't *do* anything dumb or immoral.

With these adolescent jokes I was separating myself from the world of adults, who would be appalled, and from little kids, who wouldn't be mentally tough enough to take them. I also loved these jokes as things in and of themselves—not things of beauty exactly, though I can imagine a definition of beauty that includes their linguistic efficiency, their powerful imagery, their probing of social norms, and their provoking strong, often conflicting, emotions. Because I loved them and admired them as art and as craft, my emerging sense of discretion was balanced, and all too often outweighed, by my desire to share them. Who would laugh? How far could people be pushed? How far could I push myself? I knew not to tell them to my father, but did I dare tell them to my mother?

I sprawled across the vinyl recliner, legs flung over the arm, watching my mother, who sat in a child's rocker by the sliding glass door, using the natural light to see the sock she was darning. She was petite, heavily freckled, with auburn hair that she called red. All her life—she died of leukemia before she turned fifty—she considered herself a tomboy. She loved the small, cane-bottom rocker because it was the perfect size for her small body and it was easy to pull around the living room, from the TV set to the glass door to the telephone. I was sixteen, hesitating on the edge of a joke, trying to decide if I should tell it to her. Mom liked to feign toughness since she was raising a houseful of boys, four of us that she called "rug rats," "house apes," "yard monkeys," and "carpet munchers" when we were younger—she'd heard that last phrase and absorbed it into her vocabulary, thinking it meant something other than it does. But how tough was she with jokes?

"How do you stop a kid from running in circles?" I asked her. I paused a moment to let the question sink in.

"I don't know. How?" she said, once she determined that I was not asking for advice.

"Nail his other foot to the floor," I said.

The moment between the last words of the joke and the laugh, if there is a laugh, is a fraught and complicated expanse of time. The listener has to resolve the confusion of the joke's anti-logical logic to "get" the joke and then assent to it, if she finds it funny or clever. But the teller depends totally on the listener's willingness to go along with the joke, to play with absurdity instead of rejecting it, and then to laugh with you. It's asking a lot. Even friends who know you well might suddenly, instinctively, decide a joke about abusing and mutilating a child is revolting—and that you are a pervert for telling it. I did not want my mother to think I was a perv, but damn, I wanted to tell my joke. I'd already told it to everyone I could find to tell it to and it was burning a hole in my brain.

Her blank look crumpled into laughter, which she tried to suppress. That joke shouldn't be funny! But the natural impulse won out. She laughed, stopped to sputter, "That's terrible!" and then laughed some more. The amoral logic of the joke surprised her. For a parent who'd nailed one of her child's feet to the floor, it makes sense to solve the problem of his running in circles by nailing the other one down. For me, I couldn't imagine a house in which it was acceptable to hammer nails into the floor. As a military family, we moved a lot and Mom was scrupulous in caring for the houses we rented. She wanted her entire security deposit back.

I suspect my mother also laughed because these jokes couldn't be shared with my father. The anarchy of this kind of joke troubled his sense of a moral universe. A lot of serious people assume that anybody telling a cruel joke is in fact a perv, advocating cruelty instead of flinching from it. My mother, thank God, wasn't one of those always oh-so-serious people. Actually, I've always thought jokes affirm established morality by imagining a world so amorally unaware of our deepest convictions that we can't help laughing. Without knowing it, I was testing to see if my mother and I could share a laugh behind my father's back. It was an illicit pleasure to discover that we could laugh with each other almost like adults, just for the pure joy of laughing.

I already knew I wasn't a perv, though. I'd learned that two years before when my ninth-grade world history teacher played a recording of *Medea*, and I failed at listening to it. When the scratchy LP of Euripides's play spun around to the scene in which Medea kills her children, I began to giggle. I fought the giggles, but they burst from me in snorts and liquid sputters. Soon I was laughing desperately. Holding my sides, head down on my desk, drooling, I jerked with laughter and hated myself. Why was I helpless with amusement at a mother's anguished determination to slaughter her sons and feed them to her unfaithful husband?

The teacher raised the needle from the black groove, and the whole class, already silent, stared, waiting for me to compose myself. I expected to be slapped and shipped off to a secure facility where I could not hurt myself or others. The only place I'd ever seen people laugh the way I was laughing was on movie screens, and those laughers were homicidal lunatics with spectacular and obviously flawed master plans for world domination.

The teacher, a tall woman with a pixyish face and short chic black hair, walked to my desk, paused, and gently touched my head with one finger. I was still snorting, trying to squelch my laughter. "When we hear an event too horrible for our minds to comprehend," she said to the class, "we sometimes laugh. We refuse to accept it. We treat it like a joke." Aspirating snot, still half slobbering, I sucked my humiliating cachinnations to a halt, and wiped the desktop with my shirtsleeve. She was doing me a great kindness while also teaching me something that would be useful for the rest of my life. If I could remember the name of that magnificent woman, that splendid teacher toiling at a junior high school in France for American military dependents—and I have tried for decades to call it up—I would send her a spray of white roses every year on her birthday, and then randomly from time to time, just to surprise her.

I seized her explanation gratefully; it let me off the hook and made me look good too: I had responded so crassly to the play because I was really *more* sensitive than anyone else in the room. I suspected she was right, mostly right, but later I wondered if there weren't more to it than that. I was also laughing at the stilted language of the two boys when they figure out Mom's going to chop them into stew-sized bits. It didn't sound like anything my brothers or I would scream if we saw our mother racing toward us with a sword in her hands and crazed determination in her eyes:

> *First son:* Ah me; what can I do? Whither fly to escape my
>   mother's blows?
> *Second son:* I know not, sweet brother mine; we are lost.

"Sweet brother mine" started my giggling, but I lost control entirely when the second son cried out in terror, "Even now the toils of the sword are closing round us." The boys' languid and archaic discussion of their imminent murder triggered my laughter. The ungraspable idea of an infanticidal mother kept it going.

From my involuntary laughter and the teacher's shrewd interpretation of it, I glimpsed how life and art can be horrifying and comic at the same time. The two are bound together in art, as they are in life. Most of us don't live in a literary genre, but in a world that swerves between tragedy and comedy, as it famously does at weddings, where we often find ourselves weeping when we expect to be laughing, and laughing at funerals, where we expect to cry.

The teacher's kindness when I cracked up during *Medea* opened a deeper and stranger world of laughter than I had known before. When I discovered the almost maniacal, intoxicating laughter of the desperate, I dove into it as if it were a drug. And that's what it was, an intoxicant. It altered my consciousness; it made my world larger, richer, weirder, more frightening, and truer than what I saw.

While my mother was still laughing at the joke about the boy running in circles, I asked, "What do you do with a dead dog?" "Take it out for a drag." She doubled up. The pile of blue socks, the needle, and the black thread dangling from it, slipped off her lap and onto the carpet. She was convulsed, completely lost inside the silliness of the joke, the grotesque and oddly naïve—even innocent, if deranged—image it evoked. For the next couple of days, she looked at me from time to time, said, "Take it out for a drag," and giggled.

It was risky to tell these jokes to a woman who had lost a child, something I fretted about before I told them, but my craziness to laugh and share the laughter overwhelmed my always weak sense of discretion. This time I was right. I didn't, though, ask my usual lead-in to the dead-dog joke: "What do you buy a dead baby?" "A dead puppy." And I certainly didn't ask her, "What's red and sits in a high chair?" "A baby eating razor blades." I knew these jokes were too graphic for her, but it wasn't totally a matter of sensitivity: I also know those jokes aren't that funny.

At school being insensitive was the point. Most girls winced and left the room when we boys asked one another, "What's blue and squirms?" "A baby in a plastic bag." Their gasps, their flutters of indignation, their flouncing away from us, muttering, "You're sick," confirmed our sense of being outré, of being boys, especially since the guys I hung out with weren't athletes. We didn't have the athlete's socially acceptable way of proving our masculinity on the football field or basketball court.

Not long ago, I read a piece by a critic who said that the dead-baby and mutilation jokes arose just as abortion was first being debated openly in America. The jokes, he argued, were the country's way of beginning to work through its ambivalence and unease about abortion. Perhaps. But not for me. Growing out of childhood, physically weak, uncertain of who I was, I wanted to be a tough thinker, if not a tough guy, and what better way to show you're not soft-minded than to make fun of the most sentimentalized people who exist: babies and cripples? And Helen Keller.

I was enchanted with Helen Keller jokes from the first time someone asked, "How did Helen Keller burn her fingers?" "Trying to read a waffle iron." The joke was absurd, with a cruel edge, and to this day I can't find the slightest sparkle of wit in it. The pleasure mostly resided in mocking a woman who had been used as a bludgeon to shame and taunt us kids. If Helen Keller, who was blind and deaf, could overcome all the terrible obstacles life had thrown in front of her, surely you, Andrew, with all the advantages you've had, could learn your multiplication tables. You could spell *Mississippi*, read Tolstoy, and earn at least a B+ in algebra. Even when Helen Keller's moral superiority wasn't stated—and it usually was—the point was implicit in every classroom performance of *The Miracle Worker*, every assigned reading of Keller's autobiography, and every book report on yet another children's book about her. Still, with all the praise that was heaped on her, all the saintliness attributed to her, I was never certain what Helen Keller had done other than be blind and deaf and learn how to read. What was I supposed to do? Poke my eyes out and jab a pencil in my ears so I could get credit for doing normal things? (Apparently blind kids had it even worse than the rest of us. Georgina Kleege in *Blind Rage: Letters to Helen Keller* gets down to business in her very first paragraph, telling Keller, "I hated you because you were always held up to me as a role model, and one who set such an impossibly high standard of cheerfulness in the face of adversity. . . . 'Yes, you're blind, but poor little Helen Keller was blind and deaf, and no one heard her complain.'")

Mom laughed when I told her the waffle-iron joke. As a country girl from Georgia, she bore a chip on her shoulder against the celebrated and the intellectual. So I asked if she knew how Helen Keller's parents punished her. They rearranged the furniture. How did Helen Keller burn her ear? Answering the iron. How did Helen Keller burn her other ear? The guy called back. Mom laughed less enthusiastically then. But I plowed ahead with the irritating tenacity we jokers are famous for. How did Helen Keller burn her face? Bobbing for french fries.

Mom pursed her lips and darted me a cautioning look. That joke had gone too far. Yes, that's why I liked it. It was so grotesque that it became a parody of cruelty jokes. It established a boundary by crossing it and scuffed its feet on the line as it crossed it. It showed that even jokes that make a point of going too far can go too far. But that joke inside the joke was a pleasure I didn't expect others to share.

More idiosyncratically, I laughed at the joke about Helen Keller's burned face because I was fascinated by deep-fat fryers, which are dangerous and therefore potentially funny. In high school I worked at a hamburger joint, and one of my jobs was to man the deep-fat. On my first day on the job, when I casually plopped down on a metal bench next to the fryer, the shift foreman slipped a handful of ice into the hot fat. Everyone jumped back, and before I registered what was happening, scalding grease sprayed a nasty archipelago of red islands up my left arm, to the merriment of everyone, including, eventually, me.

As new workers came on the payroll, I obsessively repeated the joke. I was a jerk about it. Hell, I'd laughed at being hurt, so could they. But in lulls between rushes of customers, I sometimes stared into the hot grease, watching it roil and sizzle around a load of frozen potatoes. The terrible image of Helen Keller plunging her face into the fryer leapt to my mind, and with it came the empathetic vision of my own face submerged in the boiling oil—and I shuddered at what the imagination was capable of, and at the frailty of human flesh.

In "What to Do with Helen Keller Jokes," Mary Klages says that telling Helen Keller jokes "makes us feel safe, adequate, and competent, as we realize that we can successfully perform tasks, like shopping and answering the phone, that left this noble American heroine completely bewildered." It's not a coincidence, I think, that jokes ridiculing the competence of a famous role model became popular just after baby boomers like me learned how to answer the phone, walk to the bathroom without a night-light, and make waffles, and right before we learned to hold jobs and make french fries. From time to time, throughout childhood and well into high school, I'd clench my eyes shut when no one was home and wander around the house—go to the bathroom, maybe try to make a bologna sandwich—testing out what it must be like to be blind, imagining I was Helen Keller. But I could never do it long. Going backward and relearning skills I'd already learned strained my sense of transparent mastery of everyday life; the exercise in infirmity was too unsettling.

The sick jokes—dead baby, Helen Keller, and mutilated-boy jokes—mock human frailty. They became popular when we boomers were, as adolescents, starting to grasp that our bodies weren't invincible and our lives would have a terminus, even if we couldn't yet see it over the horizon. Some of us, though, had to toughen our minds to that knowledge.

Those of us who grew up in evangelical churches were reminded almost every week, sometimes two and three times a week, that we were mortal and we would die. We were steeped in the apostle Paul's fierce insistence on the weakness and evils of the flesh. As a practical matter, our preachers knew they could more easily persuade apprehensive teenagers to walk down the aisle and accept

Jesus if the sermon hammered home what we were beginning to comprehend with new emotional force: life is fleeting, death eternal, and the body begins to decay while we're still in it.

We may be proud of our strength, they preached, but strength could be taken from us in an instant by a car wreck or a fall from a bike, and we could be left dead or imprisoned in a bed or a wheelchair. Even in the normal course of life we'd weaken as we aged, until even breath itself was taken from us.

We may be proud of our intelligence. Yes, we might think we were so smart that our intelligence couldn't be taken from us. But time and chance happeneth to all men. The nursing homes are full not just of broken bodies. Also there, and even sadder, are men and women with perfectly sound bodies, staring into space. They look just like you and me, but they do not possess the wit to feed or wash or wipe themselves. Everything can be taken from us in the blink of an eye.

Morbid? Sure. But true, too, and after one of these sermons I, like almost everyone I knew, staggered down the aisle, blubbering in terror, to be baptized and saved from the terrible fate of living in a body made of perishable flesh. I came almost immediately to doubt that anything was eternal, while still frantically hoping I was wrong, but I could see my body was a terribly flimsy abode for my soul, a house made of straw, not brick, and I was only renting, not owning.

Real life was every bit as morbid as my jokes. The year my family moved to Alabama, 1966, Charles Woods ran for the Democratic gubernatorial nomination against George Wallace. Woods appeared regularly on television, in rambling half-hour commercials that he bought with his own money. I watched, horrified and fascinated. Charles Woods looked like a half-melted blob of shiny, pitted pink plastic, splotched with red. I'm not sure how I extrapolated the colors. On our black-and-white TVs, Woods looked, as one of my friends said, like Mr. Potato Head without some of the plastic facial features, as he talked calmly, if stiffly, about how sound business practices would solve all of Alabama's problems.

Later, I learned he was born in a shack in Toadvine, Alabama. After his father deserted the family when Charles was five, his mother placed her two sons in a state orphanage because she could not support them. At twenty, Woods joined the Royal Canadian Air Force and later transferred to the U.S. Army Air Corps. By the time he was twenty-three, he had already piloted hundreds of trips from India to China, "flying the hump" over the Himalayas, to supply the Chinese forces of Chiang Kai-shek. It was extraordinarily hazardous duty, and on December 23, 1944, loaded with twenty-eight thousand pounds of aviation fuel, Woods crashed on takeoff and over 70 percent of his body was burned. According to his surgeon, Joseph Murray, who later received a Nobel Prize for his work in organ transplants, "The fire erased his face, destroying his nose, eyelids and ears. . . . Over the next two years, we operated twenty-four times to build Woods a new face—a new nose, eyelids, and ears—but he still looked like no one you have ever seen."

He does not say that Woods's new ears were barely more than small ridges of flesh and the black patch over his right eye was held in place with a black strap that sometimes went around and sometimes over his head. His good left eye was so oddly prominent that, when I watched him, I always thought of Poe's "The Tell-Tale Heart": "One of his eyes resembled that of a vulture—a pale blue eye with a film over it. Whenever it fell upon me my blood ran cold." Despite his terrible scars, Woods, a hero by any measure, went on to make a fortune from house construction and a television station in Dothan. He also fathered a large brood of children—seven or so—whom he once arrayed before the TV cameras, leading many of us callous souls to speculate how one particular appendage survived the fire.

Only fifteen years old and new to Alabama, I failed to grasp that he was running to unseat George Wallace, which would have been a service to America greater even than his military service. What I knew was that a man who looked like Death's own horrifying self took over our TV from time to time. So I was not surprised when one of my friends at school asked, "Why can Charles Woods never be governor?"

"I don't know."

"Nobody'll let him kiss their baby."

Another friend showed me a joke that I liked so much I took it over as my own. I drew an eye patch on my thumb with a jagged mouth under it. Holding my inked thumb before people, I said, "Hi, I'm Charles Woods. Friends, Alabamians, countrymen, lend me your ears." Mom, shocked, chuckled at that.

Now I'm nearly appalled at my callousness. Any joker has to be worried about the truth behind Goethe's chilling judgment that "Nothing shows a man's character more than what he laughs at." But I'm only *nearly* appalled because I remember what I was thinking then. I could have *been* Helen Keller. I could *still* be Charles Woods. I could be the dead baby or the armless and legless boy whose parents tossed him on the porch and called him Matt, hung him on the wall and called him Art, threw him in the pool and called him Bob. Anything that happened to them could happen to me. By telling the jokes, I sneaked up on acknowledging that life was harsh, unfair, and temporary—and that my time in the world was unlikely to culminate on a positive note. By laughing at cruelty and fate, you could pretend to be superior to it, and yet what fueled the laughter was the absurdity of laughing: nothing tames death. So you might as well laugh, brother, and strengthen your mind against your own vanishing.

Three

Gladly, the Cross-Eyed Bear

There must be no foul or salacious talk or coarse jokes—all this is
wrong for you; there should rather be thanksgiving.

Ephesians 5:4

My mother loved to tell me about the boy who wanted a puppy for
Christmas, and I brooded on the anecdote as if it were the medita-
tion of the day from *Guideposts* or *The Upper Room*, the monthly
devotional magazines that my father left on the back of the toilet for
me and my brothers to read.

If the little boy really wanted a puppy, his mother said, he
should get down on his knees and ask God to give him one. Night
after night, before going to bed, the boy besieged heaven, praying
for a puppy, praying fervently and long, confident that God was
hearing him.

But at Christmas there was no puppy under the tree. As the
boy played contentedly with the toys he did get, his mother said, "I
guess God didn't answer your prayers."

"He answered me," the boy told her. "He just said no."

"That's a cute story, don't you think?" my mother said, chuckling, then glancing at me to see if I got it.

I got it. It was a moral. It was an Aesop's fable for little Christians. It was her way of telling me that I wasn't going to get the puppy I'd been whining for and that I might as well stop walking around the house belting out, "How much is that doggie in the window, the one with the waggly tail?"

My mother loved the anecdote because it showed a model child bowing humbly to God's better judgment. It also conflates parents and God, because it's not God who drives to the pound and gets the mutt. It's Mom and Dad. How stupid did she think I was?

I was indignant that the mother in the story was just pushing the blame for her decision off on the Almighty. Even when I was ten, the psychological vacuity of the weakly humorous anecdote and the emotional manipulation in it left me raw with contempt. *That smarmy boy knew nothing of desire and disappointment,* I thought, though I couldn't find the words for it then. I knew what it was like to have balked passions—or at least, balked greed—and I knew that even on those rare times when I accepted disappointment with seeming grace, I did it only after swallowing a bitter mouthful of resentment. The little plaster saint of Mom's joke infuriated me, but he also admonished me irrefutably, and I bowed to the point: Prayers were not always granted. We are guaranteed only that God will listen, not that he will oblige. I hated the joke for making me see what no sermon, no matter how compelling, would ever make me acknowledge, much less understand.

At least the pious anecdote gave me something to chew over. Humor and religion were married, it seemed, but not altogether faithfully. Behind religion's back, the really funny jokes went on savage benders every Saturday night with punch lines of easy virtue, and then on Sunday morning they slumped in the back row of church, nursing a hangover, and worrying if they had caught a dose.

The jokes I heard in Sunday school, by contrast, were so insipid that I didn't even groan when I heard them.

Where is baseball first mentioned in the Bible? In the big inning, Eve stole first, Adam stole second, and Cain struck out Abel.

Where is tennis first mentioned in the Bible? When Joseph served in Pharaoh's court.

Who was the greatest comedian in the Bible? Samson. He brought the house down.

Where is cannibalism first mentioned? 2 Kings 8:1.

Who is the fastest man in the Bible? Adam. He was first in the human race.

Who was the first person to drive a sports car in the Bible? Joshua. His Triumph was heard throughout the land.

Where was Solomon's temple located? On the side of his head.

What kind of car did Jesus drive? He drove the moneychangers out of his father's house in his Fury.

(I have to admit, though, that I was fond of the imaginary Christian plush toy we joked about: "Gladly, the Cross-Eyed Bear"—a pun on the hymn "Gladly the Cross I'd Bear.")

Still, the bad jokes in Sunday school topped the torpor of sitting in church, waiting for something interesting to happen. No matter what I did, I was bored, bored, bored. I read the bulletin till I was furious with tedium. Who cared when the Adult Bible Study group was meeting and who had donated the lovely floral displays at the front of the church? If I kicked the pew in front of me or jostled my brother, trying to claim more space, Mom pinched me, thumped me with her finger, popped my thigh, or jabbed me in the side with her elbow. "Sit still and pay attention," she hissed. "Just wait till I get you home, young man!"

Momentarily chastened, I studied the pictures in my Bible of Jesus blessing the children, Jesus feeding the hungry multitudes, Jesus bearing the cross to Golgotha, and then I quietly creased the bulletin into a minutely pleated accordion and silently tore it into one-eighth-inch strips. Sometimes I chewed the strips as I tore them off. Sometimes I took the damp paper out of my mouth and studied the impressions my teeth had clenched into the sodden wad of pulp. *Maybe I am destined to be a dentist*, I thought.

The preacher's microscopically close analysis of Bible verses went on and on. The state of our souls—miserable—was too depressing to contemplate. And the terrors of judgment and the increasing likelihood of my burning eternally in perdition—"like a pork roast on a grill"—disturbed me so much that I concentrated on not hearing them. But early in the sermon, warming us up for the brimstone to follow, the preacher often paused and smiled self-deprecatingly, letting us know he was going to tell a story. I stopped fidgeting and listened. Sometimes he simply told a cute anecdote about something that had happened in the news that week, but often he told a joke. And then I knew I'd have something to think about for the rest of the sermon.

Many times I heard from Baptist pulpits the story—it was a great crowd pleaser—of the farmer caught in a flood. As the waters rose around his isolated farmhouse, the farmer moved to the second story of his house and then onto the roof, where he perched, prayed, and waited for God to save him.

His neighbors rowed over in their fishing skiff and asked if he wanted to get in with them, but he replied no, he had prayed to God for help and God was going to save him.

They left, and as the waters kept rising, the farmer prayed even more fervently. The sheriff's department puttered up in a motorboat, rescuing stranded flood victims, and again the farmer sent them away. He had asked God to save him and he was waiting for God.

Swirling brown water now lapped onto the roof, and a National Guard helicopter circled overhead. Through a loudspeaker, the guardsmen offered to send down a ladder. But once more the pious old farmer, who had climbed onto the chimney, waved them off.

As the water sucked at his boots and then started creeping up the legs of his overalls, the farmer, giving way to doubt, called up to the sky, "God, I thought you were going to rescue me."

The sky opened. A bright light shined out of the sky, and God said, "I've already sent two boats and a helicopter. . . ."

When I first heard the story of the stranded farmer, I laughed and thought what I was supposed to think: *Yeah, why can't the old guy just accept the way God has answered his prayer? God helps those who help themselves.* But as the preacher moved on into his sermon, I kept pondering the story, worrying over it. I knew I was supposed to take the obvious lesson from it and move on. But I saw the farmer's point of view. When God admonished the presumptuous farmer, he was also correcting our definition of grace. Was the story telling us that the days of direct, divine intervention in our lives were over and we could only count on each other? Did God now only work through people? Why wouldn't the farmer, after a lifetime of belief and obedience to God, want the Almighty to reveal himself in his servant's time of greatest need? I was only twelve, but I wanted to see God. I wanted that reassurance. If God only worked through people, maybe there was no God. Maybe those saviors in boats and helicopters weren't God's agents but just people doing their jobs. That was a hard and frightening idea for a boy brought up as a believer.

Hadn't God sent this flood, as he had sent the flood in Genesis and then intervened to save the one good man, Noah, in his ark filled with animals? But instead of being Noah, as he had imagined, this poor proud farmer found himself to be Job, a man endangered so he would ask for help and be taught a lesson that would edify others. Under all my thinking lay the Calvinist understanding that everything is a test from God. And that led to an inescapable and terrifying corollary: God's grace and God's malice are often indistinguishable. If the farmer hadn't asked, would God have let him drown? And what about all the other people who were flooded out of their houses—what did they learn?

Maybe I wouldn't have worried over this joke so much, but these questions about who and what God is and how he works in the world were exactly the questions troubling me daily. I was surrounded by believers who never seemed anguished in their faith. The gap between the hard, obvious God of the Old Testament and the vague God of the modern world troubled me. The chasm between story and actuality, joke and the real world, was what I was struggling to plumb. Where did the one stop and the other begin? Where did they overlap and what did it mean when and that they did?

Nobody raised questions about the preacher's jokes and anecdotes. Nobody else, so far as I could tell, even had these questions waft through their minds, like eye-floaters drifting through their field of vision, so I assumed my mind was aberrant. In fact, the apostle Paul told me that I was a sinner for thinking such thoughts, so I kept quiet. But I could not stop my mind from thinking, and I began to perceive its processes as both the essence of myself and somehow autonomous, beyond my control.

If you think I'm making too much of a simple joke, you are of course right—and wrong. The preachers analyzed the parables of Jesus much more closely, and that joke is nothing if not a parable. Biblical exegesis considers everything. As a boy, I heard—twice, from different preachers in different states—sermons that explicated the Lord's Prayer one phrase at a time over a year. Week One: a thirty-minute sermon on the phrase "Our Father." Week Two: "Who Art in Heaven." Week Fifty-two: "Amen." I have heard Christ's parables analyzed from just about every angle imaginable, including the story of the prodigal son considered from the viewpoint of the pigs in their sty as the destitute drunk settles down next to them for the night. "Whoa," said the pigs, "why is this Jew, a man who has abjured pork in all its forms, sleeping here in the mud with us? Is he trying to steal our slop? There must be something wrong with him." I learned the same kind of close reading from a book suggested by my pastor, who had noticed my susceptibility to jokes: *The Gospel According to Peanuts*.

The congregation always laughed at the joke about the farmer in the flood, though, and I laughed with them. So did my father. In church, my father relaxed. At a joke from the pulpit, his round pink face lit up. Jokes told in the sanctuary would not be sexual or violent, and they always made a point, a point that was instructive, moral, and, at least on the surface, tame. The anarchy of pointless wordplay and bizarre imagery was left outside the vestibule. Church humor did not tear down; it built up.

When my father chuckled, I studied how his lips drew upward as the cheek muscles lifted toward his eyes and the flow of blood into his cheeks made his face glow rosy and soft, unlike the vibrant red flush when he got angry. The near silence of his amusement fascinated me. I laughed from my gut. I was an hysterical laugher. I laughed till I wept. But my father controlled his laughs as he controlled everything but his temper. In church, an amused chuckle wouldn't diminish his dignity and authority in the eyes of his children. When he smiled in church, he relaxed his jaw enough that I could see the blue breach where one of his molars had been extracted.

The death of my sister sowed such hidden sorrow that I grew up in a house deeply deficient in what Arthur Koestler called the "luxury reflex" of laughter. But when my father's brothers, Uncle Herschel and Uncle Bob, blew through town, mild anarchy was loosed upon our home. Though Herschel was a Methodist minister and Bob later became one, they always said it was my father who was the religious Hudgins, the one who everyone assumed would be a preacher, a possible life that bewildered me with its unsuitability. Dad had the faith and the intensity of a preacher, but he entirely lacked the glad-handing gifts of the salesman, the ease with other people, and the stage presence that good preachers relish. Around his brothers and their faith, though, he relaxed and laughed, knowing their humor, like church humor, was safe. In fact, their humor often *was* church humor.

Most preachers I've known possess a finely articulated, if circumscribed, sense of humor. Humor is a staple of the pulpit, of course, but it's also social grease for people in the public eye—genial humor that is, not too judgmental, more or less harmless. It's wordplay for well-educated people who love words, stories, and public speaking, but know the bounds in which they work. Like his brothers, Dad was raised Methodist, but my mother's family was Baptist. During a Baptist service in Southern California, I was convinced of the magnitude of my sins and staggered, blubbering, down the aisle to join the church. Dad took my salvation as a sign that he should become a Baptist. After that, my Uncle Herschel, the Methodist minister, delighted in telling his newly Baptist brother the joke about the Baptist who argued that anything less than a full dunking did not count as baptism in his eyes or in the eyes of God.

A Methodist replied that he thought a little sprinkle of water on the top of the head would do the job just fine.

The outraged Baptist responded that that was ridiculous. Jesus was fully immersed by John the Baptist in the River Jordan, and we had to take Jesus as our model.

"Wouldn't it be okay to take someone in the water only up to his chest?" the Methodist asked.

"No!"

"How about to the neck?"

"No!"

"Well, how about if you held him in the water till he was almost completely immersed, with just his head barely sticking out?

"No!"

"See!" cries the Methodist, triumphantly. "I told you that the sprinkle on the top was what counted."

You have to be pretty deeply involved in church doctrine to appreciate the wit. The joke toys good-naturedly with doctrinal issues that churches and denominations split over, but, because it pokes almost as much fun at the Methodist's skewed logic as the Baptist's doctrinal vehemence, the joke's real point is that such minor issues aren't worth fighting over. While seeming to tweak my father for becoming a Baptist while his brothers had remained Methodists, Herschel was actually saying it didn't matter, and they all shared a companionable laugh.

My uncles looked like my father, but without his austere expression. Bald men with large noses, they had pink faces creased with pleasure. Would I grow up to look like them or like my father? A few years ago a friend I hadn't seen in twenty years mentioned that he had enjoyed watching my genial face age through the years in the author photos on my books. He was worried I'd be offended by his describing me as "aging," but what caught my ear was "genial." I've turned into a version of my uncles.

On the road between Herschel's parsonage and his church, there was a factory with the company's name painted on the side in huge white block letters: SMITH MANUFACTURING COMPANY. Every time we drove past—and I mean every single time—Herschel said, "So that's why there are so many of them!" He said it with such compulsive consistency that I'd bet my next paycheck he said it even when he was in the car by himself. He chuckled at his own joke, which was in fact not his but something one of his parishioners had told him years before, as he freely admitted. But he had taken it over and it never failed to amuse him. When he was moved to another church in another town, he continued to share his parishioner's witticism whenever joke-telling time came around.

When I was young I couldn't fathom why he loved this joke. But the tidiness of the pun lodged it in my head, and I've come to see how it must have pleased Herschel to drive each day past the perfect setup to a good little joke, a witticism that a preacher could tell even the stiffest starched shirt in his congregation. With each retelling, he must have enjoyed recalling the first time he heard it: there he was, driving past the factory with his friend, relishing again that half-panicked moment when he looked around to see why his friend should say, out of the blue, "So that's why there are so many of them!" Then seeing the sign, making the connection: Suddenly nonsense turned into sense. His laugh was part admiration at the understated elegance of the wordplay, part relief that his friend wasn't a nut, and part satisfaction at solving the puzzle. Now he shared and relived that aesthetic convergence. Do I exaggerate? I don't think so. That's how *my* mind works.

For all my adolescent superiority to Herschel's pun, not only have I remembered it for forty years, I've thought about it every time I see a Smith or a Jones or a Johnson or a Williams Manufacturing Company. There are more of them than you'd think.

Herschel told a different joke one day while I was sitting with my brothers, squeezed onto his and my Aunt Hazel's small sofa, flipping through one of their magazines while sunlight flooded the small parsonage. A boy and girl are kissing in the back of a car, and when they break their clench, the boy says, "Honey, that was some powerful kiss! I ended up with your gum."

"Dum? Dat's dot dum. I dot a told."

I cringed, twisted my lips, and laughed involuntarily while swatting my hands in front of my face, as if I were trying to keep a fly from landing on my nose. Herschel roared with delight at my boyish prissiness. The idea of another person's snot in my mouth excited such a strong response that I twitched and shivered for the next fifteen minutes, and every time I did, Herschel laughed again. I'd never heard a gross-out joke from an adult before, much less from a minister—and a minister who acknowledged without judgment that a boy and girl would make out in the back of a car! This was heady talk! I was almost dizzy.

I sneaked a glance at my father. Was this joke going to mean trouble? Would he scold me later for laughing? He chuckled at my histrionic revulsion, but he looked uneasy, indecisive. Then he seemed to let his unease go, and I could almost see him think, "That's just Herschel. He likes to push at the boundaries a bit, but he never goes too far. His heart is pure." If I had told that joke to Herschel, I'd be in hot water. My heart was not pure, and we all knew it.

Throughout junior high and into college, though, I had great success telling the joke, if, as I do, you consider making your friends lose their appetite a success. My cousin Julie, Uncle Bob's daughter and a Methodist minister now herself, was scandalized as a girl by Herschel's joke about the cannibal who passed his brother in the woods, though now she laughs both at the joke and her old squeamishness. The joke seemed astonishingly racy then to both of us, the allusion to the natural function more shocking than the double taboo of fraternal cannibalism. Why? Because cannibalism was impossible to take seriously, we were free to imagine it, but talking about doing dooty was dirty and not to be discussed, though it was an act we performed every day, or at least on good days.

Another joke that Herschel got away with was telling us that when he, Bob, and Dad were kids they couldn't afford to keep a Sears Roebuck catalog in the outhouse like the rich folks, much less toilet paper. They kept a bushel basket of corncobs. You wiped yourself, he explained, first with a red corncob and then a white corncob. Did I know why?

No.

To see if you needed to use another red corncob.

I liked the joke because I knew Herschel was making fun of the you-kids-have-it-so-easy-now banter that kept erupting when the families got together—while hammering it home. He was also reminding us that indoor plumbing was a late arrival in their lives, a luxury they did not enjoy until adulthood. My parents didn't mind the joke because Herschel was telling us something they wanted us to know. The joke slightly puzzled me, though. I understood the need for more wiping would reveal itself more clearly on the white cob than the red, and that texture was at the essence of the joke. "Rough as a cob" was how everyone described a country boy with no manners. But was there another detail of country life that I was missing? Were red cobs coarser and better for scrubbing than white ones? My aunt always shuddered at the punch line.

I was even more finicky about sex, which was a mystery to me. It scared me, and like most kids I freaked out when I tried to comprehend my elders doing it. Once while I was visiting my Uncle Bob in Toledo—I must have been fifteen—my cousin Jane handed me a thin, dusty box her father had hidden on the top of one of his bookshelves. Herschel had sent it to him—a gift from one minister to another.

"Look inside," my cousin said. I lifted the lid, and pulled out a sheet of paper announcing the box contained a monokini, the male answer to the bikini, which was then new and getting a lot of press coverage. The gag gift from Florida was a skimpy polyester man's bathing suit with an eight-inch tube sewn to the front, hanging down like an empty sausage casing.

My cousin laughed and looked at me, waiting for me to laugh. Because I didn't want her to see I was creeped out, I squeezed loose a weak laugh before I hurriedly replaced the monokini in the box and shoved it back into her hands. Why was I repulsed by this silly gag gift? I'd been telling dead-baby jokes with utter delight for years.

I was shocked that a minister would indulge in sexual humor, but mostly my prissy adolescent modesty was ruffled. The vaguely transsexual merging of men's and women's clothing perturbed me, and so did the faux-silk slipperiness of the fabric, which cheapened sex with a tawdry lubricity that still troubles me. As soon as I looked at this thing that was clearly never meant to be worn, that existed only for the concept, the joke of it, I imagined my uncle pulling the panties up his legs, stuffing his penis into the polyester tube in the front of the thong, and walking around the room. And that led me to imagine myself doing it. To a boy who'd never come close to having sex, those images were so threatening, so disruptive of my sense of an ordered sexual world, that I couldn't see the humor in the monokini, and the fact that two ministers could laugh at what I couldn't disturbed me even more.

My own body was frightening. Week after week, the preachers, citing the apostle Paul, railed from the pulpit about the "works of the flesh." The flesh was a depraved substance our souls were trapped in, and I absorbed Paul's contempt. The body was dirty. I could see that. Over and above the evacuations that I never once wiped away with a corncob, my body peed, spat, and blew boogers out its nose. Each night, while I slept, crust formed in my eyes. My mother scraped brown wax from my ears. Zits erupted on my face and squirted onto the mirror when I squeezed them. My body blistered and oozed. Even something as comically innocent as my belly button collected loose fibers from my shirt—and when I swabbed my finger around in the puckered hole, gray lint stuck to it and stank. And what about farts? Sometimes they were laughingly called "poots" and "toots," and my brothers and I sang out, "He who first smelt it, dealt it!" Sometimes, a fart got us backhanded out of the chair at the dinner table. As a result, I grew up with a Puritan fascination with, and mistrust of, bodily functions that my mother derided as "nice-nasty."

I was as thrilled by this impermanent substance my soul occupied as I was wary of it. I instinctively understood Paul's Platonic contempt for transient flesh that distracts our souls from the eternal. And yet God had put me in it, and even before sex arrived and made both pleasure and shame more intense, I loved the flesh's passing pleasures. I raced to open the blue can of Maxwell House because I was enraptured by the first blast of coffee fragrance when the can opener breached the vacuum seal with a brusque *psst*. I sat in the tub for hours, reading comic books, luxuriating in the warm water till all my digits were wrinkled and tender, as if they were melting, and my mother forced me to dry off and put my pajamas on.

It seems natural to me that a boy so attuned to the competing tugs of flesh and spirit would find that dirty jokes, with their emphasis on bodily pleasures and mortality, possess a power that edges into the theological. The gap between what we want to be true and what we find to be true, between the ideal and the real, between soul and flesh, is so huge that when we reduce it to concrete examples we laugh. The romantically deluded boy who's kissed his girlfriend so passionately that he thinks he's snorkled up her gum is informed brusquely that his romanticism has blinded him to what he actually has in his mouth. The body itself continually undercuts our inclination to romanticize our desires. Similarly, the farmer stranded on his roof has a concept of the divine that he is forced to redefine. In the world of perfect forms there are no floods. But if there were, God himself would rescue us from them. The deluded farmer is trying, by will and faith, to turn this world into the perfect world, and he is slapped down for it. But why should that happen? Christ himself ordered us, "Be perfect," the most startling of all his commandments and the only one that always makes me laugh. *As if.*

God watched everything I did, judged it good or bad, and kept a running total. More attentive to the bad than the good, God, as I understood him, was not very good at communicating positive reinforcement. I grew tired of being watched, distraught at being judged, and resentful of being instructed. Why did every story have just one moral? And was the moral always the whole of what the story was telling? I was, I thought, like the six-year-old boy in Sunday school, when the preacher's wife is instructing the class about planning for hard times ahead:

"I'm going to describe something, and I want you to raise your hands as soon as you know what it is. This thing lives in trees," she says, and pauses, waiting to see if anyone is willing to guess yet.

"It eats nuts." She pauses again. "And it's gray."

No one raises a hand.

"It has a long bushy gray tail. . . ."

The children look at one another nervously, but no one says anything or raises a hand. The teacher is getting exasperated.

"And it jumps from branch to branch . . . ? And stores acorns for the winter . . . ?"

Finally, one boy raises his hand and says, "Well, I know the answer has to be Jesus—but it sure as hell sounds like a squirrel to me!"

Montgomery, Alabama—where I attended high school and college—is one of many places in the South that proudly dub themselves "the buckle of the Bible Belt." Its religiosity is airless and pervasive. Disregarding the Supreme Court's ruling against school prayer, Sidney Lanier High's popularly elected student chaplain read weekly devotionals over the intercom. Some homeroom teachers, including mine in my senior year, passed the Bible around the class every day for students to read a verse to the class. Pep rallies and student-body meetings began with a prayer led by the chaplain or a minister invited in from the community. One invocation, led by a local Baptist preacher, turned into a full-fledged revival meeting complete with an altar call for those wishing to be saved, to the astonishment of some students and the muttered rage and amazement of the Catholics and Jews.

As an adolescent in revolt against the unreflective pieties of my time and place, I was astounded that our teachers, who hammered at us to be good citizens and obey the law, so blithely thumbed their noses at the separation of church and state. But Christianity began as an oppressed religion, and its holy writings are steeped in oppression and defiance of authority. Paranoia often persists among believers because reading scripture leads us to identify with the early Church. Yet even I, a boy who went to church at least once and often twice a week, saw that the people who were loudly proclaiming their oppression were in fact the oppressors, a disparity both amusing and infuriating. In the Montgomery of my youth, the Christians were the Romans.

"Why don't Baptists screw standing up?" asked a kid in my gym class. "They're afraid someone will think they're dancing," he sneered, an answer that delighted me; I was fascinated to see my faith judged with a jaundiced eye. The non-Baptists mocked us Baptists as hypocrites who sinned in private but didn't want to be seen committing the lesser but more public lapse of dancing. The Baptists I grew up with, though, danced every time they could get a date to any of the Sidney Lanier socials: the Junior–Senior prom, the homecoming dance, or the ROTC Ball. I know because I saw them on the dance floor every time I worked up the courage to ask a girl out. In Sunday school, we talked openly about the girls we had invited and where we had bought their corsages. For suburban Baptist teenagers like us, the joke was about rural believers who still thought dancing was a sin, though our elders, with tetchy wit, called dancing "the horizontal expression of a vertical desire."

If you want to jolt yourself with your own daring and unconventional sense of humor, religion is one of the few places to go after dead-baby, Helen Keller, and mutilation jokes. Only those alert to the sacred can truly appreciate, I suspect, the various uses of blasphemy, and only those who respect taboos can enjoy the bone-deep electric charge of toying with them. Because I was a serious boy raised in a serious faith, surrounded by rational adults with a rigid sense of the supernatural, I still feel a diminishing frisson of sinfulness when I pull a cork from a bottle of Sauvignon blanc, tell a dirty joke, dance, or say "goddamn." I like to test my own sense of religious trepidation, poke it with a stick, thump it on the head as I walk by. The agitation keeps me alive to my old faith and—who knows?—maybe it to me.

The first time I heard a joke about Jesus, the thrill of blasphemy was intoxicating, and it didn't involve, as I'd imagined, witches gathering in the darkest piney woods to summon Lucifer or a warlock drawing a pentagram in blood on the floor of a deserted shack. It was simply three boys huddled in the back row of a tenth-grade world-history class after the teacher had stepped out of the room. We were supposed to be doing our homework.

Carl Blegen, a military brat like me, with black plastic glasses and lank brown hair swept across his forehead, leaned into the aisle. Elbows propped on his thighs, he motioned with his head for me and Gary Sandig to lean toward him. He looked around, and when he was sure no one else could hear, he whispered, "Jesus is on the cross."

He paused a second and stared at us, making sure we had absorbed that this sentence was the beginning of a joke. He held his hands out loosely from his shoulders to suggest Christ nailed to the cross, but not wide enough that a casual onlooker would recognize what he was doing. He looked like he was imitating a chicken spreading its flightless wings.

I was so puzzled, tense, and suddenly afraid I could barely listen. Just listening seemed dangerous.

"Jesus looks out over the crowd and says, 'Peter, come to me.'

"Peter hears Jesus calling him, so he starts walking through the crowd toward the cross, but the Roman soldiers see him and drive him back with whips.

"Jesus calls out again, 'Peter, come to me. I want you.'

"Again Peter starts toward the cross and again the Roman soldiers whip him and beat him and punch him until he gives up.

"For the third time, Jesus calls out, 'Peter, come to me. I want you.'" As he spoke Jesus's words, Carl used a dreamy, disconnected sing song voice, as if Jesus, lost in his own thoughts, had not seen what had happened to Peter.

On his third attempt, determined to make it to the foot of the cross, Peter launches himself into the crowd. The Romans lash him bloody with their whips. They club him to the ground and kick him. But Peter claws his way to the base of the cross and calls up, "I'm here, Lord."

Still using that dreamy voice, but with lilting childish glee in it, Jesus says, "Peter, I can see your house from up here."

I laughed so hard I clung to the side of my desk to keep from falling on the floor. I put my face on my desk and laughed until I slobbered on my notebook paper. Other students turned and stared.

"What's so funny?" they asked.

"Nothing," I said, and kept laughing. Carl, red in the face with pleasure at his own joke, shushed me. He was nervous I'd repeat the joke and other students, offended, would tell the teacher.

I held my side and racked for air till I finally calmed down. But as soon as I thought, *I can see your house from up here*, air again exploded from my lips in a wet snort, and I was off again. Carl kept saying, "Come on, man, stop." He made a lowering gesture with his hands, palms facing the floor. "Stop it. Everybody's looking at us."

Like that was going to make me stop? Everybody looking?

"What's so funny?" the students near me demanded, frustrated and a little angry. Again I just said, "Nothing," and kept laughing. It must have taken me five minutes before I could shut up.

The joke had raised me to a height of nervous expectation, and just as I was expecting something violent, gross, or sexually vile, it swooped beneath what I was prepared for. The eerie innocence of Jesus's answer exploded in my head. Tortured, dying on the cross, this Jesus spoke with the "Gee whiz" amazement of a boy who had climbed a tree for the first time. The joke takes the pivotal event in Christianity and turns it into a childish thrill. This Christ isn't interested in redeeming sinful mankind with the sacrifice of his life. He's just a dumb kid in a tree who wants to share knowledge that others already have. I could remember being that kid. At fifteen, I still remembered the first time I had climbed a tall tree and looked to find the roof of my house. I am embarrassed now by my excitement then, and I was embarrassed for the naïve Christ of the joke who was as innocently delighted as I had been.

The joke was dynamite. I knew I had to be very careful with it. I couldn't tell it to any adults at all, ever. Only my friends who saw themselves as outsiders were possible audiences, and even then I'd have to think twice. But I knew I was going to tell it. There was never any doubt in my mind about that.

In homeroom the next day, as I told the joke to my friend Tom, a girl overheard me and turned around. From her hesitant manner and the determined set of her jaw, I could see she didn't really want to say anything, but her faith compelled her. The mockers of the Lord must be both admonished for their sin and offered the chance to repent.

She curled a strand of blond hair nervously behind her right ear. "When I think of all that Jesus has meant to me and all he suffered for my sake . . ." she said, her voice trembling. Unable to finish the sentence, she turned back around and faced the front of the class, opened her algebra textbook, and stared at it, lips trembling.

Tom shrugged at me. I shrugged back. I felt small and mean, and yet aggrieved too. She had turned to hear the joke without being invited. What right did she have to complain? But she hadn't complained. She had been hurt. She was a bystander who had edged between the knife thrower and the woman strapped to the spinning wheel. A wounded civilian. Collateral damage.

Every time I told the joke, someone, between laughs, said, "You're going to get struck by lightning," and I shrugged with false audacity. For my blasphemy, I *did* expect a bolt of cosmic electricity to blast me into a stinking circle of charred earth, and for this magical thinking I held myself in contempt. It was not the sort of sophisticated, post-Christian thought I wanted to be thinking. Even if I were to remain a Christian, I didn't want to understand God so primitively. But deep in my brain, a terrified king ruling over a shrinking desert kingdom knew he deserved to have his fields destroyed by floods, drought, and locusts, and his starving people afflicted with plagues. The rest of my brain laughed at the superstitious minor king, so far from the intellectual agora of Greece and the great public baths of imperial Rome.

Had the Jesus jokes been around for a long time and I just started to hear them when, in high school, I was going through my crisis of faith? Or were they something new? Whatever the case, they were there when I needed them. Perhaps it's natural that the thing that has been drilled into us all our lives as holy should, when it is finally questioned, provoke an extreme response. This was certainly true for me. Attempting to understand intellectually and psychologically what we find funny comforts us after we have stopped laughing and the stitch in our sides has loosened. But laughter is not intellectual, thank God; it's visceral. And my favorite Jesus joke while I was in high school was wordless.

I'd throw my arms wide and stop long enough for my listener to grasp that I was Christ on the cross. Then, grimacing with feigned pain, I'd yank my right arm free of an imaginary nail. I'd do the same with my left hand. I hesitated for a moment, my eyes widened, and I windmilled them backward, as if to keep myself from falling. The audience would make the leap and imagine Christ collapsing forward, still pinned to the cross by the spike in his ankles. If the joke is funny at all, and I found it very funny, it's because it's so wrenchingly horrible to imagine the torture of crucifixion being taken to a new and surprising level, and that because Jesus, the perfect man, a man and a god, makes an elementary mistake of physics.

The joke always makes me flinch. I feel a slight psychosomatic twinge in my ankles whenever I tell it. Oddly, the joke reminds us of Jesus's humanity and torment in the body at the same time it mocks the gravity of the moment. Like the cruelty jokes and Helen Keller jokes, it reminds us of the vulnerability of our bodies and pushes fear into laughter. The person enacting the joke is Christ, but a stupid Christ, a mortal who is not going to return from the dead. Who, then, is the joke on?

Four

What Did the Devil Ever Do for You?

The more trouble I had sustaining the simple faith I yearned for, the harder I tried. That's one reason I became a camp counselor for the Royal Ambassadors the summer before beginning college, at a camp affiliated with the Shocco Springs Baptist Conference Center in the woods outside Talladega, Alabama. The Royal Ambassadors were the Southern Baptist approximation of the Boy Scouts.

It all started the previous March, when Mr. Baldwin, the camp director, addressed the Sunday night prayer meeting at my family's church and urged parents to send their boys to camp. After the meeting, my father hurried forward, buttonholed him, and pushed him to interview me. Dad was practically chattering! And it worked. Later that week, Mr. Baldwin drove over to our house one evening to size me up.

"I really prefer college men," Mr. B said, dubiously eyeing the scrawny, affectless eighteen-year-old sitting on the couch next to his father. Across from us, Mr. B perched on my mother's red velvet Queen Anne chair. I'd never seen anyone actually sit on that chair before.

"Who are your counselors?" Dad asked.

"College students," Mr. B said. "Some of them are on their way to seminary at Southern Baptist Theological Seminary in Louisville." Not the relatively liberal Southwestern Theological Seminary in Fort Worth, he meant for us to understand. "All of them are men with a strong sense of Christian vocation."

"College men? That's just a technicality," Dad said. "He'll be in college three months from now."

For every objection Mr. B raised, my father, suddenly voluble, had an answer prepared.

"Have you been active in the Royal Ambassadors program?

"He's been in Cub Scouts, Webelos, and Boy Scouts."

"Is your family active in the church?"

"Two of his uncles, my brothers, are ministers. I'm a deacon. He's at services two or three times a week, regular as clockwork, and he goes to all the revivals."

I jerked my head. Revivals? I'd gone to a lot, but not to all of them; they sometimes fell on school nights.

My father talked eagerly about what a fine counselor I would make, what a wonderful leader of men I would be. Except when directly asked, I said nothing. Where was my father's almost frantic passion to get me this job coming from? The one time I'd complained to Dad that all my friends' fathers helped them find summer jobs, he'd told me to go put my shoes on. He'd get me a job.

Suspicious, I asked him where and he told me that he'd be happy to drive me to the recruiting office himself. I'd have a job by the end of the day.

"Thanks," I'd said. "I can join the army by myself."

Yet here he was falling all over himself to get me a job that, as Mr. B explained, paid fifteen dollars for a week that began at 10:00 AM. Monday morning, when the campers arrived, and lasted until noon Saturday, when they left. The rest of Saturday and all day Sunday were free, though I would of course be expected to attend Baptist services Sunday morning and evening, both for my own spiritual good and to assure the local churches that we were working with them, not competing with them, in the saving of adolescent souls.

As Mr. B and my father talked, I saw Dad wasn't concerned about the money. He wanted to immerse me in a Christian world so I could be saved. Saved again. Perhaps he'd seen how I'd twisted myself into bowlines and clove hitches (not just any knots) over whether God existed. Had Dad detected that reading *The Rise and Fall of the Third Reich* and Anne Frank's diary had rocked my sense of a God-ordered world? Had he overheard one of the Jesus jokes I'd been telling?

More likely he'd seen the look of contempt on my face when businessmen prayed publicly in church, their prayers making it clear to me and anyone who bothered to listen that they considered their wealth an outward and visible manifestation of inner grace. The obvious corollary was left unstated: The poor deserved their poverty. I liked to remind the boys in my Sunday school class that Jesus said a rich man is as likely to enter heaven as a camel is to pass through the eye of a needle—because, as a smartass, I took mean-spirited pleasure in listening to biblical literalists explain that Jesus was alluding to one of the gates into Jerusalem, which was called "the eye of a needle." The gate was narrow, they insisted, but a camel could, in fact, pass through if it knelt down. I did not inquire why Jesus would bother to stroll barefoot through Judea assuring the whores, publicans, and sinners that the wealthy had nothing to fear in the afterlife, as long as their camels knew how to do the limbo. The church was an important, if increasingly strained, part of my life. I yearned to be comfortable there. I secretly hoped that, by some process I could not imagine, I too would become rich and would need to ponder how to slip a camel through a needle's eye.

I don't know why I was offered the job. Maybe it was late in the year and Mr. B had a poorly paid position to fill and no ready candidate. Maybe he simply yielded to my father's ardor. As they talked around me, though, the two men entered into a tacit collaboration. I'd be a spiritual reclamation project they would share.

I took the job anyway. *I could simply ignore the pressure*, I thought, and a summer in the woods beat living in my father's house and another three months of flipping charbroiled burgers at Hardee's for ninety cents an hour.

While Mr. B himself was easygoing, the camp was intensely religious, with one service right after breakfast and one in the evening, all leading up to a Decision Service on Friday night. This was the crux of the week, when the campers were, in the preacher's altar call, exhorted to come forward and profess their faith in Jesus as their personal lord and savior. The pressure increased daily; the preachers grew more urgent, their stories more dire.

Mr. B stopped short, though, of letting the visiting preachers and missionaries tell what we counselors jokingly called "flaming car wreck stories"—lurid tales of kids dying suddenly without being saved, and therefore going straight to hell without, as we said, "passing Go." We'd all heard them and, to amuse ourselves, some of us performed elaborate and grotesque mini-sermons about church buses hit by trains, junior-high football teams wiped out when lightning strikes the goalpost, stray bullets zinging through vinyl siding and into the skulls of fourteen-year-old boys who've gone to bed without saying their prayers.

Preachers love these stories. They terrify adolescents into a facsimile of faith. It isn't faith, of course; it's a craven capitulation to eschatological extortion, and it fades as soon as the fear wears off.

But in the short term, the stories work. Trembling kids stumble sobbing, snuffling, and hiccupping down the aisle to claim the eternal life held out to them at the end of the sermon. By outlawing such a reliable tactic, Mr. B risked antagonizing the preachers whom the camp, as well as the statewide Royal Ambassadors program, depended on for support.

Only once did a preacher, desperate for converts at the end of his week in residence, violate the rule. In the outdoor chapel the campers sat on plank benches that stair-stepped down the cleared hillside to a pulpit, an oak tree cut off at chest height. Sunlight filtered through the water oaks, pines, and hickories, and at night it yielded during the course of the sermon to the flickering yellow flames of the sibilant Coleman lanterns. By the final prayer, we were snugly held against the darkness of the surrounding forest by the honey-colored cathedral light of the lanterns reflecting off the underside of the leaves spreading above us.

"You could die tonight," the preacher chanted. "You could die tonight in your tent. There's no guarantee you'll wake up tomorrow morning. Your tent mate might very well wake up and find your cold lifeless body there on the cot, dead."

I cut my eyes around to the other counselors. They looked as uncomfortable as I felt. Only when I saw another counselor with his mouth hanging open did I realize mine too was agape.

"Death comes like a thief in the night, without warning. If you accept Jesus into your heart here tonight, your soul will fly to heaven with God when you die. But if you don't, if you turn your back on Jesus, who suffered and died on the cross of iniquity with the nails driven through his hands and feet, if you turn your back on Jesus, when you stand before God the Father Almighty at judgment tonight, you'll cry out to Jesus, cry out to him for mercy, but because you turned your back on Jesus here tonight, Jesus will turn his back on you and say to God, 'I know him not.'"

The preacher paused, sucked in a deep breath, and went on, his voice now soft, confiding:

"You know what it feels like when you touch a stove, don't you? You know how bad it hurts when you burn yourself on a hot coal from the campfire?" He was leaning on the pulpit, and two ten-year-olds in the front row, eyes rapt, were nodding in agreement. Yes, they knew what it felt like.

"That's what it'll feel like all over your body, every square inch of your body covered with blazing fire, when you die outside the love of Jesus Christ. Every square inch of your skin burning, and it'll never stop. It'll burn like that forever."

I looked down my row of campers. They were squirming and several lower lips were trembling. In the row behind me, two boys were sobbing.

"Tomorrow, when you're driving home from camp, a huge Mack truck could veer across the center line of the highway into your lane. It could crash into your car, and kill you and your whole family. . . ."

Mr. B walked to the pulpit, clapped one of his powerful hands on the preacher's shoulder. The preacher, startled, fell silent, and Mr. B said cheerfully, "Thank you for such a fine sermon." He wedged himself into position behind the pulpit, forcing the preacher aside, and said quickly, "Tommy, would you come up here and lead us in 'Amazing Grace'? And I want everybody, as the second verse starts, to walk quietly and reverently back to your campsite with your counselors."

Without waiting for Tommy to finish strapping on the accordion, Mr. B pitched into the hymn, and the preacher, standing shrunken beside him, sang too.

Over the left side of his mouth Mr. B had a large flesh-colored mole, and its bee-sting fullness made his face seem lopsided and effeminate—an effect his prissy lisp did not undercut. Though a few staffers at the main Baptist camp down the road mocked him, flipping their wrists and lisping, we counselors gave them cold stares. We admired the loving attention Mr. B paid to his campers, counselors, and cooks—and we admired his muscular Christianity; it had real muscles.

During set-up week at the beginning of camp and take down week at the end, Mr. B, though nearing fifty, worked all day in the wet, one-hundred-degree Alabama heat, lugging heavy wooden tent platforms and the concrete blocks we set them on. Only a concern for us, the eighteen- to twenty-two-year-old counselors who panted with exhaustion, made him stop for precisely timed ten-minute breaks once an hour.

While living in the woods, surrounded by deep believers and very dark nights, I struggled to accept again the apocalyptic faith I'd grown up in. I was obsessed with judgment and the end-time, furious with myself for letting what I was pretty sure were fairy tales get under my skin. But apocalyptic thinking is, on one level, just a way of confusing one's fear of death with the death of everyone and everything, a self-aggrandizement natural in young men and even more natural when you walk every night to your bed through the pitch-dark piney woods of North Alabama. I was like Johnny in the story about the pastor speaking to a group of kids about being good and what a wonderful reward heaven will be if they live good lives. At the end of his talk, he asks them, "Where do you want to go?"

"Heaven!" cries Suzy.

"And what do you have to be to get there?" he asks.

"Dead!" yells little Johnny.

Over iced tea one evening after work, I listened to a group of the older counselors, seminary students, puzzle over what the Bible says about the end of the world. We all knew about the Rapture, when "the Lord Himself will descend from heaven with a shout, with the voice of an archangel, and with the trumpet of God. And the dead in Christ will rise first." We all had heard sermons about the car that would, at the Rapture, continue on driverless as the driver, a believer, vanished. Or the man who, when his wife disappeared from the breakfast table on the morning of the Second Coming, looks at her suddenly empty chair with sad understanding. But how does Paul's prophecy of the Rapture fit in with Revelation's prophecy of the thousand-year reign of the Beast, which we took to be Satan? Did the Rapture precede the thousand years or follow it? Nobody got hot under the collar, merely confused as they debated, trying to sort out what the Bible says.

As they talked, Mr. B strolled over, stepped in, and explained that the book of Revelation says history will end when the Antichrist comes to power and rules over the human race for a thousand years. But Revelation is a dream vision; it's fuzzy on whether Christ will return to earth to take the faithful with him *before* or *after* the thousand-year reign of the Beast. The pre-millennialists believe that Christ will return and take all his believers to heaven with him before the Rapture. The post-millennialists believe the Antichrist will come first, and his millennium-long reign will test the believers before Christ comes to save the faithful. The timing of the Rapture is a fearfully urgent question in end-time religions.

Though the pre-millennialists have now pretty much carried the day, the ambiguous issue then was fraught with tension: high words were exchanged among believers, and churches split. For me, the issue smacked of apocalyptic scientific fiction, which made it both slightly comic and all the more frightening—comic because I recognized the literary genre in which I was expected to live and frightening because I did, at least partially, live there.

After Mr. B finished explaining, someone asked, "What do you believe? Which are you?"

"I am," he said, chuckling and pausing for effect, "like the old preacher who declared himself a pan-millennialist."

"What's that? You didn't tell us about pan-millennialists."

"I figure that, in Christ, things'll pan out all right in the end."

We laughed, of course. It was a well-timed bit of wit, played to puncture our seriousness, and to redirect us to the essential point: God's love is more important than quibbles over doctrine.

Mr. B's good humor and humanity about something so apocalyptic as the Apocalypse itself made me deeply happy. His easy-going faith softened my revulsion to a religion that depended so much on fear and not nearly as much on love as it might have. If I were to remain a Christian, a pan-millennialist was what I wanted to be.

I admired Mr. B and I was swept up in the camaraderie of the other counselors, hard working, earnest, cheerful men to a one. They didn't curse or drink. They dated the counselors from the G.A. (Girls in Action) Camp, but, judging from the boy I saw convulsing in the locker room Saturday night after a date, hunched over, pale, writhing in pain with blue balls—vasocongestion caused by sexual frustration—they didn't have sex either. A couple of guys gathered around, talking him through his discomfort, telling him it would fade, and I, while I admired his restraint, suppressed an impatient impulse to suggest he go to his tent and masturbate.

My new friends didn't seem tormented by pessimism, depression, and doubt—just blue balls—and I wanted to be like them, although I felt like a hypocrite in their midst because I cursed, masturbated, and anguished over religious doubts and spiritual torpor. I wanted so strongly to believe, wanted so much to share their sense of divine purpose, that I half-convinced myself I did.

When camp closed down in August, I found a late high school graduation present waiting for me back home in Montgomery, a huge chrome alarm clock with an electric-blue face that I thought was beautiful. It ticked so thunderously, however, that it spent the remainder of its life in the top drawer of my dresser, swaddled in socks and underwear. In my thank-you note to Mrs. Stallings, I gushed about my renewed faith and how wonderful I felt to live a changed life, redeemed by the love of Jesus Christ. For months afterward, I flinched with embarrassment every time I imagined my mother's friend in California reading this cliché-ridden effusion from a boy she hardly knew and probably barely remembered. My embarrassment was compounded because I thought I'd blurted a compulsive, inexplicable lie. It took me a long time to understand that I wrote those words to see if, by saying them fervently enough, I could make them true.

During my freshman year at Huntingdon College, which was a mile and a half from my house, I took two required semester-long classes, one in the Old Testament and another in the New Testament, both taught by Barnes Tatum. A thin, energetic, Methodist minister, Dr. Tatum did not tread delicately on the religious preconceptions of fundamentalists. He quickly introduced us to the higher criticism of the Bible. His teaching could not have been more revolutionary if he had told the class Martin Luther King Jr. was as surely a Christian prophet as the apostle Paul—which, in fact, he did.

I had a hard time deciding what to make of my new knowledge. I saw Dr. Tatum was right when he showed us there are two different and incompatible creation stories in Genesis. How had I missed that for eighteen years? (I consoled myself by remembering that great scholars had missed it for eighteen centuries.) He showed how the four gospels tell the story of Jesus's life in significantly different ways and that the Bible certainly does assume the Earth is the unmoving center of creation, with the sun circling it. Attempting to bring us to a more complex understanding of our faith, one that acknowledged and accepted these truths, Dr. Tatum rubbed our noses in many biblical errors and irresolvable textual contradictions.

Before class one day, I mentioned to the woman sitting next to me how excited I was by what we were learning. She looked up sharply from her notes and said, her voice thin with obstinacy and loathing, "I'll put down what he wants me to on the test, but I don't have to believe it and I don't have to think about it."

I did. As much as I envied her refusal, I *had* to think about what we were learning.

Because I lived at home and commuted to school, my father required me to continue attending church with my family, which I did sullenly and with as little grace as I could get away with. I'd sit in church on Sunday as my Baptist preacher told the congregation the same thing I'd heard preachers say my entire life: that the Bible was divinely inspired and inerrant; it was literally true in all particulars. If it could be shown to be false in even one detail—"even so much as a comma, one jot or tittle"—you might as well throw the whole thing away because you could no longer trust it. The whole edifice of Christian belief would tumble down around us like the walls of Jericho. If the Book of God could be proved to have one error in it, God was a liar, Jesus was a liar, and he himself, the preacher standing before us today, was a liar worse than the lowest, most desperate murderer, blasphemer, or adulterer who had ever walked the face of the earth.

I was so saturated by all-or-nothing thinking that I thought of my classmate's sharp face, makeup caked around a mole on her chin, as if her resentful and furious "I don't have to believe it" were a voice in my head. The religious edifice she and I had spent eighteen years building depended on every brick being sound, and here was our teacher—a minister!—pointing out with more than a bit of showmanship and glee every mismatched brick, every line of crumbling mortar, every gap in the facade.

I felt like a rat caught in a double bind. If I went down one path to get to the food, I got shocked. If I went the other way, I got jolted again. So I stood in the middle, hungry and trembling, unable to move. I could neither give up the faith by which I'd understood the world for my entire life, nor could I embrace it. Though I wanted to be a sophisticated atheist, I still felt an instinctive spirituality. Yet, I knew this might be mere wishful thinking, a refusal to accept mortality. I couldn't find a middle path. And Jesus specifically warned against people like me. "Would that you were cold or hot!" he says in Revelation 3:15–16. "So, because you are lukewarm, and neither cold nor hot, I will spew you out of my mouth." I imagined myself as brackish, warm water being spat from the mouths of Jesus and the atheists both, each splattering the other and grimacing with distaste.

Besides coping with classwork, money pressure, a night job tending to a bedridden old man, and an afternoon job at a dry-goods warehouse downtown, I beat my head against these intellectual questions—or were they emotional and spiritual questions? Whatever they were, they pushed me close to a breakdown. A turning point came after my freshman year, when I took a summer class in folklore, and read epics, myths, fairy tales, and folktales with fascinated compulsion. One Sunday, bored in church, I picked up my Bible and, while the preacher droned, read it as a story, beginning at Genesis 1:1. With wonderment and despair, I saw that Genesis was like the folklore I was reading at school. Adam and Eve weren't the first couple formed by a god in a garden, or the first evicted from paradise. Moses was not the first abandoned baby found and adopted by a king's daughter. Mary wasn't the first woman impregnated by a god, and Jesus wasn't the first god-fathered hero whose birth was presaged by signs and whose childhood acts foretold his becoming a savior of his people. Greek myth was full of figures like Hercules and Orpheus, men with superhuman powers and divine fathers. The biblical stories were more polished, more complex, sure, but clearly they weren't *like* folklore; they *were* folklore. The obvious will rock you when you discover it yourself.

As I was struggling with my turmoil at this new understanding, I heard this joke:

Jesus is in heaven, when suddenly he realizes that, though he sees his mother and God himself every day around the heavenly palace, he hadn't seen his earthly father in almost two thousand years.

So he goes to St. Peter, who's standing at the pearly gates, and asks where his human father is.

"Hmm," St. Peter says. "That's a tough one. What's his name?"

Jesus thinks for a moment. "Joseph," he says, proud of himself for coming up with it.

"There're a lot of Josephs here," says Peter. "What did he do for a living?"

"He was a carpenter."

"Oh, in that case he's probably been put out in the boondocks with all the other carpenters, so their sawdust won't disturb everyone else. Let's go see if we can find him."

Jesus and Peter walk and walk until they are way out in the backwoods of heaven. After checking out every carpenter and lathe operator they run across, they finally find an old man in a small shop, sitting alone at a workbench. He's covered with sawdust and little curls of shaved wood, and Jesus thinks he looks familiar.

He says to the old man, "Did you once have a child by miraculous circumstances?"

"Yes, I did," says the old man.

"And did you then take that child and love him and raise him as your own?"

"Yes, yes, I did," says the old man, excitement rising in his voice.

"And did he have holes in his hands?"

"Yes, yes, he did!" says the old man, leaping from his workbench.

Jesus throws his arms wide to embrace the old man, and says, "Father!"

And the old man launches himself into Jesus's arms, hugs him, and yells, "Pinocchio!"

Oh, it is impossible to tell you how much I loved that joke. I don't remember where I heard it or who told it, but I laughed until I had to sit down, tears leaking down my hot cheeks. I chuckled for the rest of the day, and when I woke up the next morning my jaws ached. I made a pest of myself, telling it to everyone I thought could stomach it. The joke plays on the search of a son for his lost father—a staple of myth, drama, and popular fiction—and ends here, comically, with him finding the wrong person.

But it's more than just the wrong person. Jesus confuses this particular woodworker with Joseph, but Geppetto confuses the son of God with a puppet. If bringing down the high and mighty is funny, no descent is more vertiginous than the fall from God Incarnate to a hand-carved block of wood in a children's story. Suddenly we see in Jesus, the exemplary man, a character flaw we had not expected: vanity. He'd thought himself the only person with holes in his hands who had been brought to life by a miracle and raised by a woodworker.

I was thrilled to hear this criticism, however mild, of Jesus. But what really fueled my laughter was seeing yet another way in which the story of Jesus, the story scholars call the myth of Christianity, was similar to other stories. The comic slamming together of the historical world of Jesus with the fictional world of the puppet is charmingly disorienting. Despite his having been indisputably a living person, was Jesus, as he was portrayed in the Bible, also fundamentally fictional?

F. Scott Fizgerald famously observed that "the test of a first-rate intelligence is the ability to hold two opposed ideas in the mind at the same time and still retain the ability to function." Two opposed ideas are, with the right twist, often the source of humor, and I am grateful for the first-rate intelligence this joke embodied. It didn't solve my spiritual dilemma, but it showed me how to laugh at the forces at loggerheads in my mind. If I acknowledged that each force—faith on the one hand, skepticism on the other—was legitimate and each had a right to be there, jammed up against the other, the pressure to make a decision eased. Over time, I'd sort them out.

In the meantime I could still laugh at the excesses of the faithful. At Huntingdon, a pre-seminary student and his girlfriend began seeing extravagant, brightly colored demons perched on the shoulders of everyone who did not share their fundamentalism. I don't remember what color they told me my demon was, but I remember that it was polka-dotted.

Some believers managed to keep their faith while acknowledging they followed a flawed and sometimes unreliable holy book; I, though, had been trained *not* to have a nuanced mind, one that could tolerate inconstancy, confusion, and imperfection. I knew now I would have to develop one. I kept eyeing faith. What form would it take if I could still have it? What would I believe in this new dispensation from absolutism, and how would I believe it?

After my sophomore year at college, I returned to the Royal Ambassadors Camp as a counselor because I was between jobs and I wanted to get away from home again. Mr. B was gone, forced out of his job by political maneuvering inside the hierarchy of the Alabama Baptist Association. Mr. B's assistant, who just that year had graduated from college, now ran the camp, and he was the same age as some of the counselors. Had the camp really changed or was I merely two years older and more aware of others' failings? I got my first taste of the new regime arguing with a new counselor, a college student who insisted *Baptist* was spelled *Babtist*—the way we all pronounced it. I've seen that spelling on rural churches.

During the second week of camp, leading my squad of boys on an afternoon hike, I heard a loud rhythmic voice echoing through the hickories and loblolly pines. I told my campers to hunker down on the trail, and I crept toward the voice to see who it was. Trespassers were an occasional problem. Peering through the leaves, I saw one of the new counselors preaching to a water oak. As a teenager, Billy Graham had taught himself to preach by standing on a stump in the pasture and expounding the gospel to his father's cows. *Maybe that's what this guy is doing,* I thought. He's trying to be Billy Graham. Voice rising and falling with stiff, unpracticed fervor, he flailed his arms, slapped his Bible, and harangued the oak to abandon its worldly aspirations and accept Jesus Christ as its lord and savior. His face was upturned in what I assumed was a direct address to the Lord until I noticed his eight campers perched on the limbs of the tree, swinging their legs in the air, and listening to the sermon. Quietly, I led my own boys away.

Unlike him, I did not enjoy public testifying. My first year I'd weaseled out of giving my personal testimony at local churches because of my youth. "We are ambassadors for Christ," the apostle Paul wrote to the people of Corinth, and as an experienced, second-year Royal Ambassador counselor I could no long avoid ambassadoring. With three or four other counselors—some nervous, some raring to go—I stood before Sunday night prayer meetings in local churches throughout Talladega County and gave witness to my personal relationship with Jesus. Mumbling, hesitating, I rushed through a story cobbled together from other testimonies I'd heard, trying to make embarrassment and equivocation sound like diffident sincerity. I'd been born again in California, I said. In high school I'd fallen under the influence of bad companions but coming to work at the Royal Ambassadors Camp with good Christians had restored my faith and led me to rededicate my life to Christ. I hated standing in front of kind, earnest people, and lying about the thing that was most important to them. The first part of my story was mostly true, though I did not specify that my bad companions were Voltaire, Darwin, Clarence Darrow, and H. L. Mencken.

During the final week of camp, takedown week, all the counselors moved into the main meeting hall, the building we held services in when it rained. We used the building as a makeshift barracks while we dismantled and folded tents, stacked tent platforms, and covered them with tarps. After work one day I noticed a *Penthouse* magazine tossed in the corner of the locker room. It remained there untouched and uncommented on for several days. The longer it lay there, everyone ignoring it, the more toxic it grew. Finally, its sheer silly forbiddenness overwhelmed me, and I picked it up and ostentatiously flipped through it. I was just being bold, trying to see if I could shock anyone, including myself. Since I lived at home and my parents monitored me closely, I'd never held a girlie magazine in my hands before.

One of my friends called, "Woooo! You're going to go to hell. Straight to hell." We laughed, nervousness edging into our voices.

Thomas, a barrel-chested man who was already jackleg preaching at local churches, looked around the corner from his locker to see what we were laughing at.

"I don't think you should be doing that," he said tentatively.

"Sure we should, we're guys," I said.

He grumbled and the only phrase I could make out was "abominations before the Lord." Encouraged by his disapproval, I flipped open the centerfold, took a long leering look at it, and held it out for my friend to see.

"Whoa, ho!" he said. "Good-looking!"

Thomas jerked his head up in a small challenge, a we'll-see-about-that gesture, before he slammed his locker door and stalked out.

Defiant now and determined to get under his skin even more, I eased the centerfold off of its staples, took it upstairs, and stuck it on a nail jutting from the wall above my cot.

Lying in bed, lost in a book, I'd already forgotten about the picture when Thomas, who'd come into the room, snorted loudly twice, like a bull in a Bugs Bunny cartoon, and charged across the room toward me. He reached over my head, tore the picture from the wall, and held it crumpled in one fist. He stared at me, breathing in heavy gulps.

I leapt off my cot and snatched the wad of paper out of his hand. "What do you think you're doing? That's private property! Keep your hands off it!"

"This is blasphemy! You're desecrating the Lord's house."

"What? I'm what?"

"We hold *church* in this room." He snatched at the creased and torn centerfold, and I held it behind my back, out of reach.

"I'm not desecrating nothing. That naked body was made by God and you may find God's work disgusting, but I don't." I was tossing out clichés, egging him on, trying to goof with his head, enjoying myself. But I could feel myself slipping into real anger, unable to back down.

I unwadded the picture, smoothed it as flat as I could, and jammed it back on the nail. Thomas lunged for it, grabbing over my shoulder. I slapped his hand away, and suddenly we were chest to chest, eyes locked, breathing into each other's faces. He bumped me, and when I bounced backward a step, he grinned.

"You Nazi!" I yelled, and I jammed my chest back up against his, shouting into his face. I was afraid. He was a thick, powerful man and the zealous light in his eyes glowed even brighter than usual, but I was sure he wouldn't hit me if I didn't swing first.

The other guys rushed from their cots and stepped between us, and the camp director, who'd run upstairs from his office when he heard the yelling, ordered us to calm down. He took me aside, and when we were out of Thomas's hearing, he laughed and told me I knew better than to hang up a nudie picture at a church camp. I needed to take it down. He was right, of course, but I appreciated his laughter. It made it easier for me to walk across the room with everybody watching, and pull the mangled centerfold off the wall.

Then half-reluctantly, at the urging of the others, Thomas and I shook hands.

Back home that fall, I announced to my father that I didn't want to go to church anymore. He sat in his olive-green lounge chair and kept staring at the TV set while I sat a few feet from him in the orange swivel rocker, pivoting it back and forth nervously. I'd had to work up my courage. I was afraid of him—physically afraid and afraid too that he'd stop helping me with my college expenses. Both my parents had told me often enough, "While you live in my house, you'll play by my rules or you can leave."

Finally his silence wore me down, and I prodded him. "Did you hear me? I said I don't want . . ."

"I heard you. I'm thinking about it."

After a long silence, staring at the TV, never letting his eyes drift in my direction, he said, "No one is going to make you go to church if you don't want to go."

"Okay," I said softly, "I don't want to go."

He stood up from the lounger, leaving it open, the footrest stretched out in front of it, and walked out of the room. I was half-way up the stairs to my bedroom when my mother raced across the den, where the TV was still blaring, and at the foot of the stairs she yelled, "Just who do you think you are? Just who do you think you are not to believe in God? As long as you live in this house, you're going to get your butt up and go to church whether you want to or not. Do you hear me? Do you hear what I'm telling you?"

Her eyes were slightly unfocused and her jaw was clenched combatively. I'd expected Dad to go berserk, not her. She had always seemed to take church with a grain of salt, sometimes griping about having to go, occasionally implying that Dad made her go when she didn't want to. As I stood on the stairs gaping at her, unable to speak, I realized that Dad, as a strong believer, must have struggled with faith and could accept, though unhappily, those struggles in his son, who was still poring over C. S. Lewis, *The Lives of the Saints,* Teilhard de Chardin, and everything in print by or about Thomas Merton. But Mom, because she accepted without challenge the faith she'd been born into, was enraged by my rejection of it. I was getting too big for my britches, showing off, trying to be a smarty-pants intellectual.

Dad walked up beside her, put his arm around her shoulders, and pulled her around so she stood at an angle to the two of us.

"Roberta, you don't force somebody to go to church. That isn't what it's about."

But the next Sunday, when I didn't come down for breakfast, he knocked on my door and said, "You're going to be late for church," just as if nothing had happened. And just as if nothing had happened, I got up and I went, confused and sullen. And the next Sunday, and the next.

On the fourth Sunday, when he knocked, I called back through the door, "I don't want to go."

"You're not going to church?" He sounded surprised.

"Only if you make me," I said—one of several lines I'd practiced.

"No, I'm not going to make you," he said, and he left to dress for church.

In the hall of the church I no longer attended, I'd seen tacked on the bulletin board one of the most shocking pictures I've ever seen. It was the famous Ralph Kozak painting of Jesus, his head thrown back in manly, open-mouthed laughter, delight untouched by malice, his upper teeth in a straight pearly row, unlike any ever seen in a grown man's face in Greco-Roman Palestine. I stared at it with amazement, amazement and longing. I so wanted the picture to be true that I felt a physical craving, a craving as pure as hunger, and I didn't believe it for a second.

As G. K. Chesterton and others have pointed out, the story of Christ is technically a comedy. If his life ended with his death, it would be a tragedy. But he returns from the dead, and, if you believe in what the faith teaches, he brings eternal life to all believers. That's a lot to rejoice over. And the laughing Christ is right to see this. Yet it is impossible not to notice that in the gospels Jesus is the Man of Sorrows. He famously never laughs or jokes, and the only time he is confronted with a riddle, he doesn't answer, though his life could depend on the answer. Francis Bacon retells the story this way: "What is Truth? said jesting Pilate; and would not stay for an answer. Certainly there be that delight in giddiness, and count it a bondage to fix a belief; affecting free-will in thinking, as well as in acting." If he is who he says he is, Jesus must know, but he doesn't say. Perhaps he disdains to answer. Some answers are only for those who can hear them.

The Oxford don turned Episcopal priest M. A. Screech says in *Laughter at the Foot of the Cross* that the religious and the nonreligious will always find each other amusing because they understand the world in fundamentally different ways. The spiritually inclined value things that, to the worldly, don't exist, which makes their actions comic; and the worldly, to the sad amusement of the otherworldly, cherish evanescent delights that will cost them eternal bliss. Paul says it in almost those words, in Corinthians: "Hath God not made foolish the wisdom of the world? For since, in the wisdom of God, the world by wisdom knew not God, it pleased God by the foolishness of preaching to save them that believe."

"The secret source of humor is not joy but sorrow; there is no humor in heaven," wrote Mark Twain. Baudelaire, his contemporary, went further. Baudelaire declares that because there was no sadness in Eden, there was no laughter either. Harmony prevailed. Laughter didn't exist till disharmony provoked it: "The comic is a damnable element born of diabolic parentage." But I doubt there is much laughter in hell either. Laughter isn't demonic, but the result of our human double vision. We see both the perfect world we desire and the flawed one we live in. Believers and unbelievers live in different flawed worlds and conceive different perfections.

What we see around us is often disorderly and impossible to understand as meaningful. Christianity, like all religions, offers meaning. Jokes home in on the disordered places where meaning fails. They are drawn to chaos but they are terrified of it too because they cannot *not* see where meaning breaks down. Once they find those inconsistencies and breakdowns, they play with them, toss them in the air like a juggler keeping aloft a ball, two flaming torches, a cat, and a milking stool. Their attraction to chaos can be satanic delight or a godly attempt to heal by cauterizing a wound. They are both revolutionary and profoundly conservative. They are suspicious of systems of thought and enamored of the anomalies in them, but mostly they are content to mock, not destroy, those spindly systems.

Walking through a small town, Jesus sees a crowd milling about, preparing to stone to death a woman who has committed adultery. Just as in the Bible, he steps forward, raises his hand, and proclaims, "Let he who is without sin cast the first stone."

The crowd falls silent, abashed. They begin to disperse, and then a lightning bolt zings out of a clear sky and blasts the woman to a charred lump of flesh.

In an anguished voice, Jesus looks up at the sky and, through clenched teeth, says, "I'm trying to make a point here, Dad!"

The joke depicts people's uneasiness with forgiveness, especially for sexual sins. But more than that, it brings together as comedy the tensions of the faith. How do those two forces at the core of

Christianity—judgment and forgiveness—work in practice? For all its talk of forgiveness, and the real dedication of many believers to that ideal, the faith I grew up in often took more pleasure in the failings of others than joy at redemption. The knowing remarks about how Mr. Holcomb was going to roast in hell for all eternity and how Mrs. Sloan might be enjoying life now but she was going to be paying for it for a long time in a very warm place elicited more smiles than any confession of faith I saw. So I appreciated the beleaguered Jesus of the joke who was balked in his effort to teach compassion. And it's just fun to see one of the great trump lines of the Bible trumped, one of the great moments of enduring wisdom turned upside down.

The tension between judgment and compassion is at the base of a religion that rests on the paradoxes of its tenets. I love the Christian faith for those paradoxes. Whether we are believers or not, we make judgments; we extend or withhold forgiveness every day. The two impulses are rich, true, decent, and irresolvably in conflict. So it's impossible not to imagine that those Christians who see this life as a tragic fleshly trial and those who see it as a wonderful precursor to heaven are simply living out visions that are determined more by temperament than theology. Their preconceived worldviews determine which side of the gospel they focus their eyes on. And that, sadly enough, is something else to laugh about.

Here's how I resolve them. Here's my theology:

At the end of a powerful and emotional sermon, Billy Graham looks out over a packed arena and asks those who have felt the Lord working on their hearts to come forward and be saved.

One man slowly makes his way down the aisle. When he reaches the front, Reverend Graham holds up his hands, the music stops, silence falls over the huge hall, and into the microphone Billy Graham says, "Brother, who put those clothes on your body?"

The man replies, "The Lord did!"

"Amen!" roar a hundred thousand voices.

"And who, my brother, puts food on your table?"

The man replies, "The Lord does!"

"Amen!" roars the crowd with one voice.

"And who, my dear brother in Christ, put that smile on your face and the joy in your heart?"

"The Lord did."

"Amen! Hallelujah!" roars the crowd.

Billy raises his hands again and calls for silence. He leans in, holds the microphone closer to the flushed face of the new convert, and asks, "And, brother, what did the devil ever do for you?"

The man pauses for a second, thinking. "Nothing," he says. "Fuck him."

Amen, brother.

Five

Everybody Out of the Pool

"Get in the car. Find your brothers, and everybody get in the car! Right now!" my father yelled out the side door of my uncle's house. Behind him in the kitchen, Uncle Buddy yelled at Dad's back and kept yelling. I couldn't make out what he was saying, but as we moved in confusion through the carport to the car I heard despair in my mother's placating voice, trying to calm her husband and her brother. Then we were slamming out of the driveway, braking hard, and still slipping backward on loose gravel and red clay as Dad banged the shift lever from reverse to drive, and our green Impala wagon with the big fins accelerated furiously away.

From the backseat I studied the side of my father's face. He glared down the road in front of him, violently silent, his jaw tight, his neck rigid and flushed. Several times my mother turned to him and opened her mouth to say something. Each time she stopped herself, turned, and stared hopelessly out the window away from my father, twisting a damp Kleenex in her hands. My brothers and I were very quiet.

Only much later did I work up the courage to ask Mom what had happened. After everyone's nerves had stopped humming and I had wheedled a bit, Mom said Buddy had told a joke Dad didn't approve of. After I wheedled a bit more, she told me the joke.

A colored man collapses on the street, clutching at his heart. He thrashes around for a moment and then quits moving. Two white men dash over and kneel at his side. One man says, "I think he's having a heart attack!"

"He needs artificial respiration," the other says.

"What's that?"

"You put your lips on his and blow down into his mouth to keep him breathing."

"You do what? You put your lips on his lips? I'm not going to do that. You do it."

The second man thinks for a moment. He curled each hand till it formed a tube and stacked one atop the other.

My mother acted out the scene. She looked at me through the tube of curled fingers, letting me see that the man could breathe through them without letting his lips touch a black man's.

"Then the man," Mom said, "leaned down and put his hands next to the black man's ear," and, imitating the man in the joke, Mom put her fingers to her mouth, leaned over, and whispered through the trumpet of her fingers, "Nigger, you gonna *die!*"

The last word—*die!*—blasted through her hands with delighted triumph, propelled by the laugh she was already laughing. I laughed too, enjoying the twist in the joke and the delight Mom took when the Good Samaritan's concern for a dying man is trumped by his racism.

Dad didn't think any part of such a joke was funny. When Buddy had told it in his living room, Mom laughed, though nervously, knowing Dad was steaming. Driven over the edge by the punch line, Dad had angrily ordered Buddy not to use that kind of language in front of children. The only children in the room were my brother Mike, who was three, and my cousin Steve, who was two. What my uncle had been screaming as we rushed to the car, my mother told me later, was "This is my house! You can't tell me how to talk in my own goddamn house!"

"Nigger" would've rocketed Dad into Earth orbit. "Goddamn" would've kicked in the afterburners.

The joke sparked the first racial quarrel I'd seen, but I had begun to be wary about race a couple of years earlier, when I was six. When my father was transferred from Wright-Patterson AFB in Dayton, Ohio, to Seymour Johnson AFB in North Carolina, our family had to wait a year for a unit to open up in on-base housing. My parents rented a small brick ranch house out in the country, and I rode the bus to the county's consolidated school for first grade. The second week of school, as I hunched over the dining room table, coloring in a picture of Porky Pig with smooth, even sweeps of pink crayon, my mother asked me if any of the kids were different.

"I don't know," I said, and kept on pinking in Porky's outline while trying to decide if pigs' feet were black or brown. In real life, they seemed to be somewhere in-between. And were cartoon pigs' feet the same color as real ones? I didn't know what *different* meant. Tall or short, mean or dirty, bulge-eyed or hare-lipped? I'd been preoccupied with keeping my juice money and lunch money separate, my pencils sharp in the cracked plastic pencil box, and my sandwich unsquashed. It's very difficult not to sit on your lunch bag, step on it, or clutch it too tightly when you are six, drowsy, and your bus jounces off asphalt and down a dirt road and then back onto asphalt again five times on a forty-five-minute circuit through a North Carolina dawn.

"I mean, do any of the kids look different?" Mom asked.

"I guess."

"Well, are any of them a different color?"

I thought about it and then offered up—was this what she wanted to know?—that one of the girls was chocolate.

"Chocolate!" Mom said, laughing. "Chocolate!" After she stopped laughing, she chuckled about it, off and on, for the rest of the afternoon.

So chocolate isn't a word for describing people, I thought. She told and retold the story to my father, my grandmothers, aunts and uncles, and her friends, all of whom laughed at my charming innocence, which at that age was indistinguishable from ignorance. That's why they were laughing at me, wasn't it? I wasn't just wrong, I thought, feeling mocked and ill-used: I was so wrong it was funny. No, not just funny: hilarious. Yet from the way she'd pussyfooted around asking me, trying not to let me see there was anything charged or complicated about the color of the chocolate girl, I saw too that she was trying to protect me from the very information that she was trying to extract. But once she heard my answer, she was so amused by the cluelessness of my misunderstanding that she had to tell everyone. So I became alert to race, its secret importance, and its uneasy connection to humor.

I had not until then noticed that the characters on *Amos 'n' Andy* were black. When we got our first TV, I left the room while Mom watched *As the World Turns*, which she called "my show," as did both my grandmothers. The gloom and fraught intensity of the drama drove me away, but I always came back to sit by Mom as she ironed, smoked, and watched *Amos 'n' Andy*. I cannot think of that show without seeing it through the rickety, pincered legs of an ironing board, hearing the flick of water as Mom sprinkled the wrinkled laundry with water to moisten it, and smelling Pall Malls smoldering in an ashtray. Damp shirts sizzled under the hot iron and the stringent smell of spray starch filled the room.

I was often baffled by what was actually going on with the Kingfish, Amos, Sapphire, and the Mystic Knights of the Sea; and I puzzled mightily over why the show was called *Amos 'n' Andy*, since sweet-natured, ineffectual Amos had such a vanishingly small role. I laughed at the predicaments into which the raffish Kingfish constantly enticed Andy, and I identified with my namesake's childlike gullibility and desire to be in-the-know. But most of all, I was enchanted by the pleasure they took in rolling the words off their lips to such exaggerated effect, especially the Kingfish's affectation for pretentious words that he mispronounced: "Andy, I'se re-gusted!" Sometimes I even understood the gap between what he meant and what he said, especially when my mother repeated the mispronunciations and chuckled. That's what I really loved, the plushness of her chuckle. It is a sound that I have been susceptible to in women ever since. What a respite my mother's laugh was from the sorrow that, like standing water, dampened our house, a sorrow I could not then name. But I could recognize when laughter came in, and for a few minutes, divided the waters.

My mother's pleasure in *Amos 'n' Andy* must have been partly racist and partly, like mine, innocent, motivated by the high jinks and malapropisms of the characters, irrespective of race. Still, along with the brilliance of its comedy, *Amos 'n' Andy* was also teaching me the conventions of racist humor and the assumptions behind it. Though no one ever said so, the show was whispering, *Look at those ignorant colored folk and laugh at the comical troubles they cause for themselves by pretending to be smarter than they are.* No one ever said it out loud, except my grandmother, who growled, "I can't abide looking at that nigger foolishness."

A graduate of Spalding County High School, my mother had worked in the Dundee Mills before marrying my father in the chapel at West Point. She was uneasy with officers' wives who had Ivy

League degrees and attitudes. Part of her never left her mother's house on Vineyard Road in Griffin, Georgia.

My grandmother, her mother, was the angriest person I've ever known who wasn't actually unhinged; in fact, she might have been. Much of her explosive rage was aimed at "niggers." With every casual use of the word *nigger* she hit the short i and hard g of the word, her voice crackling with contempt, fury, and, though I was slow to see it, fear. She packed a lifetime of negation into the word. Toward the end of her life, my parents' repeated strenuous opposition forced her to modulate the word to "nigra" most of the time when we visited. She could never quite bring herself to say "negro," the polite word of the time, though occasionally she'd allow herself "colored," the polite word of her youth. But when she genuinely wanted to praise a black woman she'd unself-consciously declare that Annie or Willa was "a good nigger."

Knowing that "nigger" sometimes ruffled my mother, always infuriated my father, and jolted me, made it even more tempting to her thin lips—an orneriness I admired in general, though I was uneasy and embarrassed when it amplified her racism.

As Grandmomma grew older, her swollen legs made it harder and harder for her to walk, even with a walker. For a couple of years before my aunt and cousin moved in with her, my mother and my Uncle Buddy hired a black woman to clean the house and look after Grandmomma during the day. Angry at having to turn her house over to someone else's care, Grandmomma at first referred to the woman as "that nigger Carrie." Later, as Grandmomma warmed to her, the woman became "the nigger Carrie," and, later still, as Grandmomma grew to like the idea of having "help," she began to refer to "my nigger Carrie"—proud at last to have one, the way the rich folks did. Though I was squirmingly uncomfortable with how her pleasure expressed itself through the possessive pronoun and the word *nigger*, I was pleased, and embarrassed to be pleased, that she had found a way to enjoy her growing helplessness. When I whined to my mother, "I wish she wouldn't *say* that," Mom just laughed and answered, "Let her enjoy herself. She's not hurting anybody." It's hard not to think of Huck Finn's conversation with Aunt Sally. Huck, lying, tells her there'd been an accident on the steamboat.

"Good gracious! anybody hurt?"

"No'm. Killed a nigger."

"Well, it's lucky; because sometimes people do get hurt."

My mother and Aunt Sally's instinctive empathy extended only so far and then it ran into a wall so tall and thick and long that it seemed like the end of the earth instead of a wall. Yes, Grandmother's antipathy was monumental, but as instinctive as her empathy.

In the months after the Watts and Detroit riots, Grandmomma was so incensed by the looting and burning she'd seen on TV that she could barely talk. While I sat at her kitchen table eating grits and country ham or fried chicken and mashed potatoes with red-eye gravy, my uncle argued that the only goddamn solution was as plain as the nose on your face: line the niggers up against the wall and machine-gun them. Buddy railed that only machine guns and tanks and bodies bulldozed into mass graves would put a stop to all this nigger bullshit, and Grandmomma nodded in furious agreement, occasionally spitting out half a syllable of inarticulate rage.

I loved her.

Short, hugely squat, Grandmomma had a round bulldog face, her blunt pink features laced with broken veins and her small chin jutted forward as if to say what she often said, "Don't mess with me, boy. I'm not going to take no mess off you." Will emanated from her face the way heat emanated from the bedroom gas heater she used to overheat the whole house. It emanated even from her legs. They'd bloat till the skin was so taut it shone, and then they'd deflate slightly. The skin, distended and slack at the same time, looked like blotchy crepe de chine.

At the ends of her painful feet grew thick, dirty-yellow toenails, humped and twisted. She had to soak them for hours in warm water before she could trim them. I was fascinated. To me, a child of relative ease, those malformed nails represented an older, harder world, the physical consequences of forty years standing at a loom in the Dundee Mills making towels, and I loved to look at them because I was not supposed to. It was rude, Mom said. But Grandmomma never seemed to mind. I was her favorite, perhaps because I was a listener, and to a talker, few things are more tempting than an attentive child who is blood kin.

We lay on our bellies on her lumpy, buckled mattress and watched *Queen for a Day*, our favorite show. We had opinions. We discussed, dissected, and evaluated the relative misery of the wretched women who told their sorrows in competition for a prize that always turned out to be a Maytag washer-dryer combination.

It was nice, that Maytag washer-dryer combination, nicer than the wringer-washer Grandmomma kept on her back porch, and which she still loved because it was a magnificent improvement over a washboard and tub. When she washed, I got to turn the crank.

Because she understood the value of a new washer-dryer combo, which she did not possess, Grandmomma possessed a flawless and unchallengeable eye about what women might say to get one.

"She's lying," Grandmomma said as a woman ended her tale of woe.

"How can you tell, Grandmomma?"

"Just *look* at her! She's lying and you can see she's lying."

Grandmomma also had a sure sense of what true suffering was. "Pfft!" she said, "that's not so bad"—meaning, though I did not know it then—that she'd lived through worse. When Jack Bailey named the day's champion sufferer and draped the queen's robe on her shoulders and set the crown on her head, we sometimes teared up a bit. We tried to conceal our tears from each other because we were tough eggs, not easily fooled or satisfied. We were cynical and sentimental in exactly the proportions that Jack Bailey and Maytag required us to be. Because its life-transforming properties were deemed so evident as to need no explanation, I never had the courage to ask Grandmomma how a Maytag washer-dryer combination or, more rarely, a refrigerator, compensated for a husband crushed to death by industrial machinery (Grandmomma: "He'd been dranking. You just know he'd been dranking."), a son in reform school, and a daughter crippled with polio. Obviously something about women's lives improved spiritually as well as materially, when the burden of laundry was eased.

During the last commercial, we selected the winner, and we never disagreed. If the audience selected the hard-luck case we had selected, we knew there was justice in the world. If they did not, we poured our contempt on them, fools who were taken in by a lie or a pretty face—fools who couldn't see that a better parent would have kept her son out of reform school in the first durn place. Why, they were just rewarding some woman for raising a criminal.

As much as we agreed about *Queen for a Day*, I was prissy—"nice-nasty," was my mother's amused epithet—about Grandmomma's snuff. With a dexterity that seemed impossible, she kept a dip of Bruton's Snuff lodged between her right cheek and gums, while back on the molars on the left side of her mouth she worked a wad of gum. Overnight and during meals, the gum, used and reused, sat on the top of the red-and-white snuff tin by the sink. When, while exploring the crawl space beneath her house, I was stung by a couple of yellow jackets, Grandmomma grabbed my wrist and dragged me to the kitchen. Holding my arm out straight, she opened the tin with her free hand and scooped out a big dip of tobacco. While I struggled, trying to break her tight grip, she reached into her mouth and slapped the wad of snuff on my forearm. The pain of the yellow jacket bites vanished as I watched the brown juice stream down my raised arm. I gagged and pleaded, bucked and fought, but she didn't let go until she was satisfied that the snuff had drawn out the poison.

On bus trips or in the car, she carried her spit jar, a quart Mason jar stuffed loosely with Kleenex to keep the spit from sloshing. Sitting next to Grandmomma in the car, I tried not to look at the brown slop saturating the pink tissue. I was afraid I'd retch. But as I sat there and tried not to think about it, my eyes kept slipping back to it. I had to test my persnickety gag reflex against what I knew was her pleasure, and I wanted to train myself not to be so judgmental. I was ashamed that I could not accept her in her entirety.

My mother laughed at her mother's snuff habit and made jokes about it when Grandmomma wasn't around, but I doubt anybody ever had the temerity to suggest that she quit. It would have been a waste of breath, and an affront. Like a lot of mill workers, she got hooked on snuff because, unlike cigarettes, it left her hands free to work the looms. Once, her voice swelling with old triumph and more than a trace of lingering outrage, she asked my mother, "Sister, you remember when they tried to take the spittoons out of the mill and everybody just pulled the thread aside and spat through it onto the floor? When the foreman finally noticed the dried-up tobacco under the looms, they couldn't get them spittoons back in there fast enough." Thinking about the bosses and their stupidity, she gave an angry grunt. Mom laughed. Like me, like Dad, like all my family, she honored cussedness.

As I said, I loved her.

At the University of Alabama, I read, in a linguistics textbook of all things, the assertion, "Nobody can love a racist." Immediately I thought of my grandmother. Though I was sometimes afraid of her, I never doubted my love. At times, I wondered whether it was wrong—whether it was a *sin*—to love a woman who was often angry, bigoted, and mean. But I knew such wondering was merely forced moralizing. Grandmomma had always loved me, loved me with a hot, furious love, which frightened me almost as much as it comforted me. As I pondered the textbook's magisterial claim, all I could finally say to myself was that life is more complex than absolutists and some linguists find it to be. Love is not love that can only love those already flawless. That kind of love requires no enlargement of the self: It requires no love.

My Grandmomma's racism was the pigheaded racism of the old school—staunch, unrepentant, and all the more ferocious as it saw history turning against it. Against such racism, I saw my mother as racially enlightened. When I was about twelve my mother carried back to Grandmomma's house a pile of worn-out quilts that Grandmomma had made for her long ago. My grandmother was not sentimental about her quilts. They were quickly and sloppily pieced together, backed with cheap muslin, and quilted with long loose stitches. When they wore through or pulled apart, she didn't patch them. She simply tacked a new piece of muslin to each side and quilted the cloth sandwich together—or, as she did this time, found a black woman who lived out in the country so poor that she agreed to do the work for next to nothing.

After the quilter sent word that she was done, Mom asked Grandmomma how much she owed. "Five dollars a quilt," Gradmomma said.

"That's not enough," Mom said. "That's too much work for five dollars." I didn't know much about quilting, but I knew that if my mother wanted to pay more, something vastly unfair was happening. She was proud to call herself "tight as a tick."

"That nigger agreed to five dollars and I'm going to pay her five dollars."

"I'm going to pay her ten. Just tell me where she lives, and I'll get the quilts myself."

"Roberta, I am not going to do it. We gave her the cloth to do the work with. All she had to do was stitch it down. And I'm not going to have you spoil that nigger. She's perfectly happy to get five."

"Just tell me where she lives and I'll go get them."

"No you won't, because I'm the one who knows and I'm not going to tell you."

The fight sputtered on for a few days and ended only when Mom found someone who knew where the woman lived. She drove deep out into the country, got lost, finally found the woman's house down an unmarked dirt road, picked up the quilts, and paid ten dollars apiece for them.

Because of incidents like this, I assumed that when my mother told racist jokes she was making fun of my grandmother and racists like her. Only slowly did I come to understand that though that was true, or partly true, my mother was not immune to racism; hers was simply a more evolved species. I never saw her do a deliberately mean thing to anyone, black or white, but from time to time she surprised me with what she said. Once when I came home from high school right after it had been integrated, I mentioned to my mother that I had found myself in one of the crowded stairwells before class jammed against a girl who reeked of perfume and I had smelled it on myself the rest of the day. I mentioned this only because I had never been close enough to a girl my own age to smell her perfume and, though I didn't say so, I was disturbed to smell her musky scent later in the day on my own skin, as my own scent.

"Was she black?"

"Yes."

"Well, then be thankful she smelled like perfume," Mom said and laughed. At sixteen, and sheltered from a great deal of racism by the very woman who had just made that remark, I didn't know what to think. This racial stereotype was a new one to me. I hadn't yet heard the joke that asks, "Why do black people stink?" "So blind people can hate them too."

My mother occasionally went out of her way to speak to blacks and working-class whites with a naturalness and ease that were beyond me, distressed as I was by my developing sense of historical guilt. Original sin had merged seamlessly with the inherited sin I learned about from reading *Manchild in the Promised Land*, *The Autobiography of Malcolm X*, and *Black Like Me*. At fourteen, I couldn't walk past black people on the street without assuming they automatically disliked me because I was a member of the race that had imposed slavery on their ancestors and Jim Crow laws on them. By sixteen, I was even more self-conscious and mortified to realize that my way of thinking reduced every African-American to an undifferentiated representative of the race—and that made me a racist too, if a polite and abjectly deferential one.

Several times Mom told me she wouldn't mind in the least if I brought home a black woman and announced I wanted to marry her, as long as I "really, truly loved her." She was working hard not to be overtly prejudiced, so I've wondered if the qualification hinged on believing true love conquered all or that white men were incapable of truly loving black women. Twice, though, she added that she would have a problem if I brought home a Filipina. They started out young and attractive, sure, but they turned hard in just a couple of years, she said. They saw white men as a way out of the Philippines and into the land of the big PX. (The PX, the Post Exchange, was the army's retail store for soldiers and their families; the air force called it the BX, or Base Exchange.) This prejudice was the eccentric and unabashed distaste of a service wife who had seen a couple of friends marry Filipinas only to be dumped as soon as the wives' U.S. citizenship came through. Since I first received this warning when I was fourteen, and had only seen Filipino women at the PX or base commissary with their husbands, the proscription always tickled me. I couldn't take Mom seriously because I've never heard anyone else say anything derogatory about Filipinos, before or since.

"What about an Indian, Mom? Can I marry an Indian?"

"I don't care. Just no Filipinos."

"What about Japanese?"

"Japanese, Negroes, I told you I don't care."

"What about Mexicans? They're brown—do they get hard-looking as they get older, just like Filipinos?"

"This isn't funny anymore. I told you what I think and I mean it. Don't you bring home a Filipino girl."

"There goes my Saturday night."

"That's enough, young man."

Mom may not have cared for Filipinos, but the word *Filipino* itself had no sting to it. Grandmomma used the word *nigger* like a lash on herself as well as others. My mother softened it: "Look at this house! Clothes scattered everywhere! It looks like a bunch of Okies live here." Or "Get your bikes and toys out of the driveway. The neighbors will think we're a bunch of hillbillies." There was real despair in her voice, and something that I couldn't place. Later I came to understand it was fear. As soon as she had proclaimed us Okies or hillbillies, she pitched herself into cleaning the house, tidying the yard, polishing the silver, and I was soon on my knees washing the baseboard with a stiff-bristled brush and then scrubbing around the bathroom faucets with an old toothbrush. Only much later did I come to see that Okies and hillbillies were socially acceptable substitutions for the unacceptable word she'd grown up with. But she still needed the concept. Long before I knew what one was, I knew I didn't want to be a nigger, Okie, hillbilly, or white trash. When I was a young man, poor, angry, and depressed, I too used these words to sting myself into action. The taboo power of the words hurt and, when I used them on myself, I wanted it to.

Maybe the rage behind Grandmomma's words came from poverty, a hard life laboring at the looms of the Dundee Mills, and a fear that African-Americans, whom she had always assumed were below her, might grab the next rung of the ladder and vault past. Maybe it came from raising three children and losing a fourth during the Great Depression in rural Georgia while married to an ineffectual and self-effacing husband who drank his way through the first years of their marriage. Maybe. Even my teetotaler father once allowed that he considered drinking to be a reasonable response to being married to Daisy Mae Rodgers. Many people in her time and place suffered as much as she had, or more without becoming as fierce. Mom told me later that when she was a girl, Grandmomma would, for little or no reason, grab a razor strop or churn handle—whatever came to hand—and beat her and her brother and sister to the floor.

Grandmomma used words as she used the churn handle. For the last several years of her life, my Aunt Joyce moved into Grandmomma's house to care for her. When I visited, Grandmomma, sitting at her kitchen table and talking affectionately to me, her elbows propped on red-and-white-checked oil cloth, would suddenly turn to Joyce and snarl, "How long you gonna let that dirty skillet sit on the stove? Heavens to Betsy, Joyce, it's two o'clock and you're still slopping around in your housecoat like a nigger." *Nigger* cracked like a whip. And Joyce grumbled back, "Now, Momma, don't start on me." Or worse: "Don't start on me, *old woman.*"

A dirty house and dirty clothes were the first step toward the abyss, toward slovenliness, laziness, and despair, which would lead to being fired and to drunkenness and to living hand-to-mouth, like "white trash." Grandmomma knew full well that some people would call her that—white trash—though she wasn't. She was a worker, a church woman, a woman who kept a clean house, never took a nickel of welfare, and raised three children, all of whom had jobs or husbands and not one of whom had spent so much as one night in jail. "No matter how poor you are, you can always be clean," both she and my mother said, with more intensity and certitude than any religious sentiment I heard them utter. So Grandmomma, too disabled to clean her house, bullied Joyce into doing it: "Joyce, sweep this floor! I hate the feel of grit under my feet, I just purely hate it. There's niggers live better than we do."

There was little Grandmomma could do except ride Joyce—ride Joyce and wash the dishes. She clumped across the kitchen on her walker, jerked a cane-bottom chair up to the sink and angled it so she could wash the dishes and still be part of the conversation that was going on at the table. Sitting, she slowly washed a sinkful of dishes, a two-hour job, and she wouldn't accept help. She scraped a dirty plate, dipped it in hot soapy water, and scrubbed it over a worn bath towel folded double on her lap. She dipped the plate again, scrubbed it once more, inspected it, perhaps washed it a third time, then dried it before moving on to the next one. She was a harsh, determined, wrathful woman, whom I loved because, like God, she loved me first.

I have never heard my father say *nigger* or tolerate the word in his presence, a rare attainment for a white man born in rural Georgia in 1922. As an officer in the United States Air Force and a Christian, he despised the word and everything associated with it. Though he is not much given to talk and even less to praise, he went out of his way, especially when I was young, to compliment black officers he'd worked with. Out of the blue, he found ways to indicate that so-and-so was black, and a fine man and a fine officer, and he—my father—was proud to have served under him. He made a point to say "under." Every situation was a teaching situation, and no opportunity for a sermon on race ever went unfulfilled.

When a particularly perfervid black leader in Montgomery ranted about police violence or discrimination, most of the white folks I knew got riled up, angry, and defensive. But my father often simply said, "I'd like to think that if I were him, I'd do just what he's doing," a statement that I could only take as pedagogical since I've known few people who abhor extravagant rhetoric as much as he does. Another sermon, I thought at the time, but now I wonder if Dad was weighing himself in the balances—"I'd *like* to think"—and finding himself wanting.

In Sunday school in Montgomery, Dad took pointed enjoyment in telling the other men in his class that my high school football team, the Sidney Lanier Poets, couldn't reasonably be considered the best team in the state, despite their undefeated record, because they hadn't played a single black team.

"What'd they say?" I asked.

"They explained that the blacks had their own league and Lanier couldn't be expected to play teams outside their league." He grinned and snorted, to let me know what he thought of that excuse.

In 1970, my first year in college, Daniel "Chappie" James was promoted to major general, an air force "first" for an African-American and one that received a lot of press. "Did you ever meet him, Dad?" I asked as we watched the news after supper, and my father waxed unusually enthusiastic. He had in fact met General James, he said, and he considered him to be a superb general and everyone who had worked with him thought the same thing. Keeping a straight face, I closed my eyelids and rolled my eyes as far back in my head as I could. Even honorable sermons remain sermons.

To Dad, sermons were the entire point of life. My mother and father had grown up only a few miles apart in rural Georgia, in red-clay poverty, and my father's family was if anything poorer than my mother's. My father, his two brothers, and one sister were raised by a widow whose husband died as a delayed result of mustard gas he'd inhaled in Europe during the First World War. Still, despite the hardship, my father and his brothers went to college, and their sister, my Aunt Margie, married a man who began as a lineman for Southern Bell and worked his way into management. Both of my father's brothers became ministers, while my father was for a number of years a deacon in his Southern Baptist church. Their education and thoughtful commitment to their faiths made racist joking repulsive to them—but not to everyone on their side of the family. When my father's uncle died, a man I knew only distantly as Uncle Cisco, his children found a Ku Klux Klan robe they'd never seen before hidden in the back of his closet.

I admired the humane morality of my father's family. It made me feel safe, if bored and occasionally bullied. But *humane* is a bit abstract, more affectionate than passionate—and I was claimed by the hot-blooded love of my mother's family, a love that I was all the more aware of because it could so quickly turn to anger. The same ferocity that drove their racism and raucous squabbling with one another also seemed to drive their love, including their love for me. Their laughter was volatile with fear and love, rage and attachment, and I treasured the warmth of it while dreading the flames that often flared. I was drawn to the laughter even if it was bad laughter.

I felt I could separate the ugly, racist laughter from the misplaced rage that fueled it. But it troubled me as I sat at my grandmother's table, morally conflicted because I knew my uncle took my fitful laughter at his hair-raising racist jokes as complicity. When one of his jokes surprised me and I laughed before I could stop myself—"What's the difference between a snow tire and a black man?" "A tire doesn't sing when you put on the chains"—Buddy must have thought, *Andrew agrees with me because he's laughing.* But in the harmony of our voices blended in laughter, wherever that harmony came from and whatever it meant, I felt the anger ease, though not disappear. We were family. We had to find ways of living with each other.

One day Uncle Buddy set a bowl of water on my grandmother's table and pronounced, "That's the city swimming pool."

He jibbled up pieces of white notebook paper, scattered them on the water in the bowl, and said, "Those are the white kids playing in the pool, having fun." Oh God, I could almost see what was coming. Griffin had a large municipal pool built by the Works Project Administration, and a couple of times every summer Buddy took my brothers, cousins, and me for an afternoon of splashing, hot dogs, ice cream, and sunburn. When the federal court ordered the swimming pool integrated, the city discovered problems with the pool, problems so extensive that the pool had to be closed. Permanently. *It's really irreparable. I mean, we're a small town and we just don't have the money to waste on frills like swimming pools.*

Quickly, before the scraps of paper got waterlogged, Buddy shook black pepper over the water and said, "And when the niggers get in, it just ruins it for everybody." He slipped his finger into the edge of the water, and the paper bits and flecks of pepper fled to opposite sides of the bowl. "It's 'Everybody outta the pool!'" He laughed a scornful laugh. The pleasure of cutting off your nose to spite your face is well known to us southerners. You think you can make us do what you want? Ha, we'll shut down the pool and stop *everybody*, including me and mine, from swimming. How yuh like them apples, Mr. Federal Judge?

Buddy had smeared soap on his finger, and when he touched the water, the soap disrupted the surface tension, causing the paper and pepper to separate. I was intrigued by how the trick worked, but couldn't stop myself from pitching into the old and useless arguments about how black people were taxpayers too, were fully equal to whites, deserved equal rights, and on and on, splashing in the warm lard-bath of self-delighting sanctimony. We ended up where we always ended up. With what I thought of as withering disdain, I would say, "They didn't just line up and buy tickets for that scenic voyage across the Atlantic, you know. We kidnapped them and brought them here." And Buddy always answered that he knew that. That was all in the past. Wadn't nothing could be done about it now. But the situation we were in now was that we had a bunch of apes living alongside us and only idiots would try to treat apes as their equals. The whole country would fall apart. The arguments got nastier the tighter the circles spun.

So I made rules for myself. If the joke jolts an honest laugh out of me, I would, no matter how ugly it is, relax and enjoy the laugh, but I wouldn't fake a laugh out of politeness. It is hard, I found, to withhold the polite, wooden "heh, heh" that signals that, while you don't think the joke is funny, you are fulfilling your obligation to acknowledge that a joke has been told. Another rule was that I wouldn't criticize racist jokes. Maybe I'd say "ouch." Mostly I let the joke pass in silence. Sometimes I'd walk away. If I criticized, I'd just end up in another pointless argument, or I'd hear the defense I retreated to when challenged, "It's just a joke. I didn't mean nothing by it."

Around the same time that I made up these rules I made up another, larger rule: Never argue with people more than ten years older than yourself about race. You are never going to change their minds. They'll dig in harder. And you'll just piss everyone off, including yourself. As I said before, we were family. We had to find ways to live with both one another and ourselves.

Six

A Quart Low

"Don't tell your father," Mom said whenever she told me a racist joke. She didn't need to warn me. With this kind of humor, my mother wavered somewhere between my father's irascible probity and her brother's nasty delight. When she repeated them, I often heard my Uncle Buddy's voice in the background, as well as her own guilt at setting a bad example for her son. The human need to pass on something she found funny, compelling, or perplexing over-rode her guilt and became part of the joke's power—and part of its pleasure.

I loved her warning me to silence. It made explicit the grown-upness of our forbidden disreputable laughter, which was an adult intoxicant like her Pall Malls or the scotch she sometimes allowed herself at night while watching Johnny Carson's opening monologue on *The Tonight Show*. When she drank, she invariably sipped cheap scotch—Clan MacGregor—out of a thick glass that once held a frozen shrimp cocktail. With that bit of watered scotch and Johnny Carson cracking wise on the TV, she occasionally shared a joke she'd been mulling over till she had to tell it.

"A colored man suddenly finds himself in front of St. Peter at the pearly gates," she said, when I was thirteen.

This was an interesting beginning. We were Baptists, and we didn't believe in saints. In the radical Protestant democracy of faith, the apostle Peter had no more of a special standing with Jesus than each one of us did. From hearing hundreds of sermons and Sunday school lessons, I knew this doctrinal verity before I knew the multiplication tables. By repeating the joke, she accepted, for the purposes of the story, a premise she considered Catholic mumbo jumbo.

St. Peter asks the colored man how he died.

"I don't remember," the man tells him.

"We have to know. We have to fill out these forms and decide if you're going to heaven or the hot place," St. Peter says. He thinks for a few moments and then asks, "What's the last thing you do remember?"

"Well, I was attending this white Baptist Church. Everybody was real friendly. The preacher preached up a storm, and when he invited those who wanted to be baptized and join the church to walk down the aisle, I did.

"They was real nice about it. They dressed me in a purdy green satin robe, led me to the baptismal font, and sang a glorious hymn."

"That's all you remember?" St. Peter says. "Try harder. Something else must've happened."

"Let me see," says the black man. "Oh, yeah, just as I was being dunked in the water, the preacher said, 'Bye-bye, nigger, bye-bye.'"

My mother chanted the punch line triumphantly, her voice rising as she sang out "bye-bye," falling as she sneered "nigger," and then soaring joyously as she repeated "bye-bye" before she gave herself over to laughter.

Did I laugh? I did. We were laughing, weren't we, at hypocriti-
cal Christians who demonstrated, with homicidal glee, their lack of
true Christianity? The joke pointed out the conflict between how we
acted and how we were supposed to act. "Man is the only animal
that laughs and weeps; for he is the only animal that is struck with
the difference between what things are and what they should be,"
says William Hazlitt.

The joke could not possibly *really* imply that killing African-
American converts to keep the church segregated was a good idea,
could it? There wasn't enough wit in the joke to disguise its ugliness, if that's what it meant. Anyway, didn't our suburban church in
Montgomery, like almost all Southern Baptist churches, prohibit, by
a vote of the congregation, blacks from joining? Even today, the old
lament of that time remains true: Eleven to noon on Sunday is the
most segregated hour of the American week.

As a young teenager, in the last years of such earnest innocence, I wondered why African-Americans would care to worship
in a church that purposely excluded them. *How could you force
your way into fellowship?* I asked myself, though I knew my church
was wrong, cowardly, and un-Christian to turn anyone away. I was
confused, but my mother was adamant. She herself would rather
die, she said, than join a church that didn't want her, and she didn't
understand why the coloreds, unless they were just troublemakers,
didn't feel the same way. They had their own churches and they
should go where they were wanted. Her anger came through in the
exuberance with which she told the joke. She seemed to identify
just a bit too much with the homicidal preacher, and she took a bit
too much delight in "the colored man" getting his comeuppance for
his uppity desire to join a church that didn't want him. I was right
to understand the joke as a joke about entrenched and murderous
racists, but, because I loved her and didn't want to think badly of
her, I didn't see that she also identified with racists like her brother.

I was too young to see how someone could in good faith believe two contradictory things at the same time, especially since I knew Mom had often sat in military chapels with black worshippers and, when we were overseas, she and my father had sent me to a Sunday school class taught by a black man.

Before we moved back to the States, to Montgomery, my father was stationed at a NATO base outside Paris, and my Sunday school class at the base chapel was taught by a handsome young black NCO whom I'll call William. When William talked, softly but intently, about Jesus and the Bible, I felt as though I were in the presence of an apostle. The small storeroom where we met behind the chapel became a direct extension of Galilee. We were walking with Jesus. William possessed an otherworldly charisma, in both the theological and the popular meanings of the word, and when he taught the class his faith and passion enlarged him. My troubled questions—I was fourteen then—about evil, doubt, God's will, and God's essence never irked him as they did my father and most other adults who, when boxed into a theological corner, said with a rhetorical shrug, "Some things we just have to take on faith," an aggravating and complacent evasion. They were uncomfortable—afraid or unable to venture into the dark emotional and spiritual places where logic broke down. Those were the places I spent much of my time, and William, leaning over the table, eyes locked on mine, intent but not so intent as to make me turn away, was at ease in those intellectual dead ends.

Even when William had to resort to the take-it-on-faith line, which is an almost inevitable redoubt in theology, he was articulate and thoughtful about it. Though he didn't, as far as I remember, ever let a ray of doubt escape his orbit, he was the most (and I'm tempted to say the only) thoughtful person I'd ever met in Sunday school. The teachers were often eccentric about what aspects of the faith they emphasized. When I was eight, a honey-blond college girl told my Vacation Bible School class, with blissful longing, how much she looked forward to dying.

"Really, you want to die?" I asked. I couldn't imagine it. From as early as I can remember I've been terrified of death. Yes, she assured us third graders, she wanted very much to die. She couldn't wait to free herself of this world of strife and go to heaven, where she would be at peace in the love of God. From the overemphatic way she said "love," I wondered if she had just broken up with her boyfriend. But her longing for death, which brought tears to her eyes, was clearly real.

Seeing she had disturbed me, she later came down and bent over me while I was studying a picture on the wall of Jesus knocking on a heavy wooden door ("Behold, I stand at the door and knock"). Her hair swung against my face. She let it lie against my cheek for an uncomfortably long time, and inside the joy she was trying to radiate, I felt the unhappiness behind her proclaimed bliss. Even at eight, I thought, pleased with my own callousness, that if she were so eager to die she could, with minimal effort, fulfill her own wish. A steak knife or plastic dry-cleaning bag would do the trick. I was a boy. I knew these things.

In the hall outside the church classroom in Paris or talking to my parents in the aisle after Sunday school and before services began, William was oddly diminished, transformed into simply a trim, polite man in a blue blazer, and I was startled to notice he was shorter than my father. In our small classroom, freed from the presence of men who outranked him, he was imposing and magnetic while being enormously calm. I have never before or since desired so much to sit in someone's presence and learn from him. I would have liked to be him.

I loved William's deep pastoral interest in Gloria, the one other regular student in his class, and the callow white officer's son I knew myself to be. My father liked everything about the arrangement: my interest in religion, the sergeant's persuasive faith, and my studying with a black man. My mother didn't seem to care one way or the other, though I sensed she was slightly apprehensive about my becoming too swept up in religion. I'd never had such sustained serious attention from an adult as I had from William, though I wondered how much we were Gloria and Andrew to him and how much we were indistinct souls, impersonal obligations, he was leading to the narrow path and the strait gate.

When I told my father that William had mentioned he was planning to leave the air force and go into the ministry in the States, Dad said, almost blandly, "That's not going to be easy for him."

"How come?"

"His wife is French and they have a baby," Dad said. I'd known William lived "on the economy"—which meant off base, outside of military housing. Few people chose to do that because French real estate was expensive and complex to negotiate. By saying *French*, Dad expected me to hear *white*, which I did, and to understand that William's interracial marriage and mixed-race child would present difficulties in the States in the mid-sixties. I did understand, but I did not feel sorry for William. He was too strong in the Lord to warrant my concern, much less my pity. I never saw William's wife, though I looked for her, glancing over his shoulder as he came down the church aisle, trying to see if she was walking behind him. When he sat, I kept darting looks in his direction to see if she had come late and slipped into the pew beside him. He was always alone. I was curious about William's personal life, especially about his wife because I'd never seen a white woman with a black man. But I was also dying to see a French evangelical. Didn't William's wife have to be an evangelical too? A French evangelical fundamentalist—it was a concept so exotic I had trouble grasping it. I still do.

My un-nuanced admiration for William acquired nuance with a jolt the Sunday he brought his two-year-old daughter to class. Sarah was the first mixed race child I'd ever seen, so I'm sure I studied her with more open curiosity than was polite. She had much lighter skin than her father, his face was longer, and her brownish hair curled loosely around her head. A few minutes into class, Sarah began to squirm in her father's lap, bored and restless as William expounded biblical texts just above her head. A sharp jerk settled her for a moment, and then another jerk settled her again briefly before she started to sniffle and then cry. The sergeant, who had always been vastly patient with Gloria and me, held the child up, legs dangling in the air, glared at her, shook her, and snarled, "*Ça va, Sarah! Ça va?*"

"*Ça va, Sarah! Ça va?*" he repeated into the girl's face, and waited with savage expectancy as if the stunned child could answer. The ferocity of his voice rocked me back in my folding chair. Was William exasperated that taking care of the girl had impinged on the serious business of soul-saving? Was he simply a stern father, embarrassed that his daughter was disturbing our Bible study? Why so harsh? Was William annoyed because he'd wanted to present a model of black good behavior to us white kids? I couldn't tell and I was unhappy at letting race enter my thinking at all, but I was disturbed at a personal level and disillusioned theologically to see the messenger of God's love turn wrathful with such small provocation. I was used to this kind of transformation at home. But I believed I'd seen in William a different way for men to be men and maybe, given his patience with me, a different way for Christians to be fathers. And I'd been wrong. Or maybe only partly wrong. Anyone can lose his temper and I only saw William lose his this one memorable time. I still admired my vibrant teacher, but more guardedly, anxious now about my boyish desire to idealize people. If nothing else, the Old Testament teaches that prophets aren't distinguished by even temperaments and sensitive natures, not even when their preaching is being heeded.

After we left Paris, I never saw or heard about William again. In the way of military brats who grow used to leaving people and places behind, I didn't expect to, though I often wondered about him, his family, and his ministry in America. But William was the figure in the back of my head when I heard racist jokes, and perversely it was my admiration for him that made me unable to take the racism of these jokes completely seriously. I knew better—and so I could laugh harder.

I don't remember hearing my mother ever telling a racist joke until my father was transferred to Alabama in June 1966, two and a half years after George Wallace, in his first inauguration address, had declared: "Segregation now, segregation tomorrow, segregation forever." Taking the oath of office, Wallace stood on the bronze star marking the spot where Jefferson Davis had been sworn in as president of the Confederacy. During an American history field trip, I too stood on that star and proclaimed loudly, throwing my hands up over my head, "I feel I have the power, yes, the power to tear the United States ASUNDER!" Mrs. Warr—that was really her name—told me to stop acting like an idiot and to keep up with the rest of the class or I'd miss the bus and have to walk back to school.

Mom may not have previously told any racist jokes simply because she had not heard any on the integrated military bases. I never had. But shortly after we arrived in Montgomery, she told me the joke I think of as the racist joke of the sixties, partly because I heard it more often and from more people than any other, but also because its meaning strangely shifted the more I thought about it.

Martin Luther King Jr. gets up one morning, glances in the mirror, and notices his forehead has turned white. At first, he doesn't think much about it. He just pulls his fedora down over the pale area and goes about his business. But the next morning he looks in the mirror again and sees his face has turned white down to his nose, and the day after that he's white down to his neck. He must be sick, but more than that, he has a serious problem. Other African-Americans won't accept him as a civil rights leader if he turns into a white man.

Worried, King goes to the doctor and explains how each day he's turned a little whiter, from the top down. The doctor examines him, then goes into his back room, brings out a large jar of brown liquid, hands it to King, and says, "Drink this."

King glugs it down and then, grimacing with distaste—an expression my mother acted out—he sputters, "That tastes like bullshit!"

"It is," the doctor says. "You were a quart low."

The joke startled me. Not only wasn't it funny, I was having trouble seeing how she could find it funny. It was a kids' joke, a poop joke. Why in the world was my mother telling me a poop joke? Despite its easy and ugly punch line, I laughed shallowly. I didn't want to discourage Mom from telling me jokes.

At first, I thought the joke was about a racist doctor who dupes a not-very-bright King into drinking a bucket of shit—"bull poop" in my mother's version but not, I'm sure, in my uncle's. I'm sure Buddy was the source of the joke. I also tried to laugh at the famous preacher, already perceived as a saint and a prophet in the larger world, being taken down a peg. Was that how Mom meant the joke? Only after thinking about it for a couple of days did I realize with a jolt that she thought Martin Luther King Jr. was full of shit. That understanding, which mildly embarrassed me, led to another understanding, the more embarrassing and frightening one that I was pretty sure my uncle meant to convey: niggers are made of shit and the essence of negritude is shit. From that perspective, the only pleasure the joke offers is the grim and soulless pleasure of animosity.

Later, as I continued to hear the joke, I saw it also implies that Martin Luther King Jr. was essentially a white man. Only the civil-rights rhetoric ("bullshit") that discomfited whites made him black. If King didn't keep renewing his racial identity with racial causes and rhetoric, he'd turn into a white man. My mother would have agreed that blacks and whites are essentially the same. It was my Uncle Buddy who saw African-Americans as intrinsically inferior to whites, and a deeply held rage at their attempting to change the natural order ran through many of his jokes: What's the difference between a nigger and a bucket of shit? The bucket. Why don't niggers let their babies play in the sandbox? The cat'll bury them. And this twofer: What do you get when you cross a nigger and a Mexican? Someone too lazy to steal.

The jokes my mother told, even if they came to her from Buddy, were usually more storylike and ambiguous. They were also my mother's and my hidden, homeopathic rebellion against my father, who was right to proscribe them but typically counterproductive in his heavy-handedness. Mom and I shared, I thought at first, an understanding: While others believed the jokes denigrated blacks, we recognized the joke wasn't on the victim but on the perpetrator, the racist and not the victim of racism. But the truth is more complicated.

Once or twice Mom mentioned "Martin Luther Coon" and chuckled. I was disappointed in her, I admit, and troubled that fear had led to anger and the anger to leaden ugliness—and then I was ashamed for feeling superior to my mother. I didn't sense in her the hatred I felt when my uncle and grandmother spat out the witless epithet, not even pretending to find it funny, just relishing the old racial insult's attempt to reduce the famous man from a king to a coon. *What was Mom hearing?* I wondered. *What was making her laugh?* I think it was the phrase's bullheaded resistance—the sheer unreconstructed ugliness of it—that pleased her.

I'd long understood my uncle's jokes grew out of his loathing of black people, but I began to understand my mother's goodwill was sometimes shaded and even overshadowed by racial fear. These dreary dull-edged jokes were a church that I didn't want to join, a congregation I couldn't comfortably laugh with, a community that valued the anger of its point more than the humor in its telling. Yet adults who fiercely loved me and whom I loved, and who understood the complexities of the world better than I did, as they were quick to point out, were confirmed racists who found the jokes funny and even comforting. I didn't respect my elders' fear but I absorbed it—and sometimes I laughed at their jokes.

I assumed that my mother's racial jokes were aimed at people like her mother and brother—that she was distancing herself from their rural racism by making fun of them, and that her voice was full of a strange affection when she told these jokes because she could not separate her love for her family from their bigotry. Her rich chuckle usually seemed rueful, an acknowledgment that "Yes, people do think that way." Yet in that chuckle there was also a stubborn appreciation of the culture that fostered the racism, an understanding of it that went to acceptance and forgiveness too easily. She didn't give full weight to their malice because she loved them. I also have been guilty of that blindness. I have a hard time crediting racial malice—and I attribute this innocence to my parents' care in trying to shield me from it. And so my understanding of racism is probably a quart low.

Because they are almost the only jokes I remember my mother telling, I cherish these jokes with guilty affection. Though Mom sympathized with the plight of individual blacks, the idea that African-Americans had organized and were no longer asking for, but demanding, their rights pushed her further than her basic sympathy could extend. In retrospect that later understanding of my mother changed my reaction to this next joke, one I loved when I first heard it.

A sheriff is called to the scene when the body of a black man is pulled out of the Mississippi River. Standing on the bank, he looks down at the body wrapped head to foot in heavy chains, shakes his head sorrowfully, and says, "Ain't it just like a nigger to steal all those chains and then try to swim the river with them?"

When Mom told it, I laughed wholeheartedly, enjoying what I took to be our shared understanding that, yeah, that's just exactly what a redneck sheriff might say and even half believe. Not only was I sure that Buddy had told her the joke, but I also imagined him as the sheriff. I heard his voice in the sheriff's lascivious and vicious pleasure in refusing to acknowledge an obvious murder.

In any moral world the joke is about the inhumanity of the sheriff, and thus southern lawmen's complicity in lawlessness. But the segregated South was a world of skewed morals. If, like Buddy, you don't recognize the civil rights of African-Americans, then you identify with the sheriff's inhumane protection of his fellow racists—and your laughter at the joke celebrates the arbitrary power of white society to turn a blind eye to lynching.

My mother would not have gone nearly that far. But she appreciated the cussedness of the sheriff, his recalcitrant exhilaration in being in the wrong, and enforcing his wrongness. Mom savored the subversion of the racists in her jokes even when she disapproved of their practices in life. She liked the joke because it embodied her struggle with her own racial fears and contradictions and because she knew that the rich and educated scorned her fears, which is one of the reasons I love jokes, even some of these.

Self-defeating southern cussedness has a long cultural history. We oppose evils whose very perversity we go ahead and gloat over because they seem like the epitome of human nature at its worst. To Calvinists sin is often funny because it confirms our low opinion of ourselves. My college history professor, Dr. Chappell, said he had never voted for George Corley Wallace Jr., and he never would.

He hated the man and everything he stood for, but, said Chappell, clenching his incisors, he couldn't help relishing Wallace's electoral successes anyway just because they so flummoxed and inflamed the Yankees, driving the national commentators to paroxysms of sanctimony aimed wholesale at the South and Alabama, including those of us who resolutely opposed the governor.

While shaking our heads in honest sorrow, we also found perverse humor in the sheer mad brass of George Wallace. When a rival politician tried to use against Wallace the fact that he had been mustered out of the air force with a ten percent mental disability, the governor turned the political assault to his advantage by declaring that, unlike his opponent, he could prove he was ninety percent sane. Late in life, Wallace tried to put his racist legacy behind him, going around the state and begging the forgiveness of any African-American organization that would permit him to address them, and we laughed out loud when he earnestly told a black audience, "Sure, I look like a white man. But my heart is as black as anyone's here." It's hard not to wish the self-judgment was deliberate wit.

When I conjure in my head the sheriff in racist jokes, he is always some combination of my Uncle Buddy, as I said, and George Wallace. And therefore the sheriff who finds a thief in the river instead of a murder victim is the same one in another joke that made my mother laugh. A black man wearing an expensively tailored suit and a silk tie shows up to register to vote in rural Mississippi. Or Alabama. Or Arkansas. At the polling booth—this was when literacy tests were still common—the sheriff asks the man about his education. Wounded comic dignity filling her voice, my mother acted out, with sonorous bombast, the black man's outrage.

"I have an undergraduate degree from Harvard, a PhD from Yale, and for two years I was a Rhodes Scholar at Oxford before I returned to Harvard as a professor of Greek and Roman literature."

"Now, that's all well and good," sneered my mother in the voice of the redneck sheriff, "But tell me, boy, can ya read?"

Mom drew out the word *read*, enjoying the hick accent she gave it, the obtuseness of it, and the malicious pleasure the imagined sheriff takes in his willful abuse of authority.

At the time I was sure the butt of the joke was the redneck sheriff, who could not accept the superior attainments of a black man, and who was going to flagrantly misuse his power to frustrate the man's right to vote. In *Nigger: The Strange Career of a Troublesome Word*, Randall Kennedy recounts pretty much the same joke and says it's told by African-Americans "to satirize 'legal' disenfranchisement." That's how I wanted to understand it too.

Yet now I hear in my mother's voice something I didn't hear then. Along with her mockery of the sheriff and his redneck racism, I hear a touch of gratification at the sheriff's staunch refusal to admit the educated, successful, and apparently wealthy black man is his equal, much less his superior. My father's suits were not tailored and his ties were acetate.

Randall Kennedy tells another joke that he says black activists told to emphasize "the depth of white racism all across the United States: 'What is a negro with a PhD?' Their response? 'Doctor Nigger.'" The subtle shifts of stance and presentation are everything in jokes, aren't they? My uncle told me the exact same joke, but his point was not to satirize white racism. Buddy was educating me. I may think I knew how the world was supposed to be, he was saying, but he knew how it really was.

And then he told me a joke that went one step further, one that demonstrated that whatever African-Americans accomplished, they'd always be first and foremost niggers, not just in Buddy's eyes but as an unalterable ontological state.

"What do you called a Negro with a PhD, an MD, and a law degree from Harvard?" he asked.

Immediately, I was wary. I knew it had to be a joke because in normal conversation he never used the word *Negro*, and of course in Griffin, Georgia, in the 1960s there wasn't much chance he had actually met anyone, white or black, with those credentials. And if he had, he was not someone who'd agonize over how to address the distinguished personage.

All these thoughts plodded through my head as I pondered how to react and then took the path of least resistance. "I don't know," I said. "What?"

My uncle took a moment to look at me. He knew I wasn't going to like the answer and that meant he was going to enjoy telling it to me all the more. Within the next two years, I read the same joke in *The Autobiography of Malcolm X*, and Malcolm X savored with rage the same point my uncle savored with triumph.

Slowly growling out the hard *g*s and *r* of the word, savoring them, Buddy said it: "Nigger."

Seven

Where's the Edge?

The only racial slur I remember coming from the lips of children my own age before we moved to Alabama was in fourth grade, when some kids in the neighborhood, for a week or two, called me Nigger Lips. I was disturbed, not because of the racial epithet, but because I was sensitive about my thick lips. I was more stung when they called me Pudgins, even though I knew I wasn't pudgy.

Not until we were on our way to New York to catch a plane to Dad's new posting at an army post outside Paris did I hear a racist joke from a kid my own age, thirteen or fourteen. My folks had stopped to visit some old friends in D.C. and their son, a military brat like me, pulled my brother and me into his room and asked, furtively, if we had heard about the first black astronaut. His eyes were wide and eager. Manned space flights were big news in the sixties, and I, like many kids, had learned to count backward from ten to one so I could chant along with the launch countdowns.

"No," I said. "There's a black astronaut?"

"Yeah, this black astronaut is sitting in the capsule, waiting for the countdown, when . . ."

"Oh, it's a joke."

"Yeah, it's a joke. What'd you think it was?"

"Never mind. Tell me what happens." Since his dad was stationed at the Pentagon, I'd hoped, for a moment, he had some inside scoop that wasn't in the newspapers. Instead, I was alarmed to find myself being told a dicey joke by someone I'd just met, a stranger whose intentions, as the joke began, were inscrutable. Were we going to be racists or were we going to be making fun of racists? I couldn't tell.

"Well, the sergeant who pushes the ignition button starts counting down, but he gets excited before he gets to one: 'Ten, nine, eight, seven, six, five, four, three, two—shoot the coon to the moon!'"

Beyond the blatant racism here, I've usually found rhyming jokes too dumb to enjoy. In elementary school, boys asked, "What did Hitler say when another recruit joined the party?" "Hotsy-totsy, another Nazi!" Sometimes they goose-stepped across the playground, *sieg heil*ing with their right hands, their left index fingers curled under their noses to represent Hitler's mustache, while they chanted, "Hotsy-totsy, another Nazi!" They loved the sound of it—three double rhymes in four words!—and the disjunction of jamming the slangy *hotsy-totsy* up against the sinister *Nazi*. I just watched, unable to participate in their pleasure. Now this boy I didn't know, his face shining with amusement, was staring at me, expecting me to delight in "Shoot the coon to the moon," and I saw for the first time how demanding we jokers are in our neediness, asking others to share our pleasure, to please make pleasure with us. We are aggressively negotiating an intimacy that is often unwanted. When it came to racist jokes, I was old enough to want a joke teller who would signal that we were going to enjoy a game with words, not revel in ugliness. I wanted irony.

"Huh," I said.

That was all the encouragement he needed. "'Stop!' yells the general in charge. He glares at the sergeant, and tells him to start the countdown over and this time he'd better not say 'coon.'

"The sergeant starts the countdown again: 'Five, four, three, two—trigger the nigger!'

"'Stop!' yells the general. 'Sergeant, this kind of talk will stop right now, or I'll have you court-martialed. You understand me?'

"'Yes sir. Sorry, sir. Won't happen again, sir.'

"Again the countdown begins. The general watches the sergeant closely as he counts, 'Five, four, three, two, one,' and punches the button.

"'Now that wasn't so hard, was it, Sergeant?'

"'No sir,' says the sergeant. "'The jig's up.'"

I knew I was a bad guest when, instead of laughing, I wrinkled my face. The sniggered and insinuating way the joke was told—as if this were something I would both want to know and agree with— reminded me of the sleazy sex jokes I was just beginning to hear. The joke wanted me to agree with the cleverness of the sergeant who persists in his juvenile racist jokes despite all the efforts to stop him. I grasped the class conflict in the enlisted man's outsmarting the general (and demeaning the black astronaut, who'd have to be an officer too), and I saw that the boy who told me the joke identified with the subversive enlisted man being ordered around by an officer, as he himself was probably ordered around by his father, also an officer. The racism might have been attractive because it was forbidden by his father, something I assumed from the way he'd moved us away from the closed door and spoke in a low tone. The final pun almost works: the enlisted man is saying, "My game has been exposed and I've stopped" while persisting in it via the double meaning of *jig*. But the unvarying and unalleviated bigotry of the enlisted man's purported wit outweighs what little levity the joke musters. The racist meaning of *jig* sprawls so heavily over the other meaning it can't rise off the ground.

The boy savored either the racism or the insubordination of the sergeant—I couldn't tell which—and expected me to join him. I hadn't known him more than twenty minutes, and most of that time we'd slouched awkwardly on his family's living room couch while our parents got reacquainted. He was proffering friendship, and I didn't know what to make of it. Was he trying to pull me into his racist assumptions? Did he really find the joke funny enough to overcome its nastiness? Did he see something in it I missed? Did he see something in *me*? He was oblivious to how my distaste for the joke became dislike of him—an unhappy judgment that I, already an inveterate joker, knew well. As we jokers will, he launched into a farrago of jokes—flat and unfunny racist jokes that I don't remember, though if you told me the setups, I'm sure I could tell you the punch lines.

That was it for the next year. In France we lived in integrated military housing. I didn't hear another racist joke till we moved to Alabama.

In the fall of 1966, I plunged into tenth grade at Sidney Lanier High School, which was named after the nineteenth-century poet who'd lived briefly in the Exchange Hotel, which his brother managed in downtown Montgomery after the Civil War. Our football team was named the Sidney Lanier Poets, and at pep rallies our cheerleaders screamed out, "Who ARE the POets?"

"WE are the POets!" we shrieked back.

"What KIND of POets?" shouted the cheerleaders.

"FIGHTing POets!" we screamed back, a thousand teenagers shouting in frenzied unison through the last years of the activist sixties. Our frenzy reminded me, melodramatically, of the footage of the crowds Hitler incited to a unified hysteria in Nuremberg. After my freshman year I usually stayed in my homeroom and read books. I had a few friends who also found the cheer to be hilarious, but we were the outsiders. The locals had grown up with it. Besides, the whole idea of "school spirit" seemed moronic to most of us military brats. We are assigned to our schools by the state according to where we lived and our race, and I was at Lanier because the Pentagon had sent my father to Montgomery. To me, school spirit was a celebration of impersonal but powerful winds that had deposited me someplace I'd never have chosen.

My tenth-grade homeroom was held in the gym, and the coach, who was right out of college, didn't give a crap if the non-athletes dressed out for exercise as long as we didn't bother him while he shot baskets with the junior-varsity team, which shared the class period with us. Still wearing our street clothes, my friends and I lounged on the bleachers, studied, rushed through late homework, or told jokes. I hadn't been in school for more than a few months when a kid in the class asked me if I knew what *mung* was.

I'd heard sniggering about *smegma* and *mung*. I assumed the mystery words had something to do with sex and I was eager to learn.

Smegma, I found out from the unabridged dictionary in the school library, is the shed skin that forms under the foreskin of uncircumcised men—a mystery to us circumcised Baptists who had never seen a foreskin. As boys, we were more intrigued by the esoteric grotesquery of smegma—toe cheese of the penis—than I can now imagine.

Mung, I've since learned, has a long history. The *Oxford English Dictionary* defines *munge* as a verb meaning "to wipe (a person's nose)." Closer to our time, *mung* was World War II slang for chipped beef on toast, the famed SOS—*shit on a shingle*—that servicemen groused about. My mother also called chipped beef SOS, and when, staring at the budget extender on the plate in front of us, we asked what SOS meant, she laughed and said, "Save Our Souls." When pressed, she inched closer to the truth: "Stuff on a shingle."

We boys used *mung* as a generic gross-out word for nasty liquids or bodily oozing. But now, a kid I barely knew was offering a real definition. Of course I wanted to hear it.

"No, I don't know what it is. Tell me," I said.

"Naw, you don't really want to know," he said.

"Yeah, I do. Come on, tell me."

"Beg."

"Please tell me what mung is. I really, really want to know."

"If you're sure you really want to know . . . ?"

He made me nod before he continued.

"Okay, this is what mung is. You take a pregnant nigger bitch. . . ."

He stopped, looked at me and a couple of other boys who'd gathered to listen, and then continued in a rote tone. I could tell he was repeating a spiel he'd heard from older boys or a young uncle.

"There ain't no such thing as 'nigger lady' or 'nigger woman,' it's 'nigger bitch.' You take a pregnant *nigger bitch*, and hang her upside down from a tree. Then you beat her big black belly with a baseball bat till something brown oozes out her nose—and the stuff that drips out her nose, that's mung."

Someone guffawed, maybe in shock. I said, "That's disgusting," and turned away, a fastidious rebuff that gratified the joke teller. Maybe the one of us who laughed could divorce fiction—pray to God it was fiction—from reality enough to enjoy the imaginative perversity of the revolting image. I couldn't. Baseball bats were a preferred weapon of the Klan. The year before, during the march from Selma to Montgomery, James Reeb had been beaten by a mob armed with baseball bats. Jimmie Lee Jackson was shot. Sheriff Jim Clark unleashed attack dogs on the civil rights workers, and the picture of Amelia Boynton Robinson, beaten unconscious, sprawled on the Pettus Bridge in her dress and gloves, her head lolling back as if she were dead, had been printed in almost every national news publication. Twenty miles from where we were defining *mung*, Viola Liuzzo had been gunned down by the Ku Klux Klan on the day after the march, and the trial of one of her killers had gone to the jury in September, right after school started. Despite overwhelming evidence against him, Collie Wilkins was acquitted by a jury that fully understood he had participated in the murder but refused to convict a white man for killing a nigger-loving outside agitator. The federal government was now retrying him in Montgomery for violating Mrs. Liuzzo's rights by shooting her in the head. The story was constantly on the front page of the *Montgomery Advertiser* the first semester I was a Sidney Lanier Poet.

The boy who knew about mung had assured us that Viola Liuzzo was nobody to worry about. She was a just a Yankee whore who had left her five children behind to come down to Alabama and fuck niggers. He proclaimed it with such vehemence that it took me years to flush the lie out of my head, a lie he didn't know was a lie. The ultimate source of the defamatory falsehood about Mrs. Liuzzo, who died singing "We Shall Overcome," turned out to be local law enforcement agencies.

For several days, my classmate's definition of *mung* came back to me powerfully, and I twitched with visceral empathy with the fictional lynched woman. My imagination kept forcing the ball bat in my hands, trying to test both sides of the horror—myself as murderer, as murdered—but I always stopped before I swung. I hated the joke for tempting my suggestible imagination toward this abomination. Awake at night, the image seared into my brain, I tried to imagine who'd think up such a thing, and why. If the joker's goal was to disgust his listeners, he'd succeeded. But why did he think it was funny? It had no wit, no lightness of language, no depth of dreadful self-understanding, or even any clammy pleasure in trying to disguise hatred as humor. The joke was just sodden misogyny and bigotry exulting in its power to create a nauseating image.

Jokes like this make people hate jokes. Once the forces of un-restrained imagination and our ugly subconscious come together there's no telling how wrong they will go. Propelled by fear, they can rocket out of the gravitational pull of decency, wit, and rough fun, and zoom into the deep-space darkness of airless viciousness. People are right to fear what this union might create. *Mein Kampf* is as much a product of the human imagination as Goethe's *Faust*.

Despite my revulsion at the joke's racism, I think I'd have re-acted almost as strongly if he'd begun the joke, "You take a woman, hang her up by her feet. . . ." Our innate sense of the inviolability of pregnant women and the near sanctity of infants, combined with most people's instinctive wince at the thought of being clobbered in the belly with a bat, is ghastly enough. But the joke brings in the historical horror of slavery, lynching, and the dehumanization of African-Americans for an extra dose of nastiness. At fifteen, I pondered over why I was so repulsed by this joke while loving the gross-out joke I talked about earlier: How do you unload a truck-load of dead babies? With a pitchfork.

I found many reasons. Imagining an anonymous mass doesn't engage the emotions the way imagining one person does. In the mung joke, I had to imagine being a torturer and a murderer. ("*You*," he said to me, "*you* take a woman, *you* hang her, *you* beat her.") The joke had no point except the racist and sexist pleasure of utterly de-humanizing a pregnant African-American. I was probably too young to see the dead-baby joke's point is that corpses, despite our intrinsic reverence for them, are no longer persons, while this joke meant me to feel the ugliness of its murderous punch line. These reasons are all true, but now I think the fundamental difference between the two jokes is I didn't believe the truckload of dead babies was anything but a conceit, a fictional construct built to be played with, one that let me toy with larger issues of death and bodily integrity without thinking about actual people. But in the mung joke, I believed the atrocity could happen—might *have* happened—and the fifteen-year-old boy telling the joke might have been happy if it did.

Like any story, anecdote, or tidbit of gossip, jokes can create stereotypes or reinforce existing ones. But by playing with stereotypes, they can also reveal them for the fictional constructs they are, as I had thought my mother's jokes were doing. The taboos and ugly forces behind jokes can feed positive laughter as well as nasty laughter. They feed laughter the way an accelerant feeds a fire, a terrible thing if the fire is on the living room carpet, a good thing if you're having trouble getting charcoal briquettes glowing in the grill. With nasty racist jokes, however, it's impossible to keep the fire in the grill. The lack of any mental gymnastics, which a true joke requires, reveals what is truly driving the joke: The teller's ugly relish confirms his sense of African-Americans' inferiority.

Laughter is, as Thomas Hobbes wrote, "a sudden glory arising from some sudden conception of some eminency in ourselves." In this joke there is a conception of eminency all right but there is nothing sudden or glorious about it. And the eminency is very much in doubt. I have often, while laughing, protested, "That's not funny!" Then I am left looking backward, sometimes in shame, to figure out why I laughed. When a friend asked me, in high school, "What's long and hard on a black man?" and answered himself, "Third grade," I burst out laughing, before I turned away, ashamed, and I made a concerted effort to expunge it from my mind.

Why did I laugh? Because the punch line surprised me. The question so fills the mind with sex that even though you know that the right answer can't be "penis," you can't see around the stereotype to grasp the other meanings of *long* and *hard* until the joke reveals them. In that way, it works like the junior-high joke:

Q: What word starts with ƒ, ends with k, and has a u and a c in the middle.
A: Firetruck, of course. What word were *you* thinking of?

The long-and-hard joke also shocks by dropping the racism to an expectedly lower level—from sexual superiority to intellectual inferiority. It leads you down one racist path and then jumps to another, much worse, one. Though many people find the racism too ugly for the joke to be funny, it possesses a bit of ugly wit and a touch of audacity. When I heard it again, several years ago, encountering it as if for the first time since I'd happily forgotten it, I trusted the decency of the teller, whose voice, as she introduced the joke, implied, "You gotta hear this racist joke. You and I won't agree with what it says but we can appreciate the way it plays with racist ideas." That time I laughed without guilt, savoring the ugliness of the joke, and the nasty psychological ingenuity of it.

The first time I went to the Gulf Coast with my six-year-old nephew, he ran along the sand, chasing the waves as they pulled back into the Gulf of Mexico, then running away as they rushed up the beach. Every now and then a wave raced up farther and faster than he'd expected and rushed over his feet, surprising him, and after a few such surprises he simply stood still in the foaming water and wailed plaintively, "Where's the *edge*?" The answer of course is that the boundary changes, the answer he knew already but couldn't accept, even as he ran on, skipping in and out of the shifting water.

I understand his confusion. Just this morning, looking at an Internet listing of racist jokes, I saw the joke again, in the middle of an interminable list of sour, witless, racist jokes, and my laughter turned to wormwood and ashes in my mouth. Whatever twisted wit, surprise, or inverted understanding of racism I'd once found in it vanished in the context of an excruciating compilation collected by someone who seemed to believe the jokes were, in some way, true.

If we sense that the person telling a racist joke puts an ounce of credence in it, the lightness goes leaden because the malice is real. Who could laugh then? Those who agree with the premise of the punch line. Instead of taking the racism as an idea to make fun of, some words to play with, a construct to deconstruct, or a taboo they simply can't resist prodding, they approve of it as an accurate representation of their reality. At the moment it's taken seriously, the joke moves out of the category of joke and becomes a belief, one of the ugliest of ugly beliefs.

Maybe I first laughed at the long-and-hard joke because the fear of sexual inferiority was one that I'd begun to work through in my second year of high school. In tenth grade, I held a wooden ruler to myself and came in about a quarter of an inch under the six-inch average. At five foot six, 120 pounds, with a twenty-eight-inch waist, I was pretty pleased by the judgment of the ruler. Because I spent as little time as possible in locker rooms, the jokes and jibes about penis magnitude seemed largely metaphorical. I never heard anyone, except as a joke, mention the size of another man's penis until I was a senior in college, when a black basketball player was tossed off the Huntingdon Hawks for some indiscretion or other. To demonstrate what he thought about that, he stood across the street from the girls' dorm, I was told, and twirled his pecker like a baton. My friend, who happened to pass by before the police arrived, assured me, laughing, that it was large enough to twirl. Bigger than his by a long stretch, he said. "No kidding?" I said. We laughed, and then we settled in to study for our history test.

Not until college did I hear a follow-up to the long-and-hard joke:

Q: What's long and hard on a white man?
A: Nothing.

At first, I took the second joke as a flaccid reversal of the first, a weak attempt to show that the person telling the long-and-hard joke wasn't a racist, but an equal opportunity joker. When I repeated it, I was metaphorically tugging my forelock, attempting to embrace the stereotype and say that white men ("Like me—look, I'm mocking myself too!") can laugh at themselves too and at our purportedly paltry penises. I told it a number of times before I understood it's really slyer and funnier than I'd thought. The joke does do exactly what I thought it did, but it also implies that the attainments for which black men work long and hard come easily to white men because they live lives of untroubled privilege. I would be offended if I believed it was a sincere assessment of my life. I mostly don't, it mostly isn't, and, despite what I thought at first, it's funny, though— or is it *because*?—it has a bit of a sting to it.

Nine months after I graduated from college, I married, and my father-in-law, as he had during the four years I dated his daughter, brilliantly frustrated my ability to discern the motives of jokers. He turned my status as the wince-inducing joker on its head. He did the joke telling; my ex-wife and I did the wincing. So of course he told the same jokes over and over, delighting in discomfiting us, try-ing to provoke a response beyond my wife's pained, "Oh, Daddy!" One of his favorites involved two black professors at Alabama State University, the historically black school less than a mile from his house. As they pass each other on campus, one professor asks the other, "Is ya did ya Greek?" The pretentious professors presume themselves to be Greek scholars while the ugly (and inept) parody of rural Black English that they speak reveals them as incapable of mastering proper English, much less Greek.

Over time I came to laugh at the joke, not because I thought it was funny but because I came to love my father-in-law and trust him as a man of basic good-heartedness who wanted to be seen as an iconoclast. Much of his racism—how much I was never sure—was pretense designed to irk me. Some of it grew from his insecurity about not having gone to college. Those insights aren't the reasons I laughed, but they allowed me to enjoy the impishness with which he worked to make me laugh at something I didn't want to laugh at. Chanting the punch line in an almost incomprehensible sequence of syllables—"Izya-didya-Greek?"—he waggled his thick eyebrows and gave me a grin that hovered between mischievous and wolfish.

His pleasure in his own joke was impossible to resist. Once I determined that he was much more interested in the silly rhythm of the line than the racial message, I relaxed. Perhaps I shouldn't have. But I saw he was mostly interested in making my wife laugh while she was trying to say, "Daddy, don't tell that joke again." He was teasing us, mocking what he saw as our overfastidious liberalism. The point of the joke was no longer in the joke itself, but how we reacted. And, of course, his delight in chanting "Izya-didya-Greek?"

My father-in-law was a smart man who'd gone straight from high school graduation to supporting his family after his father died. Even after he'd suffered four heart attacks and undergone a coronary artery bypass, his skin remained walnut brown from sweat-drenched hours working bare-chested in his garden, pipe clenched in his teeth, as he mowed, shoveled, transplanted, edged, trimmed, and weeded. He grew the most elegant stand of hollyhocks I have seen outside of photographs. In an old refrigerator from which he'd stripped the rubber gaskets, he smoked turkey, chicken, and pork chops. Smoky, rich, and thoroughly desiccated, they were the best smoked meats I've ever eaten, though they took a lot of chewing. Once, shaking his head and chuckling, he told me about a friend who had tried to copy his homemade smoker but got a crucial detail wrong. When the friend finally pried open the door, fused shut by melted rubber, he found a beautifully cooked turkey infused with the flavor of burnt rubber.

His flat black hair slanted over his forehead, emphasizing the slightly Asian cast to his face that you sometimes see in very thin older southern men who spend a lot of time in the sun. From constant pipe smoking his teeth were, under a gray cast, distinctly green. His teasing was pure, complex play to him, and I came to love him over and above his joking, which played a game so deep that often I wasn't sure what the game was.

Though intimidated by people with college degrees, he was also contemptuous of them because he, a voracious reader, found they often didn't know nearly as much as he thought they should. How could I tell him that the faux black English of his joke was nothing like real black English vernacular? And why would I tell him, since he knew that better than I did? Certainly I could've told him that teachers don't do homework; students do. He told the joke because he had only been a student, not a teacher—and because it sounded funny. But why cause a family rift, especially when over time I came to know him as a man of little malice who delighted in wordplay? And the Greek joke was in tune with other, non-racist, jokes he enjoyed.

In the middle of a conversation, he casually inquired of new acquaintances if they'd heard about the two gay judges who tried each other or if they'd known the plastic surgeon who hung himself. Had they met the two gay Irishmen William Fitzpatrick and Patrick FitzWilliam?

He delighted in one-liners that disrupted the flow of conversation, especially if he suspected he was being condescended to. If someone explained to him something he already knew, he invariably responded, "'I see,' said the blind man, who picked up the hammer and saw."

The first time he used that line on me, I said, "Wha?" He looked at me as if I were a dimwit, until, blinking, I got it. After that, I watched in fascination as he lured new victims into confusion.

When the conversation veered into absurdity, the only way out was to acknowledge the absurdity, to relinquish control, to play. I couldn't help loving the zest with which he decoyed chitchat out of its appointed rounds of business, small logic, and politesse—and into pleasure. A lot of people didn't want to follow him there.

Some laughed, some groaned before laughing, and others simply groaned. Uptight listeners got huffy that he'd bollixed the flow of conversation for no good reason that they could see. He had shifted the focus from them, the explainers, to him, the one who was supposed to be listening. He delighted in small verbal anarchies and illogic, and I shared his pleasure. He made opportunities to laugh where they didn't appear to exist, and he enjoyed one-upping people whose lecturing tacitly made him their pupil.

With the same bland irony, if it was irony, he occasionally commented to me, never in public, "A blue-gum nigger'll cut your heart out." Was he warning me that the blacker a black man was—so black his gums were blue—the more dangerous he was? Was this a bit of racist folklore he'd heard as a boy and enjoyed marveling over, mocking of outdated understanding and outré wisdom? Or did he merely like to say something outrageous for the sake of being outrageous? I suspect the latter, but I wouldn't bet the house on it. He played, as I say, a deep game.

The overt racists were far blunter. Hidebound white southerners resisted, according African-Americans, the honorifics "Mr.," "Mrs.," and "Miss," and were often hostile when they insisted on it. Encroaching equality had to be squelched early and hard.

In my last year of high school, a boy in my math class told me what happened when the family maid's son called and asked for "Mrs. Johnston." My friend's father snarled into the receiver at the child, "Ain't no *Mrs. Johnston* here—just a nigger name of Bessie what works for us!" And he slammed down the receiver.

Seeing the astonishment on my face, my friend, who had

laughed at his own story and expected me to laugh too, explained. After slamming down the receiver, his father had then looked at him and said, "So far, with all her marriages, if they was marriages, she's been a Smith, a McCoy, a Peebles, and a something else. Now she's a Johnston. I can't keep 'em all straight."

This time, I barked a shocked, mean laugh. My friend was, I think, disturbed by his father's meanness and yet proud of him for standing up for racial superiority, which they both believed in, the son probably not as strongly as the father. My laugh was fueled by the depraved audacity of the comment, the gap between my world and theirs, as well as the cold insufficiency of the father's reasoning. I was repulsed by the adult's cruelty to the black child, yes. The denigration of the mother to the son and of the son himself is obviously vicious, as is the example the father set for his own son. But in my southern soul I was also deeply troubled by the man's searing and deliberate discourtesy. Not only did Mrs. Johnston likely hear her child rebuked for his good manners and then the ugly summary of her married life, the father had refused to convey the polite message the boy had wanted to tell his mother.

My friend saw everything I saw, but from the other side. Though he was aware of his father's cruelty and wanted to distance himself from it, he seemed to believe that his father was basically right in his ideas, if crudely mechanical in enforcing them. The critic Henri Bergson, one of the most important humor theorists, says that we laugh when someone turns himself into a thing by acting mechanically: "The laughable element . . . consists of a certain *mechanical inelasticity*, just where one would expect to find the wide-awake adaptability and the living pliableness of a human being." I laughed at my friend's story because his father had made himself into an automated bigot. Whatever complexities of sociology, temperament, and economics lay behind it, he was now just a racist being a racist.

Only once have I actually seen such remorseless disregard for a black man's humanity that I felt as though I were living in a racist joke. My first year at Huntingdon College I worked as a sample clerk in a dry goods wholesaler, Solomon Brothers, in downtown Montgomery. Every day at noon, I rushed out of class and drove downtown, where I sat at a table, cut cloth into small pinked rectangles, and glued them into books for the salesmen to show to buyers for retail stores. I sullenly mused that, as a beginning college student living at home, I was doing exactly what I'd done in kindergarten: cutting and pasting, though now I was doing it for a buck sixty an hour.

The firm's scrawny black janitor, Jerome, was bald, over seventy, and down to his last couple of teeth, which, when he laughed, you could observe standing like lonely sentinels stationed far apart in his gums. The first rumor I heard at Solomon Brothers was that Jerome, who was married, had a girlfriend and every day at lunch he hustled off to her place for a nooner.

For four hours a day, five days a week, we part-timers cut cloth, using the pinking machine, a yard-wide, lever-operated guillotine with a notched blade. As we separated out the pinked rectangles and pasted them on heavy, glossy paper in color-coordinated flaps, we had plenty of time to listen to local talk radio and hypothesize on Jerome's sexual capacity.

"Naw, that can't be right," protested Maury, one of the other two sample clerks.

"That's what folks say," said Ken, the boss of our little department.

"Aw man, look how old he is! It's all he can do to push that broom from one side of the warehouse to the other."

"I'm just telling you what I hear. Got a little tucked away on the side."

"Idn't he a drinker too? Keeps a pint in his overhauls?"

"Yeah, that's true. I've seen it," Ken said.

"I don't know, man. Don't sound right to me."

Like Maury, I was skeptical, not just because of Jerome's age, infirmity, and drinking. I assumed the talk was just racist speculation about a black man's sexual voracity.

Ken, though, assured us we were wrong. We simply didn't understand that black men have to have it.

One afternoon, as Jerome pushed his broom desultorily through our work area on his way to the stairs, Ken yelled out, in a loud voice aimed toward his three workers more than to the janitor, "Hey, Jerome, I hear you get some lunchtime pussy every day. That's true, ain't it?"

I was as mortified as I've ever been in my life. The racist superiority that allowed one man to address another with such egregiously false bonhomie left me stunned into silent shame. Also I'd never heard an adult talk to another about a woman so openly and vulgarly. From what little I knew of southern chivalry, Jerome, if he were white, would be within his rights to kill Ken, and maybe me too for being there.

After a long moment, Jerome chuckled and nodded. Because I'd faded into my own shocked humiliation, I do not recall exactly what Jerome said or how Ken responded. It must have been something about the size and stamina of Jerome's penis because Jerome hefted the broom, stuck the handle between his legs from behind, and waggled it in front of him at a forty-five-degree angle, lurching and staggering behind it as if it were dragging him across the room.

With a wide grin, he said, "Yessuh, when de big hog talk, I gots to listen."

Ken, Maury, and the other clerk burst out laughing. I didn't. I was still trying frantically to understand the confluence of mortifications running through me like a hot river—racial shame, sexual fear, shock at seeing an elderly man debase himself and yet aware that he was, like a jester sporting a colossal deforming codpiece, asserting his manhood through humor, the only way he could. After I sat for a moment perplexed, embarrassed, wanting to apologize, wondering if I were morally obligated to quit my job, I laughed too, though weakly, because . . . because . . . because if Jerome was laughing, I had to also. Jerome had seen my hesitation. In the middle of his minstrel act, in a moment that somehow slipped outside of time, visible to no one but him and me, he looked seriously into my face to see if I was laughing too. And I realized the complicity of laughter. If I didn't laugh at his antics, I was rebuking him and whatever compromises he had made to make his life workable, and I had no right to do that.

Eight

The Perilous Needs of the Joke Teller

In the South, sports leads where religion, intellect, decency, and the United States Constitution have failed to take us. Sitting on my future in-laws' couch, I watched the all-white 1970 University of Alabama football team begin the season with a loss to the University of Southern California. The Crimson Tide was slaughtered at home in Tuscaloosa, 41–21, and Sam "Bam" Cunningham, a black fullback for USC, ran for 135 yards and two touchdowns on just twelve carries. We stared at the TV, thunderstruck, as a team from Los Angeles manhandled our Tide. How could a football team from the land of the lotus-eaters be good enough to beat us? Beat us? Hell, they kicked the living, breathing crap out of us. And those of us in my future mother-in-law's den were not the only viewers staring at their console TV slack-jawed in disbelief.

The defeat shocked the entire state. How could surfers, hippies, suntanned rich boys—and African-Americans—so thoroughly manhandle an Alabama football team? No one outside the South, where football and personal identity are more deeply entwined than anyplace else, can quite conceive the magnitude of this loss.

But Bear Bryant, Alabama's legendary coach, understood the implications. In a widely published story, one that seems too good to be true, he invited Cunningham into the Alabama locker room after the game, pointed to the black man, and told his defeated players, "Men, this is what a football player looks like." Bryant later commented that Sam Cunningham had done more in sixty minutes for civil rights in Alabama than Martin Luther King Jr. had done in twenty years. And some observers fantasize that Bryant may have engineered the pivotal moment behind the scenes, scheduling the game with his good friend Coach John McKay of USC. Bryant knew that Alabama's inability or unwillingness to put black men in crimson jerseys had left them incapable of beating the best teams in the country. He certainly knew that he had invited to Legion Field in Birmingham the first fully integrated team to play in the state—an achievement in itself. USC was one-third African-American and frequently played with an all-black backfield at a time when Alabama, because of pressure from the state government, had avoided playing integrated teams when it could. Frustrated at losing talented black players to northern schools, Bryant was setting up his team to get clobbered by the deeply talented Southern Cal Trojans.

That's the way the story is usually told. But as Samuel Johnson observes of the tale about why John Milton was not executed after the restoration of the English monarchy, "The objection to the anecdote is its neatness. No good story is quite true." Sam Cunningham recalls that, though Bryant did take the unusual step of going into the visitors' locker room to congratulate him and other Trojan players, "It wasn't anything earth-shattering." Likewise, the famous assessment comparing Cunningham to Martin Luther King Jr. has been attributed to two different Alabama assistant coaches. When the *Wall Street Journal* asked the curator of the Bryant Museum, the poshest building on the Alabama campus, who really said it, Taylor Watson replied, "I've been here twenty years, and I've never been able to figure it out."

To complicate the story yet further, Bryant had offered scholarships to three black athletes as early as 1968, but because he did not pursue them vigorously, they went to other schools, including Auburn, Alabama's cross-state rival. Even earlier, in the spring of 1967, five black walk-on students participated in spring training. Two of them made it onto the fall squad, but never dressed out for games and were never listed in programs or media guides. Taylor Watson sums up the story this way: "The idea that the Southern Cal game meant they could integrate at Alabama is the greatest myth in college sports."

But Bryant still seized the opportunity presented by the lost game; the next fall, the university that eight years before had been integrated only with the assistance of federal troops, had three black players on its beloved football team.

A joke I heard in high school in 1966 had predicted the eventual integration of the Crimson Tide. In the joke, an Alabama talent scout approaches Bryant on the sidelines of a Crimson Tide practice. He points to a young black man and yells, "I know you're not going to like it, Coach, but way out in Pickens County, I found this running back here. He's blazing fast, he's got great hands, and he just runs over people. You gotta see him to believe it."

Bryant looks over at the potential recruit, a big raw-boned country boy, and, without speaking to him, bellows through his megaphone for the first-string defense to take the field. They line up on the twenty-yard line. Bryant flips the ball to the black kid and says, "Let's see you score a touchdown."

From the goal line, the kid races up the middle of the field, jukes one All-American, stiff-arms another, blasts right over a third, and, as he's bulling into the end zone with five defenders clinging to him, Bryant says, almost to himself, "Look at that Puerto Rican boy run!"

The joke is close enough to reality that I've seen it cited as fact on blogs. It suggests that Bryant knew he had the power and prestige to declare an African-American a Puerto Rican and make Alabamians accept the lie for the sake of the football team. In truth, when Bryant finally did put black men into games in Denney Stadium, most Alabamians, loving football more than bigotry, didn't even swallow hard.

One of the three African-Americans recruited by Bryant in 1970 was Wilbur Jackson, who became an all-SEC halfback. My future mother-in-law, my future ex-wife, and I cheered for him mightily game after game. "Wil-bur! Wil-bur!" we chanted when Jackson broke free on a long, sweet run. Then we chanted it again on the replay. After one of Jackson's touchdowns my mother-in-law crowed with pleasure, "He may be a nigger, but he's our nigger." Then she looked over her shoulder quickly to see my reaction.

I'm translating. What she said was more like, "'Ee muh be a nigwa, bu 'ee's owuh nigwa."

My mother-in-law had a cleft palate that left her with a very pronounced speech impediment. She had been born into a wealthy and, I was always told, pedigreed family with a cotton plantation in a rural county west of Montgomery, and her father, an old-fashioned martinet, wanted one of his daughters to stay home and take care of him, so he had refused to have the cleft palate repaired, figuring the deformity would leave her dependent on him. Though the surgery is fairly easy for children, it becomes much more difficult with age and the speech impediment is likely to become irreversible. By the time she could pay for the surgery herself, it was too late to do any good.

When, as a freshman in college, I first began to go over to Mrs.

Ruby's house to pick up her daughter, Mrs. Ruby sat with me in the living room and made conversation while Kathleen finished getting ready for our date.

"Ow ah oo, ahwoo?"

"I'm fine. I hope you are doing well too, Mrs. Ruby."

Once the obvious conversation paths had been trod, I was lost in a dark wood, and, for the first several months I knew her, my answer to everything else was simply, "Yes, ma'am." After Kathleen and I were married, my mother-in-law regularly invited my widowed father for Thanksgiving and Christmas, and when I passed on the invitation I could see anticipatory discomfort on his face. The dinners were a misery to him as she graciously tried to pull the reticent man into the family conversation and he tried gallantly to meet her halfway.

"Ih ure ih uh pur-ee ay, inuni? Ow oo bih oohing?" she asked, and my father would agree that indeed it sure was a pretty day and he'd been doing fine, and she was well?—though he did not entirely know what he was agreeing with. I felt sorry for him because I had long stopped hearing her impediment.

Unwilling to be her father's deformed helper for the rest of her life, Mrs. Ruby had left home, worked her way through the University of North Alabama, married, had a child, and steadily moved up to better and better, but always clerical, jobs in the Alabama State Highway Department. Like a lot of people who have overcome difficulties with dogged, routine courage and compromised aspirations, Mrs. Ruby did not exude immediate empathy for complainers, a category that to her encompassed much of the civil rights movement.

Later, when my first book came out, five or six years after my divorce, she made a point of coming to a bookstore signing I did in Montgomery. Afterward, she hugged me, chatted briefly, and when it was time to go, she took my hand, and with tears in her eyes said, "You were always my baby too." I have never stopped loving her.

When Bryant died in 1983, the principal at my friend Juliana Gray's elementary school in Anniston, Alabama, announced the death over the loudspeaker, and her teacher, sitting at her desk, cried. Students were impressed with her grief because she was known to be an Auburn fan, and Auburn and Alabama have always been bitter interstate rivals. Some state legislators proposed to rename the University of Alabama, changing it to Bryant University. The proposals had enough support that both the Montgomery and Birmingham papers felt the need to editorialize, gently, against it. One joke that's a bit too close to the truth: How many Alabama fans does it take to change a lightbulb? Only one, but the rest will spend the next month talking about how the Bear would have done it.

By dying early in the year, Bryant spared himself the angst of witnessing the 1983 Iron Bowl, the Auburn–Alabama game, in which Bo Jackson, as a sophomore, gained 256 yards on twenty carries and led Auburn to a 23–20 victory. I never heard anyone say of Bo Jackson, "He may be a nigger, but he's our nigger."

The Auburn-and-Alabama rivalry still verges on open animosity between the state land-grant "Ag" school, with its emphasis on agriculture and farming, and the "prestige," liberal arts university, where most of the state legislators, judges, and journalists went to school. Or used to. That's changing as Auburn has become stronger in the liberal arts. I married into a family of Alabama fans and then went to Alabama for graduate school. But my brothers, all three of them, went to Auburn, and my brother Mike met his wife there. Their house is full of Auburn blankets, throws, bedspreads, mugs, magazines, pictures, sweatshirts, sweatpants, sweatbands, and memorabilia—all in the school colors of navy blue and burnt orange. When Bo Jackson played tailback for Auburn, huge posters of the future Heisman Trophy winner covered my nephews' bedroom walls, which pleased and startled me. The family dog was named Bo, and when Jackson went on to star briefly for L.A. in the NFL, the next dog found himself answering to Raider. Both of my nephews have since gone to Auburn, as they always knew they would, so it was natural for them to convert their rooms into virtual Bo Jackson shrines. A new era had arrived in the state of Alabama. Except for Jimi Hendrix posters taped on the bedroom walls of high school guitarists, I'd never before seen a picture of a black man in a white person's house in Alabama.

I doubt there's an Auburn–Alabama joke my brothers and I haven't fired at one another. The jokes are pretty much the same jokes you hear about Texas–Oklahoma, Texas–Texas A&M, South Carolina–Clemson, North Carolina–North Carolina State: basically Little Moron jokes with a few regional twists whenever they can be worked in. The North seems less fond of them, but some of them attach to Ohio State–Michigan, Iowa–Iowa State, and USC–UCLA. Why was Auburn late for the game? Driving up the interstate, they kept seeing signs that said CLEAN RESTROOMS, so they did. How do you break an Alabama student's finger? Punch him in the nose.

An Alabama student sees an Auburn football player in the frozen food section of Winn-Dixie, staring without blinking through the glass window at a can of frozen orange juice. "What in the world are you doing?" asks the Alabama student, and the Auburn football player replies, "It says *concentrate*." A tornado recently went through Tuscaloosa/Auburn and did five million dollars' worth of improvements. What's the difference between a litter of puppies and an Alabama fan? The puppies stop whining after six weeks. What's a seven-course meal in Auburn? A six-pack and a possum.

When Bo was first recruited by Auburn, my father-in-law liked to tell a joke in which Bo Jackson goes into a tailor shop in Tuscaloosa. (The most famous joke about Tuscaloosa is Groucho Marx's, from *Animal Crackers*: "While shooting elephants in Africa, I found the tusks very difficult to remove. But in Alabama, the Tuscaloosa.") The tailor helps Bo select a good wool fabric, advises him on different pant styles, and measures him. The tailor makes the pants and ships them to Auburn. After Bo tries them on, he calls the tailor and complains that the pants are too tight. He can't even get them past his knees.

The tailor is surprised. He knows he measured carefully but he tells Bo to mail them back and he'll fix them. When the pants arrive, the tailor lets them out in the waist and sends them back to Auburn. But after Bo tries them on again, he calls the tailor with the same complaint: the pants are still too tight.

Once more Bo ships them back to Tuscaloosa. Once more the tailor lets them out, this time as far as they will go. Once more he ships them back to Auburn, and once more Bo calls the tailor to say they are still too tight.

"Well, Bo, you've got to remember," the tailor says, "you just ain't as big a nigger in Tuscaloosa as you are in Auburn."

As soon as I heard the word *pants*, I was nervous, positive the joke was going to be about penis size, so I suppose the joke gives a slight head fake toward sex and then runs in a different direction. But like many race jokes, it just comes to the old surly point: Bo, you are a nigger and no matter what you accomplish you will always be a nigger to me.

The joke suggests that redneck Auburn fans are "nigger lovers" who overvalue Bo Jackson. Oddly, the joke all but admits the failure of its metaphorical attempt to cut the famous black man down to size. Bo Jackson was a Heisman Trophy winner with astonishing power and speed, a pro athlete in both baseball and football, and a handsome man whose face was world-famous from Nike's "Bo Knows" ads. The joke's clear subtext is that the rest of the world may see Bo as a big shot, but I'm sticking to my mulish refusal to see what everyone else sees, even my fellow Alabamians. The strained effort to belittle Jackson reveals the littleness of the attempt. Yet, within the undeniable racism of the joke, there's something unmoored in the bigotry. It doesn't link Jackson to a racial stereotype. It just calls him a nigger. For what it's worth, this is the only racist joke I can remember about a football player, in Alabama or anywhere else. Calling an African-American a nigger remains a deep transgressive pleasure for a few people.

Once I stood in line with my father-in-law, waiting for him to buy a pair of pajamas, while the harried and inept clerk struggled to ring up customers. Mr. Ruby, who had been daydreaming, suddenly looked up, noticed I was getting antsy, and said, "What's taking that nigger so long?"

"Will you shut up?" I muttered, laughing with shock, trying to make a joke out of it. He was my father-in-law. I thought then that I was going to live with him the rest of my life. And I loved him. I didn't want him to say things like that.

"What do you mean?" he said loudly.

"She can *hear* you!"

"But she *is* a nigger—and she knows she's a nigger too." He laughed at my discomfort.

How much of this exchange was his wanting to get my goat and how much of it was true entrenched racism, I don't know. But what was tolerable and even funny teasing at home, in his house, was intolerable in public, where the overwhelmed clerk had to deal not only with her job but also racist abuse.

"Just be quiet," I said, again through tight jaw muscles. "Please. Before you get us killed."

He laughed, enjoying my anxiety and embarrassment, but he changed the subject.

Because I loved him, I am still, I know, making excuses for him, and these are some of them: He had never said anything similar before in public, and never did again. After he had been fired from the *Montgomery Advertiser*, where he had worked since high school, he fell into a depression so persistent that he submitted to several rounds of shock treatment. They altered his personality, weakening his sense of discretion, and he changed even more after four heart attacks and a coronary bypass.

My wife and I had been divorced for several years when, working in his garden in one-hundred-degree heat, my father-in-law suffered his fifth and final heart attack. He died there on the perfectly tended turf, next to the lush bed of hollyhocks bounded by monkey grass, as everyone for a decade had told him he would.

Because I happened to be in Montgomery, visiting my father, I attended the funeral service, in the Episcopal church where Mr. Ruby sang in the choir and where my ex-wife and I had married. I sat in the back row. Although it had only been three years, the family pew held several people I didn't recognize. The church was so packed with mourners that the air-conditioning system was overmatched, and I sweated through my shirt and coat. I stayed till the service ended, then quickly slipped out into the bright afternoon light of the parking lot and my car before I had to talk to anyone. The picture of my mother-in-law lost in grief haunted me. Later that night I called my friend Tom, whom I had known since high school and who knew Mr. Ruby because he had briefly dated my ex-wife in high school. From Montgomery, he went to Spokane for college because it was just about as far as he could get from Alabama. Tom observed gleefully, "That's luck, isn't it? You're in town one week a year and that's when the old guy kicks. For normal people the odds of that happening are—what?—two percent? For you it's practically inevitable."

That was the best laugh of the week.

Later the State of Alabama, because of his work for the Bureau of Tourism, named a rest area after my father-in-law. I have stopped there many times over the years, not as homage but because I have to use the restroom, and each time I try to imagine the jokes he would have made about the Warren T. Ruby Welcome Center.

When my marriage broke up, I consoled myself in another round of graduate schools, first for two years at the University of Iowa and then for a year at Stanford. In that time, the only racist jokes I heard were from joke connoisseurs, people like me who were interested in jokes as cultural artifacts or mechanisms to be examined, appreciated, and chuckled over. Of course we joke tellers always displayed a bit of wariness as they approached the border of taboo and then, with mutual assent, crossed over. Ugly jokes make you wonder about the people who tell them. We serious jokers have to sort out the motives of the teller, our own responses, and the cleverness of the joke all in an instant while never breaking contact with the expectant eyes of one another. Because most graduate students in creative writing are trained to look at stories objectively, I didn't feel so much like the tempter, enticing friends to laugh at things they don't want to laugh at, when I asked, "Why do a black man's eyes turn red after sex?"

I assumed, not always correctly, that other jokers would see the joke not as racist but a joke *about* racism. And when I told the joke, or one like it, I started by saying, "Now, this is a racist joke." I was trying, not always successfully, to tell the listener I was not, under the guise of humor, passing on my own beliefs. As Shakespeare has Rosaline in *Love's Labour's Lost* say:

> A jest's prosperity lies in the ear
> Of him that hears it, never in the tongue
> Of him that makes it.

It's a dicey business for a joke to prosper when it's ugly and racist in one of the worst possible ways, so I tried to make damn sure that the ears that heard it from my lips understood I was not endorsing the sentiments in the poem, but enjoying the surprise of how it juggles racism for comic effect. Why do a black man's eyes turn red after sex? Mace.

A few painful and aggravating times I was accused of racism because I told jokes like this, and a few times I walked away from conversations where they were being told by people I didn't trust, but no one ever succeeded in completely turning the tables on me—until the spring of 1983. I was standing in the kitchen of a house on the Stanford campus, where a bunch of my friends were hosting a large dance party. I was telling jokes with friends, all men, when a poised and well-dressed black woman entered the house to a flurry of whispers. "Look who that is!" "She did come." "I didn't think she would. She just said she'd see if she could make it." There had been some gossip, some hope, and now here she was, vibrant in the excitement her presence elicited. Already a star in academe, she was the future provost of Stanford, the highest academic officer of the university, Condoleezza Rice.

She joined the small cluster I was in, probably because we were nearest the door. I don't remember what jokes I was telling, but they must have included two time-bound ones I was infatuated with then.

Q: Why did Menachem Begin really invade Lebanon?
A: He wanted to impress Jodie Foster.

From the moment an old girlfriend posed the riddle, I loved the audacity of the comparison. Who wouldn't be intrigued by a joke that conflates the 1982 Israeli invasion of Lebanon, at the order of Prime Minister Menachem Begin, and John Hinckley's attempted assassination of Ronald Reagan in 1981? It takes Hinckley's insane motive for his attempted murder of the president and applies it to a decision in which it's even crazier. The joke suggests Begin's decision, like Hinckley's, was motivated by deranged macho posturing. Whether one agrees with that assessment or not, the joke elegantly makes a complicated critique in just over a dozen words.

The other joke is more complex, and requires remembering that in the early, confusing days of the AIDS epidemic many of the first victims were Haitians who had come to America in the Haitian boatlift in 1980. At first, briefly, the illness was considered a Haitian problem. Then, before scientific understanding enlarged to include drug injectors and finally anyone sexually active, AIDS was thought to be primarily restricted to gay men. Here's the joke I probably told Condoleezza Rice:

Q: What's the most difficult thing about having AIDS?
A: Trying to convince your parents you are Haitian.

When I first repeated the joke, a stranger at a dinner party, alert to my accent, sneered, "That may be true in Alabama, but it's not true here in San Francisco." Then he asked my girlfriend if she'd like to go boating with him that weekend. He twisted my obvious relish for the joke to imply that I was an insensitive redneck with no regard for the suffering of AIDS victims. I replied that I didn't think it was easy to come out of the closet in either San Francisco or Alabama—an answer that nonplussed him into silence—and made my girlfriend laugh.

He was right that the joke suggests a victim, even in the face of death, would try to hide his homosexuality. I heard that in the joke, just as he did. But to my ear, the joke supposes sweet and terrible empathy with the victim. It's saying, *Not only is this poor imaginary bastard dying, but he is dying in a hostile world that forces him to deny his sexual orientation by telling a desperate and humiliating lie to the people least likely to believe it.*

I remain certain that these jokes, representative of my geopolitical acumen, drew the future secretary of state into our all-male group of joke tellers.

She listened for a minute, laughing easily, until I got to, I'm sorry to confess, the one about the group of leprechauns who knock on the door of the convent. When the mother superior answers, the leprechauns shove one member of their group toward her, and say, "Dewey here has a question for you."

"Sister," says Dewey shyly, "are there any nuns in the convent here about my height?"

"No," says the mother superior. "There aren't any nuns here as short as you."

Behind Dewey, the other leprechauns begin to titter, but he ignores them and says, "Now, Mother, surely you know of at least one nun somewhere in the whole of Ireland who would be about my height, wouldn't you say?"

"No," says the mother superior. "I know all the nuns in Ireland and there's not one who isn't at least two feet taller than you."

The other leprechauns are laughing openly now, but Dewey continues, wheedling desperately.

"But surely you'll agree that in the whole of the world it is theoretically possible that there's one nun who is as short as I am, wouldn't you now, Mother?"

The mother superior thinks for a moment and then says, "As a matter of fact, I know, from international conferences, all the nuns in the world and there isn't one as short as you."

All the other leprechauns burst into raucous laughter, and chant, "Dewey fucked a penguin! Dewey fucked a penguin!"

The men in the group laughed cheerfully at the deluded and

lusty leprechaun, but Ms. Poised pursed her lips and flashed me an aggrieved look.

Man, had I called it wrong. She was a prude, and the punch line, mild by my debased standards, had earned me the skunk eye.

The joking foundered for a moment, and then Condoleezza stepped in to fill the awkwardness she had imposed.

"Why is September fifteenth a national holiday for blacks?"

I'd heard the joke but couldn't come up with the answer, my memory fuddled by the music pumping in from the living room. Also, I was trying to figure out how to catch her attention, exquisitely aware she was three years younger than I and already famous, while I was a thirty-one-year-old graduate student living hand to mouth, nervous, poorly dressed, about a quarter drunk, and sporting a bad haircut and a black plastic digital watch I'd bought at Safeway for two bucks after my Timex stopped.

"I don't know. Why?" someone said, as I stared off at the wall, face scrunched in concentration, still trying to remember the answer—as if biglooting her punch line was going to impress her.

"That's the day the new Cadillacs are introduced." She smiled broadly. We laughed politely at the old joke. I studied her smile, trying to see if she was playing with us, leading us white men down a racist path so she could turn on us once we had committed ourselves to laughter. No, that wasn't right. Her laugh was open, if temperate. She enjoyed her joke. But she also enjoyed making the men nervous, clearing out a space for herself in our group, taking charge.

"What's a definition of *mass confusion*?" she asked.

This one I knew, and I wasn't about to answer it. I was only a *quarter*-drunk.

"Father's Day in Harlem," she said, and laughed more deeply, more openly than before. I laughed unhappily. Her first joke was relatively benign, turning only on African-Americans' supposed predilection for Cadillacs, but it made me squirm. The second joke was more treacherous. It mocks the serious social problem of unmarried and often teenaged African-American mothers raising children by different fathers, a charged subject to say the least—and all the slipperier when told by a highly accomplished black woman who had herself avoided that fate. I'd first heard the joke told with triumphant contempt by my uncle. To him, it was a devastating commentary on the moral degeneracy of African-Americans, and now I was hearing it from a woman who might be implying that she too felt superior to women who had made less careful choices than she had. But didn't she deserve to feel superior? If she did, was it okay to say so? Or was she just telling a joke?

Sipping my jug wine, trying to look amiable and encouraging, the way a good sport must with a joke teller, I was myself the definition of mass confusion. Not for the first time, I was in the precarious position I'd often put people in. I was like the character in Walker Percy's *The Last Gentleman*: "Jokes always made him nervous. He had to attend to the perilous needs of the joke teller."

If she could tell mildly racist jokes, could I reciprocate with similar ones? I wanted to banter, maybe flirt, with the good-looking woman with a sense of humor, the one I'd already offended once. Would she see it as intruding on turf I had no right to walk on? What would my jokes sound like to her when told in my Alabama accent? I might easily step over whatever line she had drawn for herself. And what was it in her jokes that she found funny? That they were scornful of black men? Or were they jokes about class? Were they her way of saying, however obliquely, "I'm not like those people. I don't act or think like them"? That was certainly one of the reasons my friends and I told redneck and hillbilly jokes. Were her jokes her way of showing she was at ease with herself? Was she showing us she was as tough in her way as we were in ours? Was her motivation some volatile combination of all these reasons, plus others I couldn't see?

Or, again, did she simply like jokes?

I listened while someone else told a joke and then drifted back to the jug of wine and refilled my glass. I felt like poor Dewey. But instead of fucking a penguin, I'd simply screwed the pooch: I'd failed completely. I was seeing the future diplomat at work. She entered the room, deftly sized up the group of men she found herself in, and redirected the joking toward a place where she was completely in charge.

In the years since 1983, I've heard exactly three new-to-me racist jokes. Maybe I'd have heard more if I still lived in Alabama, though I haven't heard any when visiting my father and brother there. I've worked for the last twenty-five years in universities, and academics, while they value wit, get squirmy around the atavistic psychology that drives most jokes. But I think racist jokes have mostly died out because the social stigma has become greater and more onerous in every stratum of America, and that intensifying of the taboo has been facilitated by the jokes' migration to the Internet. I very seldom hear a joke anymore. Or tell one. I receive and forward them as e-mail, but they are not racist jokes, coming or going. Very few of us want to risk forwarding a scurrilous joke that might be traced back to us. Besides, writing out an ugly joke makes it even uglier. In person, we can judge how it's being heard and change it as we tell it. We can signal with a shrug, a raised eyebrow, or a grimace how we feel about different aspects of what we are saying. If worse comes to worst, we can simply explain why we are telling it. The printed page and the pixilated screen permit none of these ameliorations.

So, in the mid-eighties, when I was visiting my friend Sara in Tuscaloosa, I had a good idea of what was coming when she asked, "What's the definition of *renege?*"

"A shift change at McDonald's," she answered quickly, before I could work out where the riddle had to go. Her eyes were shining with pleasure, and I laughed a little, buoyed by her irresistible delight in puns and trespassed taboos. It wasn't her telling the joke that troubled me, but the joke itself. It's clearly racist; it links blacks with low-paying, crappy jobs, and the premise wildly at odds with reality: McDonald's work crews are not all black. It's hard not to guess someone saw the possible pun buried in *renege* and contrived a way to bring it forth, rather than observing a situation that sparked ugly wit. The very real racism embedded in the joke is used to make the joke; the joke is not formed to advance racism, even though it does.

In other words, it's a forced pun. The ins and outs of effective punning were brilliantly dissected by Charles Lamb, the great nineteenth-century essayist, who admits to loving a bit of wordplay found in the writings of Jonathan Swift. Lamb's logic is too tight and too charming to condense:

An Oxford scholar, meeting a porter who was carrying a hare through the streets, accosts him with this extraordinary question: "Prithee, friend, is that thy own hare, or a wig?"

There is no excusing this, and no resisting it. A man might blur ten sides of paper in attempting a defence of it against a critic who should be laughter-proof. The quibble in itself is not considerable. It is only a new turn given, by a little false pronunciation, to a very common, though not very courteous inquiry. Put by one gentleman to another at a dinner-party, it would have been vapid; to the mistress of the house, it would have shown much less wit than rudeness. We must take in the totality of time, place, and person; the pert look of the inquiring scholar, the desponding looks of the puzzled porter; the one stopping at leisure, the other hurrying on with his burthen; the innocent though rather abrupt tendency of the first member of the question, with the utter and inextricable irrelevancy of the second; the place—a

public street, not favourable to frivolous investigations; the af-
frontive quality of the primitive inquiry (the common question)
invidiously transferred to the derivative (the new turn given to it)
in the implied satire; namely, that few of that tribe are expected to
eat of the good things which they carry, they being in most countries considered rather as the temporary trustees than owners of
such dainties,—which the fellow was beginning to understand;
but then the wig again comes in, and he can make nothing of it:
all put together constitute a picture: Hogarth could have made it
intelligible on canvass

Lamb contrasts this spur-of-the-moment pun with others in which
the pun is "too good to be natural": "One cannot help suspecting
that the incident was invented to fit the line." Just so *renege*. With
racist jokes that's a good thing because it exposes the distortion of
reality racism depends on. But it makes a bad joke.

I encountered the next of these three jokes in a joke book, an un-
common experience. I don't remember what book or when it was
published, only that one joke in it jolted an amoral laugh out of me.

Q: What comes out of a cocoon?
A: A n-n-n-n-nigger.

I stared at the joke for a few seconds and, when the coin finally
dropped, I barked out a laugh before, in embarrassment and shame,
I caught myself. The joke effortlessly transported me back to an idealized childhood I never lived—*What comes out of a cocoon, children,
is a beautiful butterfly!*—and then turned old, mean, and strange,
shocking me into laughter. The strangeness is the stutter. *Cocoon* is
revealed, presto-changeo, to be a stutterer's attempt to say *coon*. The
joke not only corrupts innocence, it puts the *nigger* and *coon* in the

mouth of someone with an actual affliction who hates black people for their imagined racial inferiority, invoking and then undercutting our tendency to infantilize the disabled, imagining them more innocent than the rest of us. About wordplay, Charles Lamb says:

> A pun is not bound by the laws which limit nicer wit. It is a pistol let off at the ear; not a feather to tickle the intellect. It is an antic which does not stand upon manners, but comes bounding into the presence, and does not show the less comic for being dragged in sometimes by the head and shoulders.

This pun is more of a howitzer by the ear than a pistol.

Because I was so troubled by having laughed at the joke, however briefly, I have told the joke at a couple of dinner parties, prefacing it with the question, "Is this joke racist?" Or "What's racist about this joke?" For some hearers, the n-word blots out any subtleties about implied speakers. For them, the stuttering speaker is just an excuse for the joke teller to say *nigger* for a cheap startle response that sometimes jars loose an uneasy laugh. And that is the truest measure of the joke, I think.

But the joke also possesses curiosities worth parsing. Even though it was a new joke to me, it sounds as if it's at least forty years old, dating back to a time when *coon*, the antiquated slur, was common. It doesn't sound contemporary. But at one level the joke is not deeply racist: The butt of the joke is the supposed racist stutterer who must not be very bright since he's never heard of a *cocoon*. And the joke does not really advance any stereotype or criticism of African-Americans, though one may, by squinting, glimpse a bit of the old recalcitrant slam that niggers will always and only be niggers, and, even more tenuously, perhaps a distaste for African-American sexuality and reproduction. In the main, the racism is bound up in the history and connotations of one word, about which Randall

Kennedy patiently explains, "The word nigger, you see, sums up for those of us who are colored all the bitter years of insult and struggle in America." The joke exploits the electric jolt, the transgressive power, of "that fucking devastating word," as Richard Pryor called it, to shock the hearer, the electricity sparking the volatile mix of pun-pleasure and guilt into complicated laughter.

Something similar happens in the one other new racist joke I've heard. Actually I didn't hear it. It may be the only racist joke I've ever received via e-mail.

An old man from out in the country drives into town to a divorce attorney and announces, "I want one of them DEE-vorces."

The divorce attorney is surprised. Wondering if the old man might be addled, he starts questioning him.

"How old are you?" he asks.

"Eighty-six."

"Well, if you want a divorce, I need to know if you have grounds."

"Sure do. About a hundred acres."

"No, I mean, do you have a case?"

"Don't have no Case. Got me a John Deere, though."

"No, I mean do you have a grudge?"

"Yes sir, that's where I park the John Deere."

"No, no, no. Does your wife beat you up?"

"Can't say as she does. We both get up at four thirty."

"Is she a snorer?"

"No."

"Is she a nagger?"

"No, no—little bitty white woman." Pause. "But my new son's a nagger. That's why I want a DEE-vorce."

Spins the head around, that joke, which is why I laugh.

The power of the joke comes from the shock of the "fucking devastating word," which is never explicitly used. The cuckold's advanced age is simply misdirection, diverting our attention from the possibility he could father a child and leading us to assume his wife is as old as he is.

Is the joke racist? In the main, it isn't, I don't think, except for its evocation of *nigger*. There may be some racism about black male sexuality buried in a black man's fathering the child, but that's a stretch. Race is evoked only to let us know that he figured out his wife was unfaithful when he saw his dark son.

We can argue that the character himself is a racist, but it's a peculiarly passive racism. He certainly responds to the lawyer's use of what he assumes is the taboo word, taking it as giving him license to use it too. To his ears, the lawyer has indicated "Racism spoken here," and that he is free to reveal his own. But interestingly, he brings no anger to the question "Is she a nagger?" If he were a dyed-in-the-wool racist, wouldn't he be angered, offended, or at least miffed by the misheard suggestion that his wife was black? His stolid insistence on a divorce is driven by his wife's infidelity, rather than unhappiness with whom she was unfaithful.

If these three jokes are not new, the fact that they are the only new-to-me ones a joke-magnet like me has heard over the last twenty years tells us something. My friends' experiences parallel mine. My fellow jokers very, very rarely hear—or see in their e-mail inboxes—racist jokes anymore, and when they do the jokes depend more on the taboo power of the word *nigger* than they do in perpetuating any particular invidious stereotypes. Actual racist jokes, the ones driven by animosity, are disappearing, though the taboo of the word is still being exploited. We are arguing to what degree and how the jokes are racist. No one I know is arguing that they are true.

But still, by repeating the jokes I perpetuate the stereotypes even as I hope to mock them, and affirm the power of the taboo word as I attempt to vitiate it. I've told jokes to people who have been comforted by the joke's racism, or more often, been offended. In the first instance, I've been an agent, though not by design, of perpetuating racism. And in the second case I've been perceived as a racist who has tried to lure the listener into racist agreement with me, a miserable position to be in. Can a case be made that laughing at stereotypes is a step on the way to transcending them? Yes, but there are a lot of missteps along the way.

Racial humor, like most humor, tries to draw you into its world, but it has two worlds. One is the world of the absurd, the illogical, the disjunctive, the incongruous—the world of jokes. But the other is the world of racial superiority, and superiority, according to Aristotle, is the realm in which jokes thrive, the smart mocking the stupid, the strong the weak, the attractive the ugly, the white the black. Is it possible to be drawn into one and not the other? I think so, but it's not always easy. A joke creates a bond between the joker and the audience that gets the joke, but what of the victim of the joke, the listener who just doesn't get it, or the listener who gets it and thinks, sometimes correctly, the joker cherishes the stereotype and delights in taunting the victim? Jokes depend on (and reinforce) a structure of insiders and outsiders, one that's particularly powerful and offensive with racist jokes because it's a structure of values. Even when racist jokes don't work—because of the failures of the joke, the joker, or the listener—the value being declared is still racism, even if the joker means to attack it.

Rather than risk abetting racism or being perceived as a racist, why not stop telling these jokes entirely? I pretty much have, except for a few friends whom I can absolutely trust to understand the jokes as a sort of pure aestheticism, though jokes are never pure and rarely aesthetic. I tell fewer and fewer jokes to fewer and fewer people these days. Most people won't even listen to a joke that looks like it's going to veer into racial territory; only bad things can happen there. And though I am attracted to the boundaries, the outlawed, the verboten, I too back off when it comes to race, the last true taboo, or at least the strongest current one.

Nietzsche says that a joke is "an epitaph on an emotion." For racist jokes, I think we are seeing the death throes and we are hearing the epitaph being written.

If you have a new racist joke, I'll listen, but the odds are I won't laugh.

Nine

Never Lose Your Head over a Piece of Tail

This is what my parents told me about sex: nothing. Not one word. Ever.

My brother Roger was so perturbed by my parents' omission that one day when he was home from medical school he went into our youngest brother's bedroom, closed the door, and explained to eleven-year-old Tim in dispassionate, clinical detail the physiology of human sexual reproduction.

When he was done, he came back to the living room, resumed watching football on television, and mentioned to my brother Mike what he'd done. Mike, who is closer to Tim's age, waited till Roger left and then he too went into Tim's bedroom and closed the door behind him. He'd heard, Mike said, that Roger and Tim had had a little talk and he just thought he'd come in and see if Tim had any questions. Did he?

"No," Tim said.

"You understood everything Roger told you?"

"Yeah, I think so."

"Any time you have any questions, just come to me and I'll do my best to answer them. You sure you don't have any questions?"

"I'm sure."

"Any time, just let me know," Mike said as he stood up and reached for the doorknob.

"Uh, maybe I do have a question."

"Yeah?"

"What's a vagina?"

Good question, Tim! One I myself had long pondered. And I learned about sex in an even weirder way than you did.

In seventh grade at Del Vallejo Junior High in San Bernardino, California, two boys and I regularly slipped away from P.E. We saw no reason to exhaust ourselves racing after a soccer ball that we seldom got close enough to kick. In red gym shorts, white T-shirts, and sockless Keds, we dawdled around the edges of the playing field, trying to stay out of the coach's line of vision as we talked, argued about our favorite TV shows, and told jokes.

One morning we edged along the outside of a fence along a concrete drainage culvert, curled our fingers into the fence's chain links, our sole source of support as we leaned back, watching the exertions of our classmates. While we hung there, the hard California sun rebounding off the dry field and the concrete, one of our trio, a chubby kid with a blond crew cut whose name I've forgotten, asked us if we'd heard about the dog that was walking along the railroad track when the train roared by and cut off his tail.

The dog was very upset by this. What is a dog's tail but his glory? Desperately searching for his tail, the dog sniffed and sniffed along the track, so engrossed he didn't hear another train coming from the opposite direction. The train blasted over him, cut off his head, and killed him.

"And what's the moral of this story?" the crew-cut boy asked.

"Beats me," I said.

"Never lose your head over a piece of tail."

The two of them laughed, hanging over the culvert by their fingers, while I pulled myself up to the fence, uncomprehending, stupid, left out. I chewed it over, but got nowhere. The dog had lost its head while worried about its tail. Was the point of the joke that we shouldn't let small losses lead to greater ones? The cute moralism didn't jibe with the hilarity of my friends.

"I don't get it," I said.

They explained to me that *tail* had a meaning other than the one I already knew. Then they explained their explanation.

Jesus, did they think I was so stupid I'd believe something like *that*?

The year before, my parents, after much whispered debate, had signed a consent form permitting me to watch a sex-education filmstrip with the rest of the boys in my sixth-grade class at Del Rosa Elementary. The decision had been a close one, and I was exultant that I didn't have to scuttle out of the room and sit outside the door with the unfortunate dork whose parents had elevated him to iconic dorkdom. I spent the first several minutes of the filmstrip wondering whether, if I'd been out sitting on the green bench with him, we'd have talked to each other.

The film itself was so discreet that, though I understood that seed left the boy, entered the girl, and fertilized one of her eggs, I was unclear how the transfer took place. Extrapolating from the shapeless representations of the implicated organs, I developed a vague idea that the boy shoved sperm from his mouth into the girl's mouth with his tongue, and it then somehow slid downhill to her fallopian tubes. How it got to the boy's mouth to begin with was a puzzlement. I was puzzled too that women, like chickens, carried around inside them a clutch of eggs, and that the eggs could still be eggs though they were not—I asked this—covered with a hard brown shell or suitable for frying. Not that they couldn't be fried, they just *weren't*.

I knew my junior high friends were goofing with me now because I'd read "Ask Ann Landers" and "Dear Abby." For years, I'd pondered letters from pregnant girls who claimed they did not understand how they'd come to that delicate situation thanks to a boyfriend who'd taken off without leaving behind a forwarding address. My pre-adolescent heart went out to them. I could easily imagine how an impassioned kiss might lead to an accidental transfer of sperm. But as I learned more I began to wonder. If a girl had assumed a posture inelegant enough to facilitate a boy's inserting his barely mentionable into her truly unmentionable, she could hardly assert she did not know how she'd been fertilized.

Nope, I wasn't buying it. My friends were always feeding me some line so they could make fun of me when I went along with them, but I wasn't falling for this one. As I pointed out triumphantly, how could they call it *tail* when it was in the *front*? They had no answer for that one.

As we walked back to take showers and then headed to class, the discussion nagged at me. The curly-headed boy had asked in exasperation if I hadn't ever seen two dogs screwing, the boy dog on top, trying to stab his penis into the girl dog. I had, and I'd thought it was a peculiar way to wrestle. Now I was troubled to find myself wondering if humans might possibly make love—and babies—the same way that dogs might possibly make puppies. This new and startling understanding of procreation meshed so neatly with other stray bits of information that I couldn't brush it aside. And my friends' persistent derision of the sexually ignorant moron in their midst kept my anguished turmoil alive.

The crew-cut kid's joke was what tipped the balance for me. He was obviously repeating a joke he'd heard, not one invented just to fool me. Didn't there, then, have to be a core of common knowledge embedded in the punch line? But my still-immature body did not corroborate either the scientific information on the half-remembered filmstrip or the debauched version hooted at me by my friends.

Before the end of the week, I worked up my courage. As casually as I could, I sidled up to my mother as she shredded cabbage and carrots for coleslaw, and blurted out my question. I had composed and recomposed it to be sensitive to the feelings of a woman who might resent the insinuation she was an egg-bearing mammal who had squeezed three boys out of the darkness of her tinkle place nine months after having copulated like a wild dog. But the question also had to be so clearly stated she couldn't weasel out of answering it.

"Do we have babies the same way dogs do?"

"No," my mother said. "Not exactly." Long pause. "Don't you have homework to do?"

"No ma'am. Done done it."

"All of it? Even your math?"

"Yes ma'am."

"Then work on next week's homework."

The following afternoon when I returned home from school there were two library books on the end of my bed. One, by a Jesuit, was an introduction to sex that limited itself to instructions about remaining pure, respecting women, saving myself for marriage, and restricting intercourse to the making of babies—many, many babies. At twelve, without the benefit of puberty to provide a countervailing dialectic, I found Father O'Whosit's arguments compelling. He also railed against the spiritual and mental degeneracy that were the inevitable consequence of young men touching and pulling on themselves where they shouldn't. The curled-lip disdain with which he used the words *touch* and *pull* leapt off the page, and touched and pulled at my curiosity.

Since I had never handled myself in the shouldn't area except to pee, I stood over the toilet and touched. Nothing. Pulled. Nothing. Yanked. Ouch. Five or six ouches were all it took to make me stop. I could see why the priest called it self-abuse, though given the pain, it was difficult to imagine the attraction. Father O'Whatsis made self-abuse sound like a sort of exquisitely filthy urination, but the dark secret of how the illuminati unleash the sinister magic was yet closed to me.

The other book lying on my beige Roy Rogers bedspread that afternoon was a college-level physiology textbook, with an emphasis on sexual reproduction. For hours, I meditated over the plastic overlays of the male and female skeletal, muscular, nervous, lymphatic, and reproductive systems. The knowledge that women possess ovaries, fallopian tubes, and cervixes did nothing to enlighten me about my original question: whether they screwed like dogs. A concomitant question that arrived late and that I did not welcome was whether at some point I'd be expected to accommodate one of them in this process, like a dog myself. Woof.

For a boy raised on biblical Platonism, the idea of being a good animal was not something I could easily grasp. I was as naïve as the young wife who constantly refuses to have doggy-style sex with her husband, no matter how he asks. None of her friends do it. It's not something a lady should do. It's undignified. But finally, one day, worn down by his begging and pleading, threatening and groveling, she relents. She doesn't really want to do it doggy-style, but to keep him happy she will. But first he has to promise her one thing.

"Sure, sure, I agree. What is it you want me to promise?"

"No matter how excited you are, no matter how out of control you get when we are stuck together, promise not to drag me past the beauty salon where all my friends can see us."

She was worried he was just another dog who'd lose his head over a piece of tail.

Hoping to lose just such innocence, I pored over the two sex books my mother left on my bed. I read them as I read all books then: I spread them on the floor at the foot of my bed and lay on my stomach on my bed with my head hanging off the mattress. One night I left the physiology text there when I went to sleep and didn't think to pick it up before leaving for school the next morning. When I got home in the afternoon, I leaned my bike against the wall of the carport, gathered my books from the metal baskets hanging over the back wheel, and as I reached for the doorknob, the door flew open. Screaming, my mother grabbed my outstretched hand, jerked me into the house, and shoved the book in my face as I flinched from it.

"Do you see what you've done? Do you see? Do you know what this will cost? Do you have any idea what this means?"

The book was so close to my face that actually I couldn't see what I'd done. Only when she threw it to the floor and stood in front of me, heaving with sobs, could I see that it had been eaten.

The terrier puppy we'd owned for two months had consumed the lower right quadrant of the book. The rest of the book was ragged and soggy. My mother could no longer, as she'd planned, slip it anonymously into the return slot by the front door of the library. Thanks to my carelessness, she'd have to stand at the desk, where the librarian—and every other bum with nothing better to do than hang around the library!—could see she'd checked out a book with the words *human sexuality* printed in black letters down what remained of its moist spine.

Within forty-eight hours, the terrier puppy went to live with "a nice family in the country who had room for him to run," which means, as I know now and suspected then, that he got returned to the pound. It's not much of a stretch into metaphor to say that, like the dog in the joke, he had also lost his head over a piece of tail.

All in all I received a profound education in Eros and Thanatos from the little fictional dog that met his death by the railroad track, de-tailed and then decapitated by the Super Chief. Eros and Thanatos!—from the first moment of my understanding they were intertwined. Tail can kill you, the joke says. As I grew into a normal unhealthy obsession with girls, the joke, or at least its punch line, haunted me, though I knew little of sex beyond the primal impulse and the idea that fallopian tubes were involved. Implicit in the joke is the understanding, true enough, that love and lust are different, though occasionally overlapping, desires, and that lust is dangerous. This Aesop's fable for pubescent boys also assumes, doesn't it, that some women are tail and some are not? Or, dear God, is it that all women are tail and can fatally entrance you?

An urge that powerful terrified me. When I at last experienced sex, would logic, decency, and life itself be swept away by uncontrollable passion? Would I go crazy? Would I lose my head over a piece of tail?

The joke led me to an indispensable, embargoed truth that could smuggle itself into my consciousness only through the insinuating dreamscape of jokes. Inherent in the jokes were assumptions about sex that I'd taken in before I understood the jokes themselves.

Only in retrospect did I begin to understand a joke my mother loved, and it was a racy joke for a woman who could not bear to talk about sex. I'm pretty sure that she never told it when my father could hear. It began: *A woman is out swimming in the ocean when a wave sweeps in and washes away her bikini top.* The opening grabbed my attention not because it was titillating, but because at the pool on Seymour Johnson Air Force Base my mother wore one-piece bathing suits with little skirts on them. Bikinis were immoral and provocative. She didn't want her eight-year-old boy to know about them, much less to imagine what was under them. But now, for the purposes of her joke, she was telling me non-judgmentally, even gleefully, about a woman who not only wore a bikini but couldn't keep it on. What was up with that?

The woman doesn't know what to do, so she crosses her arms and turns her back to the beach. Mom clutched her elbows, hugged her chest, and half turned toward the wall, imitating the woman in the joke, and I refused the impulse to imagine my mother's naked breasts. That is probably why the imaginary woman in the water is incised into my memory. She is tall, brunette, broad-shouldered, and tan. Her bikini top, which has been swept away, is red. Solid dark burgundy red—no dots, no flowers, no stripes. I didn't have to create her; she appeared in my mind fully formed. My mother was short, henna-haired, petite, and freckled.

The topless woman stands up to her belly button in the ocean, her back still to the beach, and stares out toward the horizon. She doesn't know what to do. While she's considering her predicament, a little boy swims over, dog-paddles around in front of her, and stares at her breasts. Mom always stopped and laughed here, and I laughed with her. She laughed, I think, because the boy's curiosity and blithe bad manners seemed to her the epitome of boyness; maybe she was tickled at the woman's discomfort as the boy studied her. I laughed because I imagined the little boy was me although he was nothing like me and I knew it. If I had ever tried to peek at Mom's breasts she would have, in a phrase she was fond of, slapped me till my head was humming—or knocked me into the middle of next week, another threat she liked the sound of. I imagined I was the boy because, though he wasn't real, he made her laugh.

"Hey, lady," the boy says, "if you're going to drown those puppies, can I have one?"

Oh, how we laughed then, our voices in near harmony, hers leading, mine following a quarter beat behind because I wasn't sure why we were laughing. At eight, I thought the joke had something to do with death. I'd heard of people drowning unwanted animals in lakes, rivers, abandoned wells, rain barrels, and buckets, and I figured the joke might be alluding to that, as of course it is. Or maybe it was about dogs. My mother was much more tolerant of the joke-boy's desire for a dog than she was of mine. The book-chewing terrier was to be her only brief wavering.

I knew the boy's ignorance was central to the joke: How weird to confuse part of a woman's body with a dog! The boy was so dog-crazy that he saw puppies everywhere. If I'd ever seen a nipple, I might have grasped the image that makes the elements of the joke fall into place. To the boy's eyes, the woman's nipples, which she has obviously not covered as well as she thinks she has, look like dogs' noses poking over her crossed arms. But I lacked that knowledge, the crucial bit of knowledge that makes the joke work, and my mother, with astonishing parental double think, both knew I didn't know and hoped I did so she wouldn't have to educate me.

The joke is about sexual ignorance that, like mine, does the best it can with the facts it has. Now I understand that my mother's laughter was propelled by having a houseful of boys whom she knew would one day ask her about sex. In the joke, what seems to be the boy's sexual curiosity and incipient desire are revealed to be the epitome of innocence: a boy's desire for a puppy. Seeking to understand the joke without the tools necessary for the task, I made it even more disturbing. Since I didn't know enough to mistake nipples for noses, I imagined a woman's breasts covered with fur, the slightly coarse yellow-brown coat of German shepherd puppies. That picture in my head gave me the heebie-jeebies for weeks. I thought heebie-jeebies might be the point.

I'd received another lesson in sex education in seventh grade, but unfortunately it took place before I'd heard about the headless dog, so I didn't have a firm educational foundation on which to build. But still I learned something. When the social studies teacher left the room, I leaned into the aisle and listened to a girl tell a joke to her friends. I was so grateful to be allowed into the audience that I remember to this moment the California sunlight pouring through the high, transom-level windows near the ceiling and illuminating the girl's thin face, which suddenly seemed older, almost mature, and slyly ingratiating. She, who had always been haughty, was now bending forward, eager for us to hear her joke.

A little boy comes home from the circus, hysterical. He can't stop crying. The fortune teller at the circus had stared into her crystal ball and finally, sadly, informed the boy that his father would die before midnight the next day.

"Don't worry about what some stupid Gypsy tells you in exchange for a quarter," the father says, and laughs. The mother laughs too.

The father tries to put the prophecy out of his mind, but all the next day at work he worries about it. Maybe the old Gypsy knows something he doesn't, so he drives home from work early to avoid traffic and eats supper chewing each bite thoroughly so he won't choke. The later it gets, the more nervous he becomes, so he goes to bed at eight o'clock, figuring he'll be safe there. As the night wears on and the clock on the mantel strikes nine, ten, eleven, eleven thirty, quarter of twelve, he grows more and more frantic. Finally, as the clock begins striking the twelve ding-dongs of midnight, he jumps out of bed, races downstairs in a panic, throws open the door, bolts across the lawn—and trips over the dead mailman.

The other students rocked in their seats with laughter, and I laughed too, but hesitantly, working my way through the joke. The dead mailman was the boy's biological father, sure, but why was that funny? Since I didn't understand sex, I couldn't understand the shock of sexual betrayal. I understood the mechanism of the joke—that the father's fatherhood, in the biological sense, was revealed to be a delusion—but the psychological power of the reversal was missing and thus, so was most of the humor. Not sure why I should laugh at the joke, I tried to locate something funny in the unexplored future of the characters. How would the husband and wife explain to the police and neighbors the dead mailman lurking around their house at midnight? How would the man and wife get along now that her unfaithfulness had been mystically revealed? In my frantic and inadequate attempt to find the source of humor in the joke, I grasped for the first time that sexual infidelity was not something that happened only in the Bible, with David and Bathsheba. I was so scrupulously churched and vigilantly sheltered that I had not understood adultery could happen in suburban homes like mine, stucco or clapboard boxes to which uniformed government employees delivered the mail and maybe a little special-delivery loving too.

As the other students laughed, all these half-formed notions pinballed around my head, and the girl who'd told the joke noticed my half hearted laughter. "Don't you get it?" she asked with theatrical incredulity. "The mailman was the kid's real father!"

"Yeah, I get it," I said. But by then I'd lost the point of the joke, caught up as I was in trying to fathom the reality it grew out of. Or was it fear? I was being educated about sex by unknowing teachers unaware of what they were teaching. I was being taught, through the oral culture of jokes, the terrors of the tribe. Long before I grasped the passion behind sexual betrayal and the mechanics involved in infidelity, I was learning that women were dangerously desirable and often untrustworthy. Men, in the millennia before genetic testing, could never know for certain they were really their sons' fathers. Here was probably the oldest male fear and certainly the stuff of both great comedy and great tragedy in literature, as well as many billions of agitated nights and angry days off the page. Jokes like this one foster a deeply unhealthy suspicion and distrust of women, but in mocking the pain, laughing at it, they also suggest a philosophical and emotional distancing that may, in time, be psychologically useful for cuckolded husbands. To laugh at the betrayed man is to rehearse for the moment you become him. Humor at the expense of others is always on the verge of becoming the rueful laugh of hard-earned wisdom. But the first time we hear the joke, our laughter at the dead mailman on the lawn is more atavistic than wise; it's apotropaic laughter, laughter that since antiquity has been used to "turn away" or ward off (from the Greek *apotropaios* "averting evil") any evil spirits the joke has summoned.

Over time I brooded over the implications of the many lessons I learned from jokes like the one about the decapitated dog. Frequently, ignorance had led me to mirth for the wrong reasons. When I was fifteen and my mother was pregnant with Tim, my youngest brother, I repondered the story of the Oof-oof bird, an ornithological curiosity I was much taken with when I was eight. On a remote island in Polynesia, scientists had just recently discovered this rara avis and named it the Oof-oof bird. Because it lays square eggs, and every time a corner of an egg emerges, the bird goes "Oof-oof!"

I'd assumed the joke was about constipation, a family affliction, and therefore the one bodily process we joked about. To me, at eight, the joke was about the visceral empathy I felt wincing in sympathy with the imaginary bird. I'm not exaggerating when I say that I could almost *feel* the eight sharp corners of the square eggs move through and out of my body. I understood the joke the only way I could. *But maybe that isn't quite what it's really about,* I thought, with my new knowledge of sex simmering. Watching my mother waddle around our military apartment outside Paris, her hands clasped under her belly as she moaned, "I'm forty years old. I'm too old to have a baby. I'm too old to go through this," I wondered if the joke about the Oof-oof bird might just be as much about childbirth as constipation. At eight, I hadn't comprehended the obvious fact that any creature laying an egg has to be a female and the *oof-oofs* were avian birth pains.

So entertained was my mother by the Oof-oof bird that for days after she first laughed at it, my brothers and I acted it out again and again. As she was ironing in the living room, fixing dinner, leaving the bathroom, or just sitting, staring into space, we stooped in front of her, flapped our elbows, scrunched up our faces in imitation pain, and grunted, "Oof! Oof!" Her mirth must have taken on a strange richness when she saw boys to whom she'd given birth imitate childbirth in front of her, utterly uncomprehending what they were doing—while pretending to be birds. But perhaps those disguises—and the distancing of laughter—are what it takes for a boy to begin to feel in his own abdomen a flinching twinge of what his mother felt bringing him into the world.

By the time I got to high school, I joked about childbirth, belaboring its similarities to another way to drop a load. On the way to the school restroom, I joked about giving birth to a baby so big I'd have to buy it a puppy. Once in the restroom stall, I read graffiti that commanded, "Squeeze hard, you are giving birth to a state trooper." And I remember with pleasure a restroom rhyme from the sixties: "Here I sit, butt a flexin' / Giving birth to another Texan." Jokes, like St. Augustine, know we are *inter urinas et faeces nascimur*, born between urine and feces, and as Freud understood, the pleasures of sex and elimination are often, in the adolescent mind, inseparable: tail is tail is tail.

Though I was slow to catch on, even children know it.

Several years ago, a friend who is a single mom was invited on the spur of the moment to a dinner with some important men in her field. Unable to line up a babysitter so quickly, she swallowed hard and took her son along with her to the up-market steakhouse.

The meal went swimmingly until the main course was served

and the conversation was getting down to serious business. The boy leaned over in his high chair and whispered, "Mom!"

"Hush, Marc," she whispered. "Mommy's busy. Eat your french fries."

She turned back to her colleagues, pleased to see that Marc had not disrupted the conversation.

But only a few minutes went by before Marc called again, "Mom! Mom!"

"Honey, just be quiet—okay?—and I'll get you some ice cream in a minute."

The next time that Marc interrupted, though, he wasn't going to be deflected by french fries or ice cream.

"Mom! Moooom! Mooooooooom! I got to tell you something!" Marc's voice was now loud and commanding, and he had the attention of the whole table.

"Mom, you know when you go to the bathroom. You know? You know?"

"Yes, I know."

"It feels so *gooooood!*"

Marc was stating a truth that the not-so-stuffed shirts at the table uproariously agreed is universal. But Marc, whose fiber needs were obviously better tended to than mine, might not take as much glee in the Oof-oof bird's travails as my family did.

In *Moby Dick*, Herman Melville's Ishmael states that whale ships were "my Yale College and my Harvard." The Yale and Harvard of my sexual instruction were, in one of the oldest traditions of American Puritanism, small groups of pimply boys giggling at half-understood filth as they walked to and from school. At home, I both anguished in shame at being an amoral mammal and exulted at having uncovered an essential secret that adults had tried to conceal. Camille Paglia is absolutely right when she describes the discordant mind, which I thought unique to me, as an irreducible fact of life: "Sex has always been girt round with taboo, irrespective of culture. Sex is the point of contact between man and nature, where morality and good intentions fall to primitive urges. . . . It is the place beyond the pale, both cursed and enchanted." That irreducible contradiction is the engine of much humor, some of it enchanted ("When she was good, she was very, very good—and when she was bad she was *wuuuunderful!*") and some of it simply ugly.

Like debauched salts on one of Melville's seaborne Harvards, we boys, to prove our worldliness, strove to outdo one another at flouting taboos, though our flouting was entirely verbal and imaginary, and perhaps the more debauched without the constraints of the physical world to limit us. Once one breaches the border of a taboo, it's not only possible to go too far: It's inevitable.

On most school mornings, on my way to my seventh- and eighth-grade classes, I met Jack Burkett at the end of my street and we walked the rest of the way to Del Vallejo Junior High together. The walk took only twenty minutes, but to a thirteen-year-old, it seemed interminable without someone to talk to. Nothing at school drew my feet eagerly toward the classroom.

With his long, angular face, large teeth that tilted forward so that his lips couldn't quite cover them, a shock of dirty blond hair that swept down over his forehead, and a harsh equine laugh, Burkett looked like an adolescent facsimile of Francis the Talking Mule. But Burkett had fallen in love with some quirks of Renaissance diction that made him sound more like Mr. Ed, the talking horse. He never said no. It was always "Nay, nay, wretch. Nay, nay!"

He punctuated his punch lines with a sharp punch to my shoulder.

"Where were you born?" he asked one morning as we dawdled on our way to school.

"Texas," I said.

"Me, I was born in a hospital. Did your mom stick her ass out the window?" *Har, har, har*—the last *har* emphasized with a stinging overhand right to my deltoid.

The image created by this ugly and nonsensical joke—nonsensical because the hospital was in Texas and my mother was in both—has never left me: my mother's naked legs and torso hanging out the eighth floor of a hospital as I fell from it. I assume the point was to draw attention to the speaker's knowledge of sex and the fact that we humans are mammals, a fact we learned to recite in school but the details of which we don't usually care to dwell on.

"How," Burkett asked on another morning, "is a tribe of Pygmies different from the girls' track team?"

Groups of something—what? I couldn't figure it out. "I don't know," I said.

"One is a bunch of cunning runts, the other is . . ." His voice lifted insinuatingly.

"Is what?"

"Figure it out, asshole."

"Running girls?"

"Nay, nay!" he crowed, and punched my shoulder. "One is a bunch of cunning runts, and the other is a bunch of running cunts."

When I asked him what *cunt* meant, I got called "asshole" again, along with "rube," "farmer," "baby," "moron," and, one more time, "asshole" before he paused for breath. I had to beg—"Come on, just tell me what it means"—before he consented to enlighten me. I instinctively knew the word was one that I had better not repeat. Maybe it was the way he said it. Maybe it's the way the word has to be said. The hard *k* sound, the short *u*, and the ugly *nt* almost force you to sneer.

The word is famously sneered in *Hamlet*. The prince, mad or feigning it, bullies and humiliates Ophelia with sexual innuendo so explicit that it's barely innuendo at all. Shakespeare was centuries ahead of country singer Carlene Carter, who, not knowing that June Carter Cash and Johnny Cash, her mother and stepfather were in the audience, introduced a song by saying, "If this song doesn't put the cunt back in country, nothing will." Carlene's pronouncement is truer than she knew. As Shakespeare was well aware, *nothing* is also slang for *vagina*:

Hamlet: Lady, shall I lie in your lap?

Ophelia: No, my lord.

Hamlet: I mean, my head upon your lap?

Ophelia: Ay, my lord.

Hamlet: Did you think I meant country matters?

Ophelia: I think nothing, my lord.

Hamlet: That's a fair thought to lie between maids' legs.

Ophelia: What is, my lord?

Hamlet: Nothing.

Another day, as we walked home from seventh grade, Burkett asked me if I'd heard about the guy who went to the morgue and asked to see Marilyn Monroe's corpse. This must have been in 1963, the year after her death.

Once more my answer, as it almost always was to Burkett's questions, was no.

"See, this guy goes to the morgue and asks to look at Marilyn Monroe's body before she's buried. The guy working at the morgue tells him to go away, but then the guy offers him a hundred dollars just to look at her body, and so the guy says okay. He pulls out the tray with Marilyn Monroe on it, and the man looks at it kind of dreamily for a couple of minutes and then asks the guy if he can touch her breasts and offers him five hundred dollars if he'll let him.

"The morgue guy says, 'You must be some sort of creep,' but he takes the five hundred dollars and lets him touch her breasts. Then he takes a thousand dollars to let the man kiss them. Finally the man says, 'I'll give you one hundred thousand dollars if you'll let me take one breast home with me.'

"The morgue guy says, 'That's just sick, you pervert. Get out of here.'

"'Okay, I'll give you two hundred thousand dollars.'

"'Man, you really are sick. No way. Get the hell out of here.'

"'All right, all right—one million dollars. But that's all I got. Take it or leave it.'

"The morgue guy cuts off Marilyn Monroe's breast and says sarcastically, "'You want me to wrap it for you?'

"'No thanks,' says the man, 'I'll eat it here.'"

Har, har, har, hard smack to my shoulder.

"That's it? That's the joke?" I asked. I felt ill.

"Yeah, that's it. What do you want?"

I wanted it to be funny. The joke spirals downward through layers of depravity, passing through insane sexual obsession and necrophilia on its way to cannibalism, but it finally reveals itself to be simply a shaggy dog story, one that goes on at length, dragging the reader along on a pointlessly degrading trip to a deliberately flat ending—a child's attachment to the breast taken to a ghoulish conclusion. For all its horror, the joke has no wit, other than to juxtapose the escalating horror with the banal language of a customer and a cashier transacting business at a hamburger stand.

I did not like Burkett or his jokes, and I doubt he liked me. We were just boys who were thrown together at school. Because he had a couple of older brothers who'd been to juvie, he had a window and probably a doorway into a world strange to me. He knew words, jokes, and stories about sex so outlandish they had to be real, didn't they? To the naïve, the most corrupt person seems the most knowing. Forbidden knowledge seems the most real because it's forbidden—and that is why Satan was so effortlessly able to lead

Adam and Eve to the Tree of the Knowledge of Good and Evil and entice them to sup. I knew that the more I asked Burkett to explain his jokes the more I was treading innocence underfoot, and I was happy enough to trample it because innocence seemed more and more like stupidity, though stupidity possessed the charm of not nauseating me.

The curse of taboos is that pointless vulgarity and perversion are hard to distinguish from suppressed truths. Vulgarity has the thrill of uncovering truth because, in the beginning, tabooed truth *was* vulgarity, and the more outré something is, the more sophisticated it seems because few others know it. Like incipient adepts of the occult, we intuited that the weirder and more improbable something was, the realer it probably was.

On that same Polynesian island inhabited by the Oof-oof bird, there's yet another rara avis, sharing the tropical canopy. Back in 1961, when I was ten, an expedition of European explorers was hacking its way through the jungle when a large bird that they had never seen before flew across the sky and, as they were looking up at it in wonder, let loose with an enormous load. It coated one explorer, who, gagging, started to scrape it off his head, but the guide, who was beaming with excitement, ran up and told him to stop. The Foo bird is magical. To be crapped on by the Foo bird means wealth, fame, knowledge, and a lifetime of good luck. But the befouled explorer is too disgusted to listen to the guide who he suspects is having fun at his expense. He can all too easily imagine the guide returning to camp and telling the other natives about the stupid explorer he convinced to walk around with bird crap on his head. He dumps his canteen over his head, scrubs off the Foo bird excrement, looks haughtily at the guide, and falls over dead.

The next day, after the funeral, the expedition continues and again the fabulous Foo bird flies overhead and covers a second explorer from head to foot. Again the guide runs up, smiling with pleasure, and tells the explorer he is lucky to be singled out for fame, wealth, and knowledge by the divine Foo bird.

"Don't give me that primitive nonsense!" says the explorer. "Yesterday was just a coincidence. I'm not going to traipse all over this wretched island with dried bird crap on my head." He scrapes it out of his hair with his fingernails, flicks it to the ground, and instantly keels over.

After yet another funeral, the third and only remaining explorer sets off into the jungle, and before he takes three steps into the wilderness the Foo bird soars overhead and unleashes a third direct hit. This explorer, having learned by the deaths of his colleagues, leaves the feces untouched on his head and continues with his expedition. He discovers species of animals unknown to science, unearths hitherto unknown civilizations, discovers hidden treasure, and returns home as the most famous and richest explorer in history, though he is widely considered eccentric because he never bathes. The moral of this story? If the Foo shits, wear it.

That's how I felt about a lot of the knowledge I had dumped on me. Enlightened but tainted. Dirtied in an essential, mostly magical, way. And even if I wanted to, I couldn't undirty myself.

Scripture has long known the moral the Foo bird embodies. In one of its stranger moods, the Bible tells us, in Proverbs 14:4: "Where no oxen are, the crib is clean, but there is much increase by the strength of the ox."

Ten

I Just Want to Make Sure He Knows I'm a Bull

In the chill before eight o'clock, as we two twelve-year-olds walked to Del Vallejo Junior High to participate sullenly and minimally in another day of American schooling, Burkett asked me, "Did you wake up this morning with cream in your mouth and a nickel in your hand?"

"Cream? We don't drink cream in our house."

"Just answer the question, you motard! Did you wake up this morning with cream in your mouth and a nickel in your hand?"

"No."

"Oh, sorry—I forgot to pay you!" he brayed, and pointed at me, chanting, "You, you, you!" as if he'd scored a devastating put-down.

"What are you talking about?" I hadn't understood he was telling a joke, and when I understood, I didn't get it. I felt stupid, and Burkett relished his superiority.

"You, you, you!"

"Stop being a creep and just tell me what you're talking about."

"The stuff that comes out of your dick when somebody sucks it, it looks like cream."

"Like whipped cream? Wouldn't that hurt?"

"No, it feels good."

"How do you know? You ever had it come out of yours?"

"No. But my brother has and he says it feels good."

His brother had humiliated him with the joke the night before, and Burkett had been eager to pass along the pain. Because I'd just learned of the penis's unexpected role in baby making, I kept my doubts to myself. And because I was still struggling to comprehend heterosexual sex, I couldn't even begin to grasp gay sex. My mother had already made it beyond clear that men did not, under any circumstance, do such things.

She made her point with a joke. Two men are camping. One takes his clothes off and slips into his sleeping bag. A rattlesnake, curled up inside the bag, sinks its fangs into the member that in our house was called the peenie. (Pee. Knee. Diminutive of penis. Cute-ification of it. I was sure my mother did not know any vulgarisms for the male member till I remembered she used to chant a little rhyme, "A woodpecker pecked on the schoolhouse door / and he pecked and he pecked till his beak was sore." Why did she laugh when she said it? What was funny about that? In her version, nothing. When I later heard the unbowdlerlized version, I realized she was laughing at what she omitted: "A woodpecker pecked on the schoolhouse door. / He pecked and pecked till his pecker was sore.")

"Oww, that hurts," screams the snake-bit man as he jumps out of his sleeping bag, holding his privates.

"What's the matter with you?" asks his friend.

"A snake bit my peenie. Do something. You've got to save me."

The friend rummages urgently in his backpack, pulls out his old first-aid manual, and quickly comes to the page about snakebites: to save a snakebite victim, you have to suck the poison out of the wound.

"Hurry up. What's it say?" asks the snakebite victim, moaning and rolling on the ground, holding himself with both hands.

"It says right here in this book, *You gonna die!*"

My mother laughed and I laughed with her. The idea that one man would put his mouth on the peenie of another man was so unimaginable we found it hilarious. Confronted with the dilemma of taking his friend's dirty part into his mouth or letting him die, this man doesn't see a dilemma. *You gonna die!*

I'm pretty sure my mother did not see the joke as homophobic, but in the same somewhat innocent way I did: don't put dirty things in your mouth! When I was in college in the early seventies, I was sitting on the kitchen counter of our house in Montgomery when Mom said, agitated, "You know, I've heard all this talk about men and men and women and women, you know, being together, you know. But I don't believe it. What would they *do?*"

For a few lunatic moments, I considered telling her. CUNNILINGUS and FELLATIO flew across my mind like advertising slogans on a banner behind a plane. Then another, smaller plane followed, trailing a banner reading BLOW JOB and CARPET MUNCHER. I waited for a third plane but the sky was blue and endless. I said, "Jeez, Mom, I've heard that too, and I have no idea either, no idea at all."

I realized Mom wasn't the only one so ill informed when I read that Lydia Lopokova hadn't quite puzzled out the conundrum either. In 1973, about the same time my mother and I had our conversation, Lopokova, who danced with the Diaghilev ballet, partnered with Nijinsky, and posed frequently for Picasso before marrying John Maynard Keynes and becoming Lady Keynes, wrote: "I can understand two men. There's something to get hold of. But how do two insides make love?"

As a kid, I worried about letting a snakebite victim die because of my squeamishness, and in an ethical decision that consumed several nights of tormented deliberation, I decided I was morally compelled, no matter how revolting it was, to save the life of any man I encountered who had been bitten on the dick by a rattlesnake. I was grateful, however, that we did not go camping very often. Secretly, I thought Jesus would be proud of my audacity and sacrifice, even though I was beginning to understand the dirtiness of the peenie was not just physical, but also moral. Together, the two jokes—Burkett's and my mother's—brought me to some rudimentary concept of homosexuality. And it was about time too. My father had flinched away from the task earlier in the year.

The week before I started junior high, Dad called me into the living room at bedtime, when the house was quiet, and sat beside me on the couch. The lights were low and the room dark with obligation. This was the time and place of our depressing heart-to-hearts about how I was not working up to my potential at school, failing to help my mother around the house, sitting alone in my room too much, not making friends, not trying hard enough at sports, and not developing a positive attitude. I was expecting another round of the same when my father said, "You know you'll be starting junior high in a couple of weeks. . . ."

Yep, I thought, *chance for a new start. A fresh opportunity to get off on the right foot. I need to find something I really care about and stick to it.*

"In gym class you are going to be taking showers with all the other boys."

"Sir?"

"If anybody touches you while you are in the shower I want you to tell the coach immediately."

I'd been in boys' showers before. Sharing showerheads, we jostled for position under the spray, and sent one another sprawling with a casual shove if the one clumsy enough to drop the soap was also stupid enough to bend over to pick it up. Crouching and dropping one's face to butt or crotch level was unimaginable. Best solution: kick the soap into the corner and then go get it, away from everyone. Or slide it up the wall with your foot until you can reach it without bending. I had no idea what Dad was talking about. It was impossible to shower without bumping into other boys or being bumped.

"I mean if another boy touches you, you should get out of the shower, find the coach, and tell him what happened."

"Touch me, like how?"

"Just any way at all. Any kind of touching. I want you to tell the coach and then tell me. Just promise me that."

"Yes, sir," I said. I had no intention of keeping this promise because I had no idea what I was promising.

"Good. I'm glad we had this talk. Some boys do bad things with other boys in the shower."

I thought he meant the bigger guys would beat you up when you were wet and naked. In the junior high locker room, the most frequent pain inflicted on me emanated from the welts scored on my butt and hips by a blocky, swarthy boy who delighted in whipping a wet towel against the flesh of smaller, pinker boys. I took his right to administer this petty cruelty as natural; he was wickedly accomplished at it and his back rippled with more, thicker, and blacker hair than I'd ever seen on a biped outside the primate cages at the San Diego Zoo.

My reticent father must have been troubled by my insouciance about public showering, along with a worrying constellation of other traits. I was a boy given to solitude and unexplainable weeping between bouts of anxious rage. Boys like me, the ones interested in books, art, crafts, wordplay that I hoped was arch, and what was then called the "ladies' section" of the newspaper, tended toward effeminacy, didn't we? Since I was inept at hitting a baseball or even tracking its arc as it sailed through the darkening sky over right field and my outstretched glove, my teammates thoughtfully alerted me to the limitations of my manhood. That strikeout cost us the game, you stupid pansy! You fag, you couldn't catch your ass with both hands. That fairy's always an out for our side. Can't we just skip him? Don't be such a wuss. You aren't really hurt. You fruit, you queer, you pussy. Maybe my teammates saw something in me that I couldn't see myself. Maybe an unsuspected hankering for men's bodies would come upon me suddenly, like puberty or religious conversion. Maybe I'd suddenly find myself hanging around campgrounds and hiking trails, looking for a man who'd been snakebit on the peenie.

From roughly ages six to twelve, every several weeks, I burst out at my mother, screaming with rage. Mom drove me past blubbering to snot-sucking terror with the usual response: "Just wait till your father gets home. Once he hears the way you've been talking to me you'll *wish* you'd never been born."

One night, following one of my blowups, my father and I had another heart-to-heart on the couch in the dark living room. He'd already explained to me, he said, that my mother was just as much my parent as he was and that I should give her all the courtesy and respect that I did him, but somehow that had not gotten through to me. Neither had whipping me. Neither had grounding me. Or more whipping. He and my mother were at their wits' end. They didn't know what to do with me, and they weren't going to accept this kind of disrespect. Choking up with frustration, fear, and resignation, he said that he and my mother had decided to send me to a psychologist.

"Am I crazy?" I blurted, shaking. I was willing to believe it. I knew I was out of control when I yelled at my mother. I knew, because she wasn't the one I really wanted to yell at. I was too frightened of my father to yell at him. When he didn't like what I did, what I said, how I said it, or how I looked at him, he jerked his belt off, making four or five machine-gun pops as the leather whipped backward through the belt loops. He ordered me to take my pants off and kneel beside the bed with my butt in the air, and then he slashed the belt up and down my naked rear or thighs. My brothers and I kept a close eye on what was holding up his pants, especially the thin black civilian belt, the one that bit the hardest. Because I was apoplectic at his mean and arbitrary rages, and terrified too, I shrieked at my mother while he was at work, and she, seeing what looked to her like unmotivated derangement, ratted me out, trying to use his anger to make me act civilly to her, which at least gave me a legitimate reason to be furious with her.

"No, doll, you're not crazy," he said, and he hugged me, clasping my cheek tight against his chest, rocking me back and forth, as he laughed shakily at my fear, which was his fear. "You just need a little help."

Every time I went to see the blond psychologist, Mrs. Miller, Mom instructed me to pay attention, do what I was told, and get my full sixty dollars' worth of counseling. Did I understand how much money that was? Did I know we could buy the whole family's back-to-school shoes with sixty dollars and have money left over for notebooks? I imagined that, unlike the boy in the jokes whose father took him to a whorehouse on his eighteenth birthday and paid a woman to "make him a man," my parents paid a woman to listen to me talk and make me normal—an auditory prostitute, a talk whore. My God, I must be pathetic if it cost sixty dollars to entice someone to talk to me.

As it turned out, I liked to talk. Mrs. Miller always began our sessions by spreading cards across her desk, each with a different black-and-white photo of a face on it. The people were dressed in the clothes of an earlier time and they seemed European. I guessed they might be postwar French or Dutch. From each grouping of cards, I chose the two faces I liked best and least, and by my choices Mrs. Miller diagnosed my mood.

After I got comfortable with Mrs. Miller and her office, I asked what the cards said about me. I liked asking her questions. The explanations were a bit thick with psychological jargon, but unlike at home, I could ask and she would answer.

She flipped the first series of cards back on the desk and said, "See that man? You always pick him."

The young man had an open, unblemished face, full lips, light hair, and he wore an almost jaunty plaid sport coat. In retrospect I see a young version of the poet Hart Crane.

"He's a homosexual," she said, and hurried to add, "That's nothing to worry about. It doesn't mean you're like him. Most people pick him. It just means you may be open to the feminine side of yourself. We all have that side, men as well as women."

Almost magically, my fear vanished. A professional had said it was okay, maybe even good, to have a feminine side. Even her cursory explanation implied that normal sexuality included a wider range of complexity than I'd been told—and that homosexuality was part of the spectrum. It was one of the most thrilling and freeing moments in my life to realize that, despite everything I was learning at home, church, school, and on the playground, normal was a much wider category than I'd known. And sex was only part of it. Normal jobs, normal interests, normal clothes, normal food, normal fantasies, normal stories, normal jokes, normal thoughts were all suddenly commodious eight-lane highways and not the strait gate and narrow road of the gospels. Off and on for a month, I stayed awake at night, marveling at the insight, which I knew to keep to myself.

But the social opprobrium of being thought effeminate continued to haunt me. That's why throughout high school I loved the joke about the two old bulls standing in the pasture, overlooking the heifers they think of as their harem. What a great life to be a bull!

As the two bulls consider their good fortune, the rancher drives through the gate, towing a trailer. He stops, walks around to the door of the trailer, unlatches the door, and jumps back as an enormous young brute of a bull blasts out into the pasture. The young bull spots the old bulls, glares at them, and paws the ground viciously, kicking up huge clumps of grass and dirt. The older bulls just look at him blankly, so the young one ambles over to the herd of heifers and begins to service them one after the other, roaring and grunting with delight.

After the fifth heifer has collapsed in a state of bovine bliss, one of the old bulls charges toward the young bull and begins to snort, and stamp the ground.

The other old bull runs up to his companion and says, "What the hell are you doing, you idiot? That young guy'll kill you!"

"I just want to make sure he knows I'm a bull."

I told the joke repeatedly in high school, even obsessively. The world of that joke *was* high school. Sidney Lanier was a jockocracy. Coaches made much more money than teachers, and the football players, on game days, sat at tables reserved for them at the front of the cafeteria, eating steak and baked potatoes heaped with sour cream and grated cheddar cheese while the rest of us munched corndogs and Tater Tots. When I complained, I was told that since the steaks were paid for from athletic department profits, it was none of my business. When I pointed out that the steaks were fried by county employees on county-owned stoves, I was threatened.

Football players were lionized at pep rallies, celebrated in the newspaper, and cosseted through dumbed-down math and history classes conducted by coaches who didn't know what they were talking about except when they held footballs—and even that didn't always help. One coach taught history while holding a football, occasionally tossing it in the air and catching it while he talked.

In gym class, the athletes terrorized the non-athletes, smacking us around. Like a number of my friends, I occasionally wore my athletic cup to class because jocks, passing me in the hall, found it amusing to slap us in the groins. Their viciousness even extended to the team managers, boys who wanted to hang around the jocks so much that they became their servants, bringing them water and toting equipment to the field. Returning from an out-of-town game, the jocks at the back of the bus stripped the team manager, smeared his penis, testicles, and anus with Deep Heat, and then mummified him in Ace bandages. He rode the rest of the way home curled up on the floor, weeping and whimpering in agony. The football player who told me this story thought it howlingly funny and wanted to share the laughter. I was a joker, wasn't I? Isn't this story hilarious?

Tell the teachers if I was afraid? The teachers knew that the coaches made two or three or four times what they did. They knew that they were servants to the football players first and school administrators second. If they forgot, they were reminded every other Friday night when it was their turn to go to the stadium or the gym, and work without pay, selling tickets and soft drinks.

Tell the principal? If the football team had a bad season, he was as likely to be fired for it as the coach.

Tell the coaches? The coaches loved aggressive players, and they encouraged violence off the field to ensure violence on the field. A defensive back in my history class told me that on at least two weekends coaches drove him and other football players to Oak Park, and encouraged them to beat up the hippies. Before they got in the car, the coach issued them baseball bats from the school's supply room.

In the lunchroom one day, I mentioned that I had cut my hand on a loose wire on my spiral notebook. The two-hundred-and-seventy-pound offensive lineman who sat at my assigned lunch table said, "Where? Let me see."

Astounded by his concern, I held out my hand. He took it and clenched down. Looking me in the eyes, he picked up the salt shaker and salted the cut. Unable to break the grip of a boy who outweighed me by at least a hundred and thirty pounds, I bucked and yelled, trying to get free, until a teacher came over and told me to shut up.

The violence peaked two years after I graduated, when a boy in the senior class led a spur-of-the-moment pep rally in the lunch-room. Jumping up and down on a lunch table, he exhorted the crowd to cheer the Sidney Lanier Poets on to victory.

Taped on his torso, pinned up and down his legs, blue-and-white pom-poms snapped with every step he took.

Suddenly the pom-poms soared into flame.

The rumor at the time was that a football player had, as a joke, snapped a couple of wooden matches at the pom-pom boy. The newspapers said that police investigating the incident had inter-viewed eighteen witnesses and the burned boy himself. They had a pretty good idea what had happened but they wanted to interview half a dozen more people before they announced their conclusion. With that, the newspapers dropped the story like a stinging nettle. As far as I could tell, the investigation was never concluded and no charges were ever filed.

In outrage, I told this story to my friend Tom Doherty, who graduated from Lanier the year after I did. Tom, now a professor of American Studies at Brandeis, said, "Come on! Of course no charges were ever filed, Brainiac! It was a football player!"

"Yeah, that's right," I said. I'd forgotten that in Alabama football-immunity extended even to felonies.

But maybe that horror wasn't the peak. Maybe the peak was the boy, I believe he was a cornerback or safety, who, rumor had it, buried a cat up to its neck in his backyard and then mowed the grass methodically, arriving at the cat in due course. He was so vicious in attacking hippies in Oak Park that one of his victims was reputed to have driven to New Orleans and paid for a professional hit on him. The hit man—and as an animal lover I have mixed feelings about this—did not fulfill the contract.

For my entire sophomore year, at night, in bed, in fear of going back to school the next day, I imagined stealing a rifle and striking back at the football players who made my life a daily misery. Instead of counting sheep, I made lists of people I wanted to kill. I stopped my murderous fantasies because I realized if I didn't, I might actually slip out of fantasyland and then into action. I had a strong hope, even an expectation, that if I just held on till graduation, I could go to college and pursue a life not shaped by fear and humiliation. But to get there, like the old bull in the joke, I was going to have to pretend like I wasn't frightened.

You don't have to think too hard to grasp the bull joke's meaning: It's better to be defeated in a hopeless fight than to be treated like a woman, better to die than let another man use you sexually. The joke's sympathy is with the old bull, and the story stops in the nick of time for it to be funny. If the joke went one step further, only one logical thing can happen: The young bull will kill the challenger.

Like the old bull, I realized that I might have to fight stupid and pointless fights, knowing I'd be whipped. If I was going to be abused by the bigger boys, I was at least going to make it as difficult for them as I could—and if I couldn't hurt them, I'd at least make them hurt me enough that they might get in trouble for it. In tenth grade, that determination, along with flailing, screaming, and unyielding panic, saved me from being stuffed into a gym locker. As the jocks shoved me into the tiny space, I kept jabbing a hand, arm, or foot out of the locker, and they had to decide if they wanted to break one of my bones to get the door shut. Two other boys were crumpled into the narrow, three-foot-tall lockers, jockstraps yanked down over their faces. With an enraged dignity that I admire to this day, one military brat—Larry Pizzi, I believe—pulled his street clothes on after he got out of the locker, walked the two miles to the police station, and filed a complaint for criminal assault. Although he'd been in town only a few months, he already knew nothing would come of complaining to the coach or principal, but he didn't yet know nothing would come of filing an official complaint with the police, who were almost to a man ex-jocks and diehard fans of their old teams. But after that, Pizzi was left alone, and after I had vowed that I would exact as much cost as I could from the bullies, legally or physically, even if it meant being maimed, so was I. I'm not sure how my determination conveyed itself. My wife tells me that when I believe I must do something, no matter what it costs me, I assume a look of fervent kamikaze resolve that makes sane people back off. You learn that look if you attend a school in which students go up in flames.

In another way, by telling the joke, my friends and I acted out the role of the combative bull, as we assured ourselves and others we were straight. The joke implicitly demeans gays, and you could say we were picking on those weaker than we, but gays at Sidney Lanier were deeply closeted, and jokers like me were one of the reasons they stayed that way. We were bullies without knowing it, our jokes reaffirming what we already believed—that it was morally wrong, personally sick, and socially unthinkable for a man to have sex with other men. The jokes relied on our boyish, visceral revulsion at gay sex to drive the humor, which only strengthened the taboo. Example: Guy orders ten shots of whiskey. Slams all ten back. Shakes head. Orders another. Bartender cuts him off.

"Ah, man, come on. I just had my first blow job."

"Oh, in that case, have one on the house before you go."

"Just forget it. If ten won't get the taste out of my mouth . . ."

I'm more ashamed of the homophobic jokes I laughed at and repeated than the racist ones. I seldom took jokes about race seriously because I never took racial superiority seriously, even when I should have listened more closely to what the jokers—and my laughter—were telling me about themselves, the world, and me. But because I dreaded other boys thinking I was gay and because I accepted the prejudices of my time, gay sex seemed absurd and therefore risible. Still, contrary to what preachers roared from the pulpit, an insistent voice inside my mind—or maybe it was simply an enlarging sense of what normal was—grew stronger and stronger, arguing that people's loves were none of my damn business.

So even as I repeated them, I was growing uneasy with the lisped jokes about limp-wristed Bruce, including the one about his attending, for some reason, Sunday services at a rural Baptist church and putting a twenty into the offering plate. The impoverished congregation is astounded by his munificence, and, as thanks, the preacher asks Bruce if he'd care to choose the next three hymns. Bruce stands up, looks around, and says that he is, in his turn, astounded by their generosity and, pointing three times around the congregation, says, "I'd like to choose him, him, and him."

Ba dum tish! A dismal *Ba dum tish.*

If there's any comic pleasure here, I can't find it in the tortured and suffering pun, God knows, or in the clash of cultural expectations between rural fundies so poor they are astounded to discover a double sawbuck in the collection plate and a citified gay so ill educated he's never heard of hymns. What sparks the humor, if there is any, is the violence that implicitly ensues after the farm boys realize what they have been selected for. Does anyone think the pastor is likely to respond with a frosty, "Sir, that is not what I meant?" The city boy is likely to get his three hims and not in the way he hopes.

Even in my revulsion at my former homophobia, though,

there's room for a laugh. I still chuckle at a joke, dated now, that my mother and I heard Johnny Carson tell on *The Tonight Show*.

Clasping his hands in front of him, rocking back slightly on his heels, Carson asked, "Did you hear about the three gay men who assaulted a woman?"

Any mention of sex while I was in the room with my mother made me anxious. Adding gayness, a category she didn't grasp, as I knew then, turned up the thermostat. Assault turned it up even higher. And of course there's the built-in tension of a riddle. Can I answer the question? Will I understand the answer when it's given? And this riddle is a poser. Why would gay men attack, presumably sexually, a woman?

When Carson began the answer, "Two held her down . . . ," the tension becomes almost excruciating. All I could think about, sitting six feet away from my mother, was gang rape.

"Two held her down." Pause. "And the third fixed her hair."

Mom and I laughed in relief, sure, but the joke is also clever in the way it sets rape so thoroughly and illogically in our head that we can't see past it, and then suddenly resolves more or less harmlessly if you aren't, as we weren't then, offended by the stereotyping. For my mother, at least a little of the humor must have resided in the esoteric concept of sissy men fixing hair. Her hair had only ever been set by women, and when I was dragged along to the beauty salon with her as a boy, I was almost always the only male in the room. Even the men who were waiting for their wives or, if it were near five, the husbands picking up the hairdressers, usually waited in their cars.

The three gay men are so offended by the woman's visible lack of beauty that, in a sort of aesthetic rape, they force beauty on her to satisfy their need for it. And the joke hints that *real* men's different needs for a woman would lead to the gang rape the joke teases us with in the beginning.

• • •

Identity is at the heart of teenage agonizing, and so a lot of the jokes I loved then were about how we define ourselves or have ourselves defined. Though I heard it often, a joke I never laughed at is the one about the man who, on the psychiatrist's couch, just happens to mention that he's been having sex with his horse.

Taken aback by this casual admission, but trying to be calm, professional, and nonjudgmental, the doctor asks, "Is it a stallion or a mare?"

"It's a female of course. What do you think I am—a queer?"

In the telling, it's necessary to get the right tone of outrage, incredulity, and contempt into the punch line. Even when I heard it told well, I rolled my eyes, not because I was offended but because the punch line is so predictable. Once the psychiatrist asks about the sex of the horse, the joke has an obvious path, and it takes it. Still, the joke has some interesting wrinkles that my contempt for its punch line blinded me to. What is worse, homosexuality or bestiality? The patient is more indignant at being thought gay than being thought a horse fucker. The joke is funny, to those who find it funny, because the man accepts with equanimity the greater taboo— he doesn't even acknowledge it is a taboo—but angrily rejects the lesser. The horse fucker clings to his dignity by insisting that there are straight horse fuckers and queer horse fuckers, and whatever else he is, he's straight! What I missed in high school is that even as the joke winks at the patient's delusions, it clearly signals that homosexuality is so outside acceptance that even horse fuckers look down on queers. The man's voice saying, "What do you think I am—a queer?" is also the voice of the joke teller, donning his terror of gayness.

But there's even more to the joke. It's the homophobic inverse of Virgil Thomson's famous quip while walking down the street with a friend. A gorgeous young woman walked by, and Thomson sighed,

"Dear, when I see a beautiful woman like that I can't help wishing I were a lesbian." At first I had dismissed this witticism as an easy reversal of expectation. Only on hearing it the fourth or fifth time (and it's unclear whether Thomson actually said it) and pondering my gay friends' affection for the quip, did I begin to understand the depth of the wit. Thomson, reveling in how his gayness defined both his sense of himself and how he wanted to be seen, understands that if he physically desired a woman he'd have to be a lesbian. Thomson's sexual desire does not lead, but follows, sexual identity.

In high school, jokes about gays, bestiality, and incest flowed together because they were all about the territories lust was forbidden to explore. Because bestiality seemed too ridiculous to take seriously, I laughed easily at the torrent of jokes about it, but I began to wonder if I shouldn't take it more seriously.

The country boys, bussed to Sidney Lanier High from the country, regaled us air force brats with stories about stump-trained heifers, receptive sheep, and chickens so ubiquitous that nobody noticed when, from time to time, a hen went missing. Since I had never seen female genitalia, I occasionally glanced at the privates of a dog or cat, and involuntarily wondered if it *would* be possible. Even those few clandestine glances made me feel like an irredeemable degenerate. So I listened avidly to the country boys' jokes. I wanted to know the things I wasn't supposed to know. What happened in the showers that left my father speechless? What happened in the barn, behind the barn, and out in the farthest pasture?

Like a lot of boys I was fascinated by the details, the know-how, of the forbidden. As Samuel Johnson once said, "There is nothing so minute or inconsiderable that I would not rather know it than not," though it's hard to envision the Great Cham listening raptly to pimply boys explain that a stump-trained heifer was one taught to stand still in front of a tree stump so they'd have easy access to her, and that if you wear hip boots you can jam a sheep's rear legs in them so she can't wander off during sex.

The country boys knew I wanted to know, so of course they refused to tell what they meant when they yelled, laughing, "Get up, wo-bak! Get up, wo-bak!" They sniggered it in gym class softly so the coach couldn't hear. They called it to one another in the hall between classes, and mumbled it in front of teachers, sure that no one would understand. It was their joke and they weren't sharing it with any of us outsiders, the air force brats who were new in town.

I was crazy to understand the farrago of incomprehensible syllables. Not until a decade ago, reading Gershon Legman's *The Rationale of the Dirty Joke*, a bravura compendium of filth and screwball Freudian interpretation, did I discover the rest of the joke. Git-up-whoa-back! Git-up! Whoa! Back! It's what the world's laziest pervert says when he's screwing a mule.

I thought bestiality was merely a joke, but in one of my classes, the boy who sat behind me claimed otherwise. He'd already bragged that he and his junior high buddies had, just the year before, hurled burning bags of their own feces at Martin Luther King Jr. and the Selma-to-Montgomery marchers, but I was even more disturbed when he hissed into my ear, with moist intimacy, "Hudgins, you ever fuck a chicken, Hudgins?" When I, incredulous, croaked, "No," he said, "Hudgins, this is what you gotta do first. You gotta snip off its legs off with wire cutters or it'll claw your thighs up something terrible.

"Oh man!" he sang to the back of my stiff neck, his voice soft with remembered ecstasy, "you ought to *feel* that dyin' quiver!"

When I jerked my head around and stared at him, trying to determine if he was telling the truth or just trying to get under my skin, he cackled. When I turned again to face the teacher, he slapped the back of my head, delighted in my shock. Some days—this is true—I actually calculated the chances that Satan had assumed human form and sat behind me in tenth-grade biology, whispering lascivious iniquities into my ear.

Now that boy reminds me of the horse fucker on the psychiatrist's couch. I'm sure he would have beaten me to the ground if I had ever suggested that he had made love with another boy. It was a hen, not a rooster. What do you think I am, a queer?

In my first-period gym class, sitting on the bleachers, trading jokes and stories, the country boys repeated, with fervent conviction, the rural legend that humans could impregnate ewes. Months after the act, a violated ewe would drop a distorted creature in the pasture, half-human, half-lamb, a ghastly, doomed mutant being that would die shortly after it was born because . . . because . . . because things like that just can't live, that's why.

In "The Sheep Child," the poet James Dickey takes the adolescent myth and points out its purpose:

> *Farm boys wild to couple*
> *With anything . . .*
> > *will keep themselves off*
> *Animals by legends of their own:*
>
> *There's this thing that's only half*
> *Sheep   like a woolly baby*
> *Pickled in alcohol . . .*

The myth of the sheep child keeps adolescent horndogs off the livestock. If during birthing season in early spring, your father finds a woolly mutant baby slipping from a ewe, your explanation that evening over the family dinner is going to be awkward.

The sheep child lived in the stories we told, laughed at, and flinched from on the gym bleachers at Sidney Lanier High. And he was very effective at his job of protecting the sheep. In Alabama, in Wyoming, in Mississippi, in Greece, in Some-Rural-Place-That-You-Don't-Like, how do they separate the men from the goats? With crowbars. And this story is a crowbar with a lot of leverage.

In that tenth-grade gym class, though I could hardly bear to think about it, I always laughed at the farmer who hated bestiality, just hated it. Why? Because when he was having sex with his mule, it was exhausting to keep running around to the front to kiss her. The tenderness inside the depravity undid me. I loved the comically pornographic Keystone Kop picture of a naked man frantically running back and forth from one end of a mule to the other so he can share the romance with her while not losing interest in his own pleasure, but I writhed in embarrassment at the stupidity of the poor, uncomprehending boob who so confused lust with love. I identified with him. The creepy poignancy of the farmer's misplaced decency inside his greater indecency upset me. It seemed the sort of idealistic mistake I'd make if I were to, um, find myself in his situation. He had lost his head over a piece of ass, and not just a figurative ass either. And not just a piece. All of her.

In high school, we learn some identities are transient, experimental, or playful. Others are ineradicable. Does anybody not know the classic joke that tells us that?

A young man sits down at a bar and falls into conversation with a grizzled old fellow. When the old guy finishes the whiskey in front of him, the young man buys him another one, clearly not the old guy's second whiskey of the day. The drink makes the old guy loquacious, and in gratitude, he wants to share the wisdom his eight decades of life have taught him.

"Look out that window there, sonny. Those eighty acres of feed corn and the eighty acres of prime pasture next to them, I made them out of scrub and nothing—but do they call me John the Farmer around here? No, they don't."

Next drink.

"And the fence around all those one-hundred-sixty acres? I built that fence with my own two hands, felling the trees, cutting the boards, setting the posts. But do they call me John the Fence Maker? No, they don't."

Next drink.

"And remember that bridge you drove over coming into town? I built it myself, standing there in the mud of the river. But do they call me John the Bridge Builder? No, they damn well don't.

"But you fuck one goat . . ."

Bestiality is a zero-tolerance offense. You do it once and you forever forfeit all your achievements and complexities and become merely, irrevocably, and comically John the Goat Fucker. It's a steep price to pay for an ephemeral, if presumably pleasurable, depravity. It was easy to extrapolate the lesson behind the joke to other sins, iniquities, and indulgences, including homosexuality and incest. Suck one cock, you're a cocksucker. Fuck one mother . . .

The closest of the intimate taboos was the one that made my friends and me flinch the most. One morning, before Analysis class began, my friend Tom observed that he had nothing against incest in the abstract. It was only when he considered his limited list of options . . . His voice trailed off and he waited for me to laugh, which I did.

Walking home that afternoon, as I cut through Sears for the blast of air-conditioning and then continued south on Court Street, tramping along the edge of people's yards because there were no sidewalks, I passed the time ticking down my own circumscribed list of possibilities. A few female cousins, not so bad, but aunts? Oh, please. After that there were, jeez, my grandmothers. That was beyond nasty. My brothers? Mom, Dad? Then I had to stop. I'd meant to entertain myself by toying with my gag reflex, but now my lips cramped from being curled so long.

Jokes love to play with visceral responses, and incest offers one of the most reliable revulsions. In the tenth grade, just as study hall was beginning, a girl I barely knew popped into the room, stopped in front of my desk, and asked, "What's the grossest thing in the world?"

Her hair was cut in a brunette pageboy, and she wore a burgundy crew neck sweater over a white blouse. Gold chain necklace. I seem to remember a green and red plaid skirt.

"I don't know," I said.

She leaned forward and looked at me intently. "It's when your eighty-year-old grandmother kisses you good night—and she slips you the tongue."

I scrunched my lips as a little bark of laughter burst through them. My mouth felt unclean. I wanted to spit. And I was also exquisitely aware that an attractive girl had just told me a joke about French kissing and laughed at my reaction. She said "slips you the tongue" as if she were nonchalantly familiar with an act I had only dreamed of.

Being a moron, I assumed that she had told me the joke only because she thought it was funny and was totally unaware that a boy might wonder if she were flirting with him. I guiltily dismissed the thought. It was unworthy of her. But the joke, I loved the joke! When she left, I whispered it to the boy on the other side of me, and kept telling it to anyone who'd listen for the next two days, until I'd exhausted my list of available listeners, gleefully telling it as a grandpa joke to girls, and to boys as a grandma joke.

Boys winced as they laughed, but girls often swatted at the air in front of their breasts, elbows held tight to their sides. They looked as though they were batting away a bee or trying to brush dust off their sweaters. The gut response is so overwhelmingly strong that listeners felt as if their minds were hijacking their nervous systems, and I was fascinated and delighted to see words exercise that much power over bodies.

The question "What's the grossest thing in the world?" sent us searching for feces, death, and mutilation, but then reversed direction when confronted with the innocent image of a grandma giving us a goodnight smack on the cheek as she tucked us in, an untainted moment of pleasure and security that we were not far removed from. Then, at the last moment, a dangerous swerve spun us into sex, incestuous sex. Was grandma a horny pervert or was she going senile? It didn't matter. We were shifting from a child's secure intimacy to an adult's riskier sexual kind, and we needed to know the rules. No matter why Grandma might do this, don't let her. Our visceral responses confirmed that we got the message.

Me, I twitched even more than my friends. My grandmomma dipped Bruton's Snuff.

But the entire time I was absorbing the warnings and prohibitions of these jokes I was also telling and thinking about a strange joke that disturbed me greatly for years. It didn't reinforce sexual categories but broke them down, challenged them, confused them. It was a joke you whispered to one person at a time, not one you gathered a bunch of friends around to hear. And my compulsive telling of it was more than a little like probing a wound, picking at a scab in my psyche.

A truck driver is taking a leak beside the road when he hears a voice farther out in the woods, crying "Help, Help!" The truck driver zips his fly, pushes through the brush into a clearing, and finds a man standing in the middle of the clearing, buck naked, with his hands tied to his ankles.

"Whoa, what happened to you?" asks the truck driver.

The man twists his head up at the truck driver and says, "I picked up a hitchhiker who pulled a gun on me and forced me to drive out here. Then he made me take off my clothes, tied me up like this, and drove off with my clothes, my money, and my car."

The truck driver kneels down beside him and says, "Those ropes look awful tight."

"Yeah, I can't move at all."

The truck driver thinks for a moment, stands up, walks behind the man, pulls down his zipper, and says, "Buddy, this just ain't your day, is it."

The cruel humor is of course that just when you think things can't get any worse and rescue is at hand, things can in fact get worse.

We enter the scene through the trucker's eyes. So we, with the trucker, walk into the clearing, see the abducted and bound man, and try to understand what we are seeing. When the trucker reaches his conclusion, we are standing with him, grasping the possibility of a free fuck, complicit because we are sharing his point of view.

Is the truck driver, usually stereotyped as hypermasculine, gay—as well as a blithe rapist? Or is he just a man seizing without scruple what chance offers, taking pleasure without anxiety for whatever category it falls in, unconcerned that his pleasure and another's horror depend on each other?

We know this amoral figure of undifferentiated desire, this embodiment of Freud's polymorphous perversity. He's the drowsy-eyed, man-womanish god Bacchus. Who'd be surprised if, in a newly discovered *Homeric Hymn*, Bacchus enters a shady grove and discovers a traveler who has been robbed, stripped, and bound, his wrists lashed to his ankles with leather thongs? Without a thought, the god takes his enjoyment and continues on his aimless way, his sleepy eyes alert for the next opportunity.

I told and retold this joke, shocking my friends as I shocked myself. The joke mocked our fears of being gay, immoral, or cruel. Bliss is bliss, and the moral categories we place on the sensual pleasures are ludicrous attempts to control a force that is, in its essence, lawless and indiscriminate. Jokes and myths can shuck our delusions of civilization right down to the cob.

Yeah, maybe—but I wasn't going to spend the rest of my life being Andrew the Goat Fucker.

Eleven

Morning, Ladies!

With her tightly permed black hair and immaculate lace-collared white blouses, my tenth-grade English teacher at Lanier, Mrs. Halliday, looked like a neurotic and perpetually confused version of Minnie Mouse. She was so timorous she often slipped from the room without explanation to cry in the restroom or sit on the couch in the teachers' lounge, rocking, smoking, waiting for her trembling to stop. She was the wife, someone said, of a big shot on the county Department of Education. That's how she kept her job.

Our list of required reading was enough to reduce anyone to tears. Established by an act of the state legislature, the list contained such zippy reads as *Green Mansions*, the story of Rima the Bird Girl, "the fiery-hearted little hummingbird," who chased her flickering shadow through the Venezuelan rain forest for mile after mile of thick green prose. "Ah, little spider-monkey—little green tree-snake—you are here!" says Abel, our hero, when he sees her, which might account for her shyness. The list included *Captains Courageous* and *The Last Days of Pompeii*—the best-selling crap of two previous generations, which possessed the literary sufficiencies of being sex-free, curse-free, and atheism-free.

One of the questions on the book test was always "What was your favorite scene?" and one boy, in his report on *The Last Days of Pompeii*, answered, "The looks on the faces of the people as they ran out of the collapsing buildings." He had read the *Classics Illustrated* version, that is to say, the comic-book version, of the novel. Though I wasn't as amused by the melodramatically panicked expressions of the soon-to-be-incinerated Romans, I admired how he brazenly let Mrs. Halliday know he hadn't bothered to read the book. She gave him a B.

I was so bored I killed class time by prying nails out of the floor's oak slats with my fingernails, scraping at the old-fashioned iron cut nails till I could get enough purchase to rock them back and forth. Each nail took weeks. Half-listening to Mrs. Halliday's trembling lectures, I had no trouble understanding the patience of Edmond Dantès, the long-suffering Count of Monte Cristo, as he scratched at the stone dungeon walls of the Château D'If. By May, I had six flat black nails in my underwear drawer at home. I'd torn my fingernails and fingertips bloody on them.

One row over and one seat up from me, a blond girl chattered constantly in a high languid Alabama drawl, sometimes cursing cheerfully under her breath when Mrs. Halliday announced a test. In the cooler months Francine often wore a sage heather angora sweater. Maybe it was a shade darker than sage. Maybe a shade and a half. I remember the sweater with disquieting clarity because I spent much time trying not to be seen studying the taut curves swelling it. One day, while Mrs. Halliday was off weeping, Francine unlatched her purse, rummaged down past her keys, gum, pens, change, and cigarettes, and pulled out a folded sheet of lined notebook paper.

"Listen to this. This is good," she said, drawling out the last word till it was well over two syllables long. She leaned into the aisle and whispered:

It's your first time. As you lie back, your muscles tighten. He asks if you're afraid and you shake your head bravely. He has had more experience, but it's the first time his finger has found the right place. He probes deeply and you shiver; your body tenses but he's gentle like he promised he'd be. He looks deeply within your eyes and tells you to trust him—he's done this many times before. His cool smile relaxes you and you open wider to give him more room for an easy entrance. You begin to plead and beg him to hurry, but he takes his time, wanting to cause you as little pain as possible.

As he presses closer, going deeper, you feel the tissue give way; pain surges throughout your body and you feel a slight trickle of blood as he continues. He looks at you, concerned, and asks you if it's too painful. Your eyes fill with tears but you shake your head and nod for him to go on. He begins moving in and out with skill, but you are now too numb to feel him within you. After a few frenzied moments, you feel something bursting within you and he pulls it out of you. You lie panting, glad to have it over. He looks at you smiling, and you smile and tell him how good you feel now.

Francine stopped and looked at us, and I too looked around to see what she was seeing. Our mouths were hanging open, I noticed, and I shut mine abruptly. The girl in front of me, Brenda Somebody, whose elegant, delectable neck I stared at every day at school, was blushing, her pimples redder than ever on a sea of pink, and she smiled with a nervous rictus that showed the entire architecture of her braces. Francine, satisfied with what she saw, took a deep suggestive breath and read the last line:

After all, it was your first time having a tooth pulled.

A few of us ponied up weak laughs of relief—courtesy chuckles, the girls' slightly closer to honest laughs than the boys', I noticed, in the moment before I blurted, "That's just stupid!"

"You don't think it's funny?" Francine said, her lip quivering just a bit. How could a girl tough enough to tell that joke in tenth grade suddenly turn as tender as Rima the Bird Girl?

"No, it's obvious," I said, knowing my objection was a lie even as I said it. I recently found Francine's joke online. Reading it brought back to me how furiously I blushed and how completely taken in I was, though I desperately pretended otherwise.

"It's just not funny. It's—I don't know—just silly or something. Forget it."

Who wouldn't make the obvious sexual interpretation, hearing these words from the lips of a luscious fifteen-year-old girl he'd been fantasizing about in nocturnal, hands-on imaginings? Night after night, I used words like these to tell my body stories that I knew nothing about, and every night, sometimes three times a night, my body believed the lies I told it. Though it was eager to hear my lies and I was eager to tell them, at the same time we were embarrassed for each other, my body and me. I was ashamed at not being able to tell it a truer story and contemptuous of, if gratified by, its gullibility. For my body, the emotions were reversed.

What a slippery and disheartening relief it was when, in her joke, the confident deflowerer became a dentist and the more-than-ready blossom transformed into his patient. I groaned at the joke, scoffing to cover my sexual unease. Francine was flirting with me and I had no idea how to flirt back. So, compulsively, without thinking, I ridiculed the joke as obvious when it hadn't been, silly when I'd taken it all too seriously, and unfunny when I'd been too agitated to laugh. I was unnerved that words whispered by a girl had caused my body to pitch an appalling erection against the fabric of my chinos—when those words, in the double-dealing way of jokes, turned out to be about a trip to the damn dentist. I felt like a fool.

Is the joke actually funny? Even now it's too wound up with the circumstances in which I heard it more than forty years ago for me to say. I can see why a pretty fifteen-year-old girl would want to tell it. And I can forgive myself my adolescent ungraciousness because boys are almost invariably laggards when it comes to emotional maturity. I'm not sure I've closed the gap yet.

Even two years later I still lagged the girls in social poise. When I wanted to attend the junior prom just so I wouldn't be one of the losers who couldn't, I looked around for a girl who I was pretty sure was in the same fix I was. After working up my courage, I dialed her number, pulled the phone cord into my room, and with my head almost touching the hollow-core door, I cleared the hurdle of her father's voice—"Hello, Mr. Reddick, this is Andrew Hudgins. May I speak to Phyllis, please?"—Then I lurched into my memorized spiel:

"Hi, Phyllis, this is Andrew Hudgins. From your history class? I was wondering if you'd like to go to the prom with me."

"Yes," she said.

"Now I understand that you might have already been invited by someone else, but I just wanted to call you to see if possibly . . .

"Yes, I'd like to go."

". . . if possibly you might still be available to go to the dance and all . . . ," my robot voice continued.

"Andrew, I've already said yes!" She was laughing.

"Oh, that's right. You did. Great!" As we talked about the date, arranging a time for me to pick her up and getting directions to her house, I imagined her getting off the phone and telling her mother about the goober who'd been so sure he'd be turned down that he hadn't heard her agree, twice, to go out with him.

That triumph of savoir faire was still two years in the future when Mrs. Halliday again fled the classroom, leaving us alone to tell jokes. Because a new student had joined the class, Francine had slipped back a seat and was now sitting next to me. Once more she pulled out a folded sheet of notebook paper, and this time she read a poem:

> *If the car broke down and we were alone,*
> *would you?*
> *If my parents were asleep and the lights were low,*
> *would you?*
> *And if the night was warm and the kisses hot,*
> *would you?*

At the end of the poem, she looked me in the eye and asked, "Would you, Andrew?"

I couldn't hold her gaze. I blushed, started to stutter, and then just shut up and smiled at her weakly. I was completely unable to come up with something light to say, anything that would deflect attention away from me. Here was a moment just like the fantasies that I told myself every night, and I was completely flummoxed because I could not speak the truth. The truth would have been to yell at the top of my lungs, "Yes, Jesus-screaming-God, yes!" Followed by a firm sotto voce, "No, not really." Or vice versa.

Her simply telling the joke made her seem so sexually aggressive that I was scared, and sure she wasn't the kind of girl I would want to be seen with. Yes. No. Yes.

No. If I said no, how could I explain that she was so experienced I felt like a six-year-old ogling the babysitter whenever I looked at her? That she was much closer to being a woman than I was to being a man? Or that, most of all, I was terrified beyond words of getting a girl pregnant and having to sack groceries at the A&P for the next thirty years to support her and our child? And that

I knew I'd quickly come to hate her, myself, and our children for all I'd given up: a life that I imagined with terrible clarity as I lay awake at night, wrestling with lust.

By the last month of the school year, I often saw her escorted through the halls by a senior in a yellow windbreaker with his initials embroidered on the left breast, collar turned up, and a Beatles comb-down over his forehead, the tips bleached blond. She laughed at everything he said, slapping his shoulder playfully as he leaned possessively over her, tall and mostly unblemished.

While my awkward encounters with girls revealed what I didn't know, my camaraderie with boys often confirmed I wasn't alone in my ignorance. If I could wheedle the Volkswagen out of my father on Saturday night, I'd drive from east Montgomery to Southlawn and pick up Tom Doherty, and we'd go out to Maxwell Air Force Base, where our fathers worked. As air force brats, we could show our ID cards, pay fifty cents at the base theater, and, along with a room full of young enlisted men, watch a movie. Often we didn't even know what we were going to see until the title rolled up on the screen. Before the show started, everyone stood, those in uniform holding a salute, the rest of us with our right hands over our hearts, while the national anthem played and a scratchy image of an American flag rippled over scenes of marines splashing onto a beach in the South Pacific, a squad of Sherman tanks rolling through a snowstorm and down a muddy road into Germany, a fleet of destroyers shepherding a convoy of transport ships through the North Atlantic corridor, and, suddenly in color, the Blue Angels, four bright blue Phantom F-4s, shooting up the screen in a terrifyingly close formation and veering apart, sketching a white, vapor-trail blossom in a flawless blue sky.

As the last martial strands faded and the lights went down, someone always yelled "Play ball" and a few people laughed at the exhausted joke, repeated now as ritual. About twice a year, a disgruntled old officer or an earnest young one wrote to the base newspaper and chastised the misguided boors who thought it funny to bellow "Play ball," as if that were the natural ending of our country's national anthem. They showed grave disrespect to the song, the flag, and the many brave men and women who had died so today's moviegoers would have the right to act like fools. Reading the letters, I was always convinced by the authors' appeals that we respect the sacrifices of our troops, until I remembered that the *men* who yelled—I never heard a female voice cry "Play ball!"—were themselves pilots and frontline mechanics prepared to follow their predecessors to the grave, if necessary, to defend the country. Some died without going near the front lines. In Vietnam, one of my father's mechanics died when the overheated brakes on an F-4C Phantom jet boiled the brake fluid and exploded in the service bay. The way I saw it, the young men were entitled to heedlessly yell "Play ball," the retired colonels were entitled to be stuffily offended, and I was entitled only to observe and keep my mouth shut.

After the movie, Tom and I drove around Montgomery, killing time before my eleven o'clock curfew. We often stopped at Bellas Hess, a discount store on the Southern Bypass between his house and mine, and wandered around the aisles, checking out paperback books and records. A few times as the elderly cashier, with excruciating exactitude, rang up my copy of *Is Paris Burning?* or the sound track to *The Graduate*, my right hand started quivering at my side. As the cashier tried not to look, my whole arm began to twitch and tremble, until, with a will of its own, it jerked at full extension, flailing spasmodically, as I politely conducted the transaction, pretending not to notice. I did a pretty good job, I think, of ignoring the hand's shenanigans because I'd stood in front of my dresser mirror and practiced twitching. Wanting the arm to seem alien to my body, I imagined it as a pelican having a seizure in midair, and I practiced looking as if I had no idea what was happening to my pelican.

I'd invented this bit of silliness after seeing—at the base the-ater—the antiwar film *Dr. Strangelove*, in which Peter Sellers as the crazed German nuclear scientist fights to keep his erratic mechani-cal right arm from launching a Heil Hitler salute. Almost every boy I knew did an impression of Dr. Strangelove and his arm. And we performed it exuberantly. We knew what it meant to have an uncon-trollable member that snapped into fascist salutes at discomfiting moments.

Behind the invention of my epileptic pelican was also a routine that the comedian David Steinberg performed on the *Smothers Broth ers Comedy Hour*. Talking about his childhood, Steinberg abruptly snatched something invisible—a huge insect? a demon?—from his right shoulder, slammed it to the ground, and stomped it, while shrieking *Get!* [snatch!], *Off!* [slam!], *Me!* [stomp!]. Then, as if noth-ing had happened, he returned calmly to his original topic. I loved the bit because it wonderfully exaggerated the sudden wrenching moments of paranoia that I, like most boys I knew, experienced, and it showed them being defeated, or at least dealt with. One of Steinberg's catchphrases was "disguised as a normal person." I took that as my motto, and I always said it with a self-mocking adenoidal drawl, just like Steinberg.

While I stood at the register, my hand jerking, Doherty was embarrassed but unable to keep from laughing. He hurried toward the front of the store and abandoned me, elbow jiggling up past my head. By the time I'd bought my book and caught up with him we were giddy with adolescent hilarity.

It was night, we were boys, which means hungry, so we stopped to stare transfixed into a glass display case of oddly large donuts. What were donuts doing here? I'd never seen them in a discount store before.

On one of the aluminum trays, amid flakes of loose frosting, a misshapen donut lay alone. It was easy to see why this one was still there at the end of the day. Stretched till the hole in the center was a thin slit, the donut was stale, the glaze thick and crusty. It looked like a scabrous vagina, the organ that Kingsley Amis would notoriously describe as "like the inside of a giraffe's ear or a tropical fruit not much prized by the locals." I giggled and Tom chuckled, as much at my amusement as at the syphilitic donut. *But does it really look like a vagina and how would you know if it did?* asked a voice inside my head, and I laughed out loud at myself being myself.

The week before, Tom had come to our first-period classroom with a dazed look on his face, as if he had seen something that had altered his sense of reality. I have never seen him so bemused before or since. Before class started, he told me that his grandmother, who was slipping into dementia, had asked him over breakfast, "What does this remind you of?"

He looked up from his cereal and saw the old woman touching the fingertip of her middle finger to the nail of her index finger. Holding her hand before her face, she stared at him through the vertical smile created by her fingers, and cackled like a crone when her grandson's eyes grew wide with reluctant understanding. Tom and I laughed with bewildered incredulity then, and now we were laughing again, with near-hysteria, at another simile of the vertical smile—the simulacrum of things unseen, the substance of things hoped for, as the Bible says in an antithetical context.

The more I laughed, the more Tom laughed, which of course made me, contagiously pixilated, laugh more. Soon we sprawled across the glass counter, holding our sides, laughing at our own laughter, laughing at our embarrassment at our laughter. Every time we almost composed ourselves, sucking chuckles back into our throats, they exploded back out as wet snorts so ludicrous that within seconds we were laughing again.

The absurd and pathetic donut was only the trigger. Seeing it as sexual revealed how sex, even in my ignorance of it, controlled my brain. We laughed in sexual fear, along with the distressing recognition that lust could reduce women to one part of their bodies, which I saw, in defiance of all good sense, in malformed pastry.

While we laughed, the middle-aged clerks, younger then than I am now, pretended to ignore us, glancing at us sideways as they went about ringing up sales. It was the late sixties. Had dopeheads wandered into their store? Tom might have been high. I was sober as a bone. Only when a woman picked up the house phone behind her register and began whispering into it, probably calling security, did Tom and I, bent over with laughter, stagger out of the store and back to my father's Volkswagen.

If girls' private parts remained, for me anyway, private, boys' were much discussed. The language itself was already in love with our uneasiness with our genitals. From the cute to the grotesque, there are dozens and dozens of names for the penis. I favor the old-fashioned *tallywhacker* for its mildly risqué, mildly embarrassing self-consciousness. *Wang* stands up to humorous repetition, as do *dong, pecker, willy, winky,* and *John Thomas,* that formal gentleman. *Baby-maker, one-eyed trouser snake, meat bayonet, tube steak, heat-seeking love missile,* and *skin flute* are funny once, maybe. There are only a few common slang names for the vagina. *Pussy,* the most common, is so pervasive it has lost almost all connection to the over-precious metaphor it grew out of. And most of the others are equally coy: *goodies, box, beaver, muff.* But *cunt* is now probably the most vulgar, contemptuous word in English, and the tense distinction between the demure profanities and the ugly one is captured perfectly in a joke I heard in tenth-grade gym class, repeatedly, from Ricky Walker, who loved it:

Q: What's the difference between a pussy and a cunt?
A: A pussy is a wonderful thing that provides unbelievable

pleasure when you cuddle up to it at night. A cunt is the woman who owns it.

The joke perfectly embodies the male adolescent rage about his own indiscriminate lust and the human consequences of it. *Cunt* is so taboo as to be almost literally unspeakable in anything like civilized company. And the thing itself is powerful almost beyond naming. In the jokes about it, which are a mishmash of desire and terror, it is often enormous.

I cannot remember how many times I heard this repulsive joke, one I have never repeated.

Did you hear about this guy that's screwing a girl and he falls all the way inside her and gets lost in the dark? He flicks on his lighter, and looking around, he sees another guy. That shocks him so bad he drops his lighter. In the darkness, he yells to the other guy, "Hey, help me find my lighter and maybe we can find our way out of here."

"Forget about your lighter," says the other guy. "Help me find my keys and we'll drive out."

The point of the joke is of course the male fear of the promiscuous woman with a vagina so accommodating as to become hugely, indiscriminately commodious. The encompassing vagina has quenched the first man's flame and stalled the second man's engine. But it's hard not to notice that the two men have more of a relationship with each other than with the woman whom they were both "making love" to, an inadvertent ménage à trois reduced to two because, although all-encompassing, the woman is hardly present. The seemingly throwaway detail of the first man's snapping on a lighter inside the most delicate part of a woman's body is viscerally unbearable; it highlights how dehumanized she is by the ancient conflict of men's desire for the sexually accommodating woman whom he then despises as a slut. Years before I knew it had a name,

I struggled with the Madonna-whore complex, blanching when boys said, "If you screw her, you'd better strap a board to your feet or you'll fall all the way in." Jokes like these, which I hated and yet absorbed, made it hard to develop a mature regard for women. But underneath everything, I heard again the male fear of becoming lost to desire, of losing one's head over a piece of tail.

Growing up in Alabama in the sixties was like growing up in a Puritan near-theocracy. For us southern Baptists, boys and girls were kept apart in church; even going to a school social was a charged religious issue during a time when our faith forbade dancing. As a result, jokes were one of the few ways to talk and learn about girls and sex. Boys were supposed to remain pure themselves and marry virgins. Even if we weren't pure ourselves, we were supposed to marry women whose purity would serve as a light and a reproach until we found the proper path. Consequently, the jokes we told emphasized the dismal consequences of defiling ourselves with tainted women. Of course, they reflected our anger that the best pleasure our bodies had to offer was forbidden us.

"What is the definition of *rape*?" Carl Blegen asked me in tenth grade as World History was dismissing for the day. "Assault with a friendly weapon," he said, grinning deviously. I laughed uproariously. The answer perfectly caught the mixed emotions of fifteen-year-old boys. We knew rape was a terrible violation of a woman, an assault that often did turn deadly. But we knew our weapons—our little soldiers, our purple-headed love monsters—as sources of the deepest bliss we had known. Who wouldn't want to share?

The jokes warned us away from loose women, but how do you know if a girl has kept herself pure? I'd been married to my first wife for four years when, thinking to amuse her, I told her the first time I'd kissed a girl I cracked my front teeth so crisply against Melanie Ames's incisors I had to squelch a yelp. I was mortified when Kathleen stopped rubbing lotion in her hands, blinked at me in surprise, and blurted, "You dated Melanie the Whore?"

Immediately I was thrown down a rabbit hole of conflicting responses. My somewhat fond memory of innocent fumbled kisses was turned upside down. I felt like a dolt who had missed the main chance. But what, in the context of the time, had it meant to be Melanie the Whore? Had she made out with a lot of guys or screwed two? Or fifty? *What right did she have to play the innocent with me?* I thought, then, abashed, I acknowledged to myself that I'd have never invited her out if she hadn't. A sense of estrangement from all women was a side effect of worrying about who was a whore and who wasn't. As a happily married man, I had hoped I was safely beyond such small-mindedness, but this question in passing showed me what I suspected: my hopes were merely yearnings.

Under the Madonna-whore complexes that plagued me and most boys, there was a deep Christian fear of ourselves as animals, creatures of flesh more than spirit. In women the division was even more startling, with childbirth and menstruation. And so our jokes emphasized the animalism of sex and the supposed ugliness of the vagina, as we tried to keep ourselves under control. When boys and men told me, as many did, many times, "Never trust anything that bleeds for seven days and doesn't die," they were in a long tradition that includes Edmund Spenser, whose Duessa is lovely to look at but a witch underneath. You don't even have to see her "secret filth" to apprehend its misshaped monstrosity:

> *A filthy foule old woman I did vew,*
> *That ever to have toucht her, I did deadly rew.*

> *Her neather partes misshapen, monstruous,*
> *Were hidd in water, that I could not see.*

But they did seeme more foule and hideous,
Then womans shape man would beleeve to bee.

Later, when the witch is stripped naked, her vagina is too foul to describe—her "secret filth good manners biddeth not be told"—though all of her other foulnesses are fair game, right down to the unintentionally charming tail she sports:

Her craftie head was altogether bald,
And as in hate of honorable eld,
Was ouergrowne with scurfe and filthy scald;
Her teeth out of her rotten gummes were feld,
And her sowre breath abhominably smeld;
Her dried dugs, like bladders lacking wind,
Hong downe, and filthy matter from them weld;
Her wrizled skin as rough, as maple rind,
So scabby was, that would haue loathd all womankind.

Her neather parts, the shame of all her kind,
My chaster Muse for shame doth blush to write;
But at her rompe she growing had behind
A foxes taile, with dong all fowly dight.

Though it might take some getting used to at first, I would love to love a woman with a fox's tail.

The animal aspect of the vagina was not limited to its looks. The first time I heard a boy say, "Morning, ladies!—as the blind man said when he passed the fish market," I had no idea what he could possibly mean. I inquired. As I'd thought, the joker, aspiring to a coarse worldliness he didn't have, was just repeating something he'd heard. His confused answer was that the blind man was confusing prostitutes with ladies, and prostitutes, from screwing a lot of different men, smelled like fish.

Fifteen years later, I heard a woman read her poems at an after-dinner get-together at a writers' colony. As was the custom, she supplied the usual bottles of cheap wine and, to everyone's surprise, a wheel of good Brie, which her audience scarfed down as she read. Her last poem, the finale of the reading, extolled at length the pleasures of performing cunnilingus. Attempting to describe the flavor of the beloved, the poem, considering and rejecting various comparisons, rose ecstatically to the end line, which the poet declaimed with loving fervor: "Not Camembert, but Brie!"

I looked around the room at the other listeners. Like mine, their mouths were poised in forced appraisal, one we had never expected to be making, and I could see people coming to the same assessment I had, "No, that's not quite right." Then, carefully making eye contact with one another, we smirked and shook our heads slightly, trying to make one another laugh. As I left the reading, I asked a woman what she thought, and, glancing to be sure she was out of earshot of the author, she exploded with rage, "Fish and cheese! Fish and cheese! That's what we're always fucking compared to and I'm fucking sick of it!"

All the joking about cavernous, ugly, odiferous vaginas was done behind the backs of adults, and almost never where girls could hear it. Public jokes about sex, especially at an event as squeaky-clean as a student-body election, broke open a window into the parallel world we all knew existed, and, once acknowledged, even the most glancingly risqué joke brought down the house.

At our high school all students were required to attend the speeches of the candidates for student council, our introduction to the stupefying cant of politics in action, the speeches as pointless as the offices the candidates were seeking. But amid the promises to work with the administration to make Lanier an even more wonderful institution, one of the students ended his speech by telling the joke about the Indian who sits on a street corner all day saying, "Chance." That's all he says, "Chance, chance, chance" to each passerby.

Finally a lady, who is more au courant on racist clichés than the Indian seems to be, stops and asks, don't you mean "How?"

"Know how. Want chance."

After a moment's indecision, the student body burst into wave after wave of laughter. I've seen the young Jay Leno perform, and he never got a laugh like that. The audience convulsed. We couldn't stop laughing at his calculated audacity. The candidate, a huge grin on his face, preened as laughter and then applause mixed with laughter washed over him. Once the hilarity died out, he unctuously applied the joke to his situation: because of his vast experience in student governance he, like the roadside Indian, knew how. All he needed was a chance. Presumably, he was not running for school chaplain, though my memory is hazy on many particulars.

The joke was perfectly considered: just impudent enough to make him seem like a rebel while emphasizing that he had been a good soldier all along. The joke was so vague he could deny any impropriety, which he knew and we clearly understood. It brought down the house, and it is absolutely the only thing about the election I remember or cared about—so slick, so perfectly placed at the limit of allowable audacity, so appropriate to the occasion that I didn't even scorn as much as I should have the cynicism behind it.

In my senior year I went out a couple of times with a girl whose open-mouthed, tooth-baring laugh I reveled in; I didn't know any other girls who laughed that way. As she laughed, though, her eyes darted around, looking for approval, a tentativeness that caught my eye and surprised me because she was friends with many of the rich kids.

Occasionally, Kelsey dropped by my homeroom and listened to us boys tell jokes, laughing her intriguing mannish laugh, and of course I was flattered that she came by to see me, often wearing a pert gray sailor dress with a red ribbon on the front and blue anchors embroidered on each side of her collar. Once, when she walked in the room before the first bell rang, a boy named Gary had just finished telling his new joke for the second time that morning and we were all chortling. Four or five of us had gathered in the front of the room, lolling in the desks of kids who didn't get to school as early as we did. The first time Gary had told the joke to me, and the second time I'd joined him in telling it to a new victim.

"What's so funny?" she asked, leaning her hips against the desk I was sitting in.

"It's just Gary's new joke," I said.

"Tell it to me. I want to hear." She slid into the desk in front of me, and turned around, expectantly.

"I don't think that's a good idea." I didn't want Gary to tell her, but I didn't think I had the right to jump in and ruin his joke. My presumed gallantry irritated her.

"Come on, I want to hear it," she said to Gary.

"You don't have to tell her," Gary told me. "It's my joke. I'll tell it."

I shrugged.

He leaned forward, locked his eyes on hers, and said, "These two queers are on an iceberg, see, all dressed for the cold—boots, hats, fur coats—when suddenly the iceberg breaks in half, and the two halves start drifting apart.

"One queer is on each half of the iceberg, standing there, looking at the other one float farther and farther away."

Gary paused for a moment and looked at Kelsey until she nodded to show she was following the story. I stared past her toward the green chalkboard at the front of the room. I had suffered many humiliations at that board, at the hands of mathematics and its earthly emissary, Mz. Gorrie, my Analysis teacher.

"The two queers can't swim across the gap because the water's too cold. It'll kill them," Gary said. "They run around looking for a kayak or raft or some way to get across the water, but they can't find anything. Finally as they start to sail out of sight on their melting icebergs, one queer runs to the edge, puts his hands to his mouth, and shouts as loud as he can, 'Radio!'"

Cupped hands held to the sides of his mouth, Gary acted out the scene, drawing out the word, *Rayyyy-deee-oh!* and we boys all exploded with raucous hilarity, some of us with our heads down on the desk, laughing, others slapping our thighs, all of us glancing at Kelsey to see what she was doing. She laughed with us, open-mouthed and wholehearted, and suddenly I was furious with her.

When Gary had told me the joke earlier in the morning, I'd disappointed him and my friends by refusing to laugh.

"I don't get it," I'd said, as they hooted.

"Sure you do," Gary said, gasping for breath. "The one queer says, 'Radio!'"

The other three boys cracked up all over again, and again I had looked at them, face scrunched with cogitation, trying to figure it out.

Now, though, I was on the other side of the joke. "Isn't that a great joke, Kelsey?" I said meanly.

"Yes," she said. Her eyes were moist at the corners with tears of laughter.

"Do you get it? Do you get the joke?"

"Yeah."

"You sure you get it?"

"Yeah, it's a good one."

"That's funny," I said, "because it doesn't make sense. It's not a joke."

As the laughter froze on her lips, the other boys erupted into real laughter. Pale, Kelsey pushed herself abruptly up out of the desk, cracking her hip hard on the edge of it as she rose, and stalked out of the room. As my friend Danny Anderson says in a poem, "It's always funny until somebody gets hurt / and then it's really funny."

The joke was a con, and as con artists supposedly say, "You can't cheat an honest man." The two-queers-on-an-iceberg opening isolates a traditionally despised minority on an arctic version of the desert island we know from many other jokes. The two men are separated by chance, and then the story arrives at a simulated punch line, one that almost makes sense. If they had radios, they could contact each other. The joke has not, however, mentioned radios before, and *radio* doesn't evoke any antigay prejudice or practice. It simply doesn't connect. The joke relies on social coercion as much as the famously infectious nature of laughter. Who wants to be the excluded, ferret-eyed mumbler who wasn't clued in enough to comprehend whatever-the-hell cleverness it is that those two gay men communicate? Or whatever-the-hell nasty antigay jibe the joke embodies?

Later that month, Kelsey abandoned me at the senior dance and spent the night dancing with the black kid whom her parents had forbidden her to date. It was a comeuppance I earned fair and square.

When I had called Kelsey and asked her to the graduation dance, she agreed, and then cheerfully informed me that she'd really wanted to go with Luther Simmons, a black student, but her parents, at the height of the Wallace era in Alabama, had forbidden it. Though she made it clear I was her second choice, I felt I had to go with her: I'd asked and she'd agreed. I did not possess the cool presence of mind to inquire, "Why are you telling me this?"

We double-dated with some friends of hers, and at her door I presented her with the requisite corsage I'd ordered two weeks before—a huge white carnation graced with a blue pipe cleaner twisted into the letter L. I'd picked it up at the florist's on Friday afternoon and kept it in the refrigerator overnight. The carnation was still cool when I lifted it out of its clear plastic box and pinned it to the strap of Kelsey's blue gown. She giggled when the back of my fingers rubbed clumsily against her pale hot shoulder.

At the old civic center downtown, Kelsey boogied with an unstable, explosive disregard. Released by the heavy beat of Billy Joe Royal's band, she shimmied her full hips and shook her pale shoulders with the self-aware sexual force of a fully grown woman, while I, practically tone deaf, shuffled around the beat. The narcissistic sexual power of her dancing left me behind, alone on the dance floor, and I was relieved that she did not expect me to follow.

After a few dances, Kelsey yelled above the music that she had to go to the ladies' room, and for fifteen or twenty minutes I stood by the stage, watching Billy Joe Royal sweat. He was famous for "Down in the Boondocks," which had reached number nine on the pop charts. The dance committee was proud to have signed a name act—one even more famous than the Classics IV, who, a month before, had played their hit "Spooky" four times at the junior-senior prom.

What was taking Kelsey so long? Had she lost me in the crowd? I pushed through dancers doing the Pony, the Frug, the Boogaloo, and when I found people I knew, I asked if they'd seen her. Betsy, a girl in my French class, said Kelsey was on the other side of the room, dancing with some black guy.

I worked my way again through the crowd, moving cautiously this time, until I saw Kelsey and Luther, whom I had never met, dancing. The other dancers had pulled back from them, and Kelsey had seized the space they'd given her, throwing her hips loosely and aggressively with the music.

Numb, affronted, I circled the outside of the crowd and sat down on one of the civic center's old swivel-bottom seats. Because the seats were higher than the dance floor, I could watch Kelsey and Luther while I tried to think of what to do. I'd never even *heard* of a girl who'd gone off with another boy at a school dance. There were several iron-clad rules, rules designed to keep fighting to a minimum, and one was that you danced with the one what brung you, as the saying goes.

I just wanted to leave the dance and go home, but because we'd double-dated I didn't have a car. I had to wait at least three hours till the dance ended, then cadge a ride with friends. Sitting there, staring at the dancers, I knew I looked pathetic and dejected. The unhappiness that showed on my face was partly real, partly adolescent histrionics that I hadn't learned to suppress—and partly I was trying to make Kelsey feel guilty. But, to my surprise, I was strangely detached, and pleased at how clearly I could understand what was happening. I could see that Kelsey didn't care about Luther any more than she cared about me. From the haughty sexual strut of her dancing and the gratified and determined look on her face, I could see she savored being the center of attention, reveled at being looked at because she was dancing with a black guy, thumbing her nose at her parents. Me? She might have been paying me back for the joke about the queers on the ice floe, but I doubted it. I had been momentarily useful and that was all. She shimmied her shoulders so hard that the corsage flew off and skittered under the feet of other dancers, which made her laugh.

Was it more humiliating for me that she had dumped me for a black guy? I wondered. Nope. Same humiliation. I felt pretty good about my liberal humanism. But didn't it make things worse in the eyes of all the other people in this dingy civic center in the heart of the Deep South? Was I expected to stomp over to the dancing couple and punch him out? I might could have. He was about my height and skinny, with thick black-rimmed glasses. He was, I believe, a trombone player in the marching band. I actually tried to work up a little racial animosity. But "My God, she's abandoned me for a black man" sounded hopelessly self-aggrandizing. What really wounded me was another great southern passion: manners. Using me as a beard and then ditching me without a word just seemed like plain bad manners.

During the dance, friends stopped by to talk to me and to offer me rides home. My friend Betsy, one of those preternaturally mature high school students who at seventeen is already a fully adult woman, stalked over to Kelsey during the band's second break, pulled her aside, and said, "Don't you know how unhappy you're making Andrew? He's your date."

"I'm not doing anything to him!" Kelsey snarled. "He can be miserable if he wants to be."

When Betsy reported the conversation to me, I laughed out loud. Even then, seventeen and wretched, I heard in Kelsey's retort the delicious theatrical wickedness of an actress who loves playing the soap opera vixen. It clarified the situation. I never saw Kelsey again. Decades ago, someone once told me she had become a nurse, but I have no idea if that's true.

I date the beginnings of my emotional maturity to that evening. Now, thinking back on it, I'm puzzled at how I sat for three hours on a rickety seat in the old civic center and seriously pondered whether my failing to punch a black guy I had never seen before and haven't seen since, over a woman I no longer even liked, would mark me forever as a coward in the eyes of people with whom I thought I'd live the rest of my life. I am very happy that time and distance have left me puzzled by what I thought. Then, I believed I understood it perfectly.

If I could go back in time to speak to the person I was then and the person Kelsey was, the only thing I'd want to say to them is: "Radio!"

Twelve

We Might as Well Leave Now, Fanny

Love is the fart of every heart:
It pains a man when 'tis kept close,
And others doth offend, when 'tis let loose.

Sir John Suckling (1609–42)

When I think of the women I have loved or almost loved, I remember the luxurious, almost lascivious, delectations of shared laughter. When a woman and I moved apart, I missed the laughter nearly as much as I missed the love, the affection, the companionship, and the sex. Laughter's plush harmonies were integral to all of the other pleasures.

When we were first dating, my ex-wife once said plaintively, "Everything's a joke to you, isn't it? Can't you be serious about anything?" We were both in college, working minimum-wage jobs, living with our parents, and learning who we were together while learning who we were individually. One evening in 1970, after finishing my shift at the dry-goods wholesaler, I picked her up at the office where she typed for a buck-sixty an hour. We decided to grab a quick supper in a small restaurant in a strip mall. We each ordered a small burger, small Coke, small fries, and I was fretting about the cost. Tuition, books, gas, the room and board my mother wanted to charge me and that I'd been ignoring—how much was this rare indulgence of dinner with my girlfriend going to cost?

We talked about what we each might do for a living. I was working on a high school teaching certificate. Kathleen wasn't sure. Maybe teach, maybe law, maybe who-knows-what? Did we want to encumber our lives with loud and dirty babies? Then the conversation went global. God, we were stunned by the wrenching pictures we'd been seeing every night on the news from a 120-mph typhoon that had blasted into the Ganges River delta and killed between 150,000 and 500,000 people. Perhaps 100,000 more were missing. To this date, no one knows the exact number, but even then everyone knew the typhoon was one of the worst natural catastrophes in history.

Even the lowest number would have been the equivalent of our entire city of Montgomery and most of the surrounding county being eradicated. The higher number would have represented the deaths of every citizen of Montgomery and Birmingham. The equivalent of our friends, our families, our high schools and college, churches, and families obliterated—and we were doing nothing. Hadn't we studied, with dread and sorrow, the famous gut-twisting photo of a man, a holocaustal specter, holding the emaciated body of his wife, daughter, or a dying woman he had picked up? She was emaciated too. A ratty shawl looped across her torso half-revealed the full swell of one breast. The other, the one against the man's chest, was fully exposed, but fuzzed out, the nipple airbrushed away so the picture, in all its poignant horror, could be published in family newspapers. Her face, tilted back over the man's arm, was reduced to a stark abstraction of disease and starvation, the high, sharp cheekbones only two ghastly steps past the gaunt beauty of a fashion model. The picture, we said, was the Pietà with the Virgin herself as Christ.

What could we do? Nothing. According to the papers, cholera was now spreading through the camps. With as straight a face as I could muster, I asked Kathleen, "Let's get serious, though. How's Alabama going to do against Oklahoma in the Bluebonnet Bowl?" Because she loved me, she laughed.

I was reeling at my own inability to do anything but lament the disaster—as earlier in the year, I had reeled from the U.S.'s expansion of the Vietnam War into Cambodia, though in July, my number in the draft lottery had come in as a relatively safe 256 out of 365. In the Black September crisis, King Hussein of Jordan attacked the Palestinian Liberation Organization and other Palestinian groups in his country with a death toll that was initially estimated to be as high as 25,000. (Current estimates vary between 3,500 and 5,000.) The month before, we Alabamians had reelected George Wallace as our governor and the trial of William Calley for the Mai Lai massacre had begun. I was unable to do anything but lament. Or unwilling. If I were a serious person, I could quit school, work full-time, and give my wages to the Red Cross, couldn't I?

In a way, my joke question was a real question. We both knew that Kathleen, her mother, and I would watch every minute of the football game, screaming so loud that Wally the dog would cower in a back bedroom for an hour after the game ended. Even then we'd have to entice him out with a Milk-Bone. If the Crimson Tide lost, we'd sink into the couch, exhausted by a grief more intense and personal than we ever could have felt for the Bangladeshis. *How many of them died*, I wondered, *during the last movie we saw, during the game, or during the week between the movie and the game?*

"How do you stop a tsunami?" I asked Kathleen. Before she could tell I was shifting from near despair to humor, I answered. "You throw half a million Bangladeshis in front of it," I said, laughing.

"Oh, Andrew," she said as she laughed, "That's terrible." Terrible.

That was the point. The answer to the joke seemed to be God's answer.

So when she then said, "Can't you be serious about anything?" I was jarred. Didn't she know I joked about terrible things because I wasn't willing to forgo my date with her to save the money and send it to the Red Cross? I wasn't going to forgo watching Alabama play Oklahoma to a 24–24 tie or my chance at graduating from college and living a more or less comfortable life. Since I couldn't, or wouldn't, do anything to help the dying thousands in Bangladesh, wasn't any kind of exaggerated concern merely histrionic hypocrisy? When I made the joke, however feeble, I knew it was on me and my failings, and on life itself, not on those poor refugees dying of dehydration and malaria. Laughter was the one way I could approach the deep, appalled fears that haunted me—a hopeless sense of helplessness, a lifelong dread of death, and—couldn't she see it?—an apprehensive and growing commitment to love.

I had a young and driven man's urgent need to conceal that I was young, driven, and frightened. Most of the time, I hid my futile empathy behind a selectively permeable membrane. Without that shield, the world's miseries would hammer me down to an oozing mound of useless guilt. Don't we all, except the saintly, learn the limits of love's jurisdiction? And don't we also feel vicious and even sinister because of our necessary callousness?

The refrain of the marriage was "Oh, Andrew . . ."

"Oh, Andrew . . ." meant she did not understand why I thought something was funny, and if I thought about it, I should have known she wouldn't laugh. But as jokers do, I persisted, knowing that if I could overcome her resistance the joke would be even funnier, provoking the moment when she would, laughing, say, "That's not funny."

Six years later, when we were moving toward divorce, Kathleen said, "What's wrong with you? You never laugh anymore." In the months before, as she'd moved out of the house and, relenting to my entreaties, returned, then moved out and then relented again, I brooded over the past we had shared. One of us alone could decide it meant nothing—or not enough—and that understanding got to be true for both of us. And the person who was moving toward and retreating from this decision for the both of us expected me to laugh?

Seven years after our divorce, I was sitting on a porch at the Bread Loaf Writers' Conference late in the evening, talking and joking with people, one of them my former teacher, the poet Don Justice. What were we talking about? Divorces? Exes? Women in general? I don't remember, but after several drinks, my tongue grew as loose as my brain, and I began to tell stories about my ex-wife.

I told them that soon after we were married, Kathleen took a job as a secretary in the Geology Department at the University of Alabama, where I was a graduate student. In the job interview, she had told the department chairman, her prospective boss, that while she was happy to attend to her secretarial responsibilities, she was not going to make coffee for the office, one of the hot-button issues at the time. Secretaries were professionals, not servants, not maids, and not substitute wives. They shouldn't be expected to clean the coffeemaker and keep it brewing unless they wanted a cup of coffee themselves, dammit. The boss was happy enough to agree since he had an office manager who already took care of the coffee, and because Kathleen could out-type the capacity of an IBM Selectric, tripping the keys so fast that the machine occasionally locked up and pitched a row of hyphens across the page.

But once the other woman quit, and Kathleen was promoted to office manager, the previous office manager's job of tending to the yellow-stained, dilapidated Mr. Coffee fell to her, a lack of respect that infuriated her. She grudgingly brewed coffee first thing every morning, while complaining about it sourly and often at home. After several months, I noticed she hadn't mentioned coffee in a while. I asked her why not. Had she trained the boss to do it for himself?

She laughed gleefully. No, she said, she still made the coffee. But she'd stopped tossing out the old damp grounds from the day before. She just threw new coffee on top of them each morning, splashed in water, and flipped the switch. By Friday, the paper filter was full, so she tossed it out and started over on Monday. Or, it being summer in Alabama, when the coffee grounds turned green. What made her laugh was this: since she'd quit washing the machine and changing the grounds daily, the boss, practicing positive-reinforcement management techniques, bragged to visitors about what a good job his office manager did making coffee.

The men I was telling the story to laughed. But one guy was disturbed. "She didn't dump the grounds unless they had *mold* on them?"

"That's what she told me."

After the anecdote of the coffee machine, I told them what she did when the geology professors in her office condescended to the secretary who couldn't be very bright because she was after all a pretty little carefully-made-up southern girl and they were Yankees with Ivy League degrees. She took their requests for travel reimbursement, slipped them into envelopes, scrawled "Physical Education" across the top, and dropped them into the university's internal mail. Sometimes the paperwork slowly found its way to where it was supposed to go; sometimes it didn't.

Did my listeners laugh at that story? They did. I'm pretty sure they did; they wanted to hear more stories.

So I told them that when she was in law school, students wrote only their student numbers on exams, not their names. Though her professors insisted class participation was important and would factor heavily in final grades, she quickly surmised that they wouldn't actually bother to do the extra work of lining up numbers and names, and reconciling class performance with grades earned on the final exam.

Not wanting to participate in the un-Socratic hazing they called the Socratic method, she refused to talk. When professors called on her, she smiled and shrugged, and they usually went on to another victim. Occasionally, though, she couldn't shrug her way out of answering. In Contract Law, the professor asked another student to lay out for the class a complex case involving a defaulted loan, and then snapped, "Mrs. Hudgins, what do you learn from this fact pattern?"

With a note of finality that made it clear she wasn't open to follow-up questions, she answered, "Neither a borrower nor a lender be." The professor was so taken aback that, after only a moment or two of silent stalemate, he moved on to the next student. He never again singled her out in class. Did he think she was stupid? She didn't care. It wasn't going to affect her grade.

If I'd had a third or fourth drink, I'd probably have gone on to tell my Bread Loaf listeners about the time the professor of constitutional law asked her to stand up and summarize a case involving a traffic stop. Bored, annoyed, and determined not to be called on again, she stood up in her law class in Syracuse, New York, and said in a nasal hillbilly accent, "Welllll, when the PO-leece stopped this WO-min in a speeding VEE-hikle, they . . ."

Slowly I noticed that although the stories I thought were riotously funny, the stone-cold determination of a woman not to be taken advantage of had made my listeners uneasy. Their laughs were fewer and strained. Understanding broke like moonlight through thick clouds when Don Justice, puzzled at the affection and skewed admiration in my voice, asked, "Andrew, why'd your ex-wife leave you?"

I was mortified at the perverse nostalgia I'd put on display. I thought we were just swapping funny stories, and Don had turned my humorous vignettes into serious conversation.

"Got a better offer, I guess," I snapped, and laughed by myself in the ensuing silence. Now I was even more mortified. My fond anecdotes, which I thought simply good stories, still held too much of the love I assumed had leached from them. And I hadn't even gotten to Kathleen's spot-on, hilarious impression of her mother's speech impediment. After a few moments, everyone stood up, seized by a sudden need to freshen recently refreshed drinks. The next day, I sought out Don and apologized, and he, still flustered, insisted on apologizing to me.

As I lamented the loss of Kathleen's and my life together, I lamented too the private jokes we had created, and I thought over and over of Ezra Pound, who, when informed that T. S. Eliot had died, said with genuine grief and some self-mockery, "And who is left to understand my jokes?" Who will understand not just the jokes but the riffs we played off the jokes, the jokes that spun us into intimacy as we tested whether we understood things in the same way? As Kathleen and I broke up, humor fled these private jokes because we no longer risked being silly, childish, or even deliberately stupid with someone we were in the process of un-loving.

Two months after we married, we drove to a stranger's house to pick up our first pets, a couple of kittens. On the way there, Kathleen, in the passenger seat, slipped her sandals off, stuck her bare feet in my face as I was driving, wiggled her phalanges, and crowed, "Toes!" Her exuberant silliness sent us into nearly uncontrollable hilarity, and to cement the moment in place, I named one of the cats, the big dumb tabby, Toes. When friends asked why the cat had such a peculiar name, they never laughed when we told the story. It wasn't funny to them or touching, just strange. Neither would they have laughed if I had told them about the exaggeratedly childish, almost retarded way she called me her Q. T. Pie.

After more than a quarter of a century, my heart tightens still just a bit when I remember Kathleen waking me in the morning, singing "Wake up, snake. Peas in the pot and the hoe cake's baking." Her mother woke her the same way when she was a child. Neither of us knew it was a corrupted (or maybe an alternative) version of a nonsense song recorded by Lead Belly called "Green Corn, Come Along Charlie": "Wake snake, day's a-breaking / Peas in the pot and hoe cake's a-baking." This lost pleasure must sound like overripe corn to anyone hearing it now. It is. That's the point.

After the marriage ended, I became enamored of a Polack joke that I changed to a Little Moron joke. The Little Moron comes home and finds his wife in bed with another man. The other man jumps out the window and runs away, while the Little Moron, enraged, pulls a pistol out of the dresser drawer and points it at his own head.

His wife, in bed, the sheets pulled up to her breasts, starts to laugh, and her laughter infuriates the Little Moron.

Still holding the pistol to his head, he snarls at her, "What are you laughing at? You're next!"

The joke captures how the self-loathing of rejection outweighs the anger of betrayal, though logically it should be the other way around. Changing the character from Polack to Little Moron eased the ethnic unpleasantness of the joke while tightening the connection between the joke and how stupid I felt.

During the year-long breakup, Kathleen, as I mentioned, said, "When we first met, you laughed at everything. Now you don't laugh at anything." True enough. But I can name the exact moment my sense of humor returned.

After the third and final time she moved out, Kathleen invited me for supper. We were going to try, she said, to be just friends.

Her apartment was in a house in an older, more fashionable, part of town than our neighborhood, where we had lived in a sixties tract house on West Vanderbilt Loop. The streets were named after elite private universities: Cornell Road, Northwestern Road, Colgate

Drive. Seeing our old furniture arranged into a comfortable and homey nest and my wife bustling out of the kitchen with the superficial gaiety of someone cooking a business dinner for a potential, but not very important, client threw me. Down the hall, I glimpsed the bedroom that was of course off-limits. We made awkward stabs at small talk. How are your parents? How is your dad? Work going all right?

I had entered her apartment with a sodden and hopeless resolve to be civil, even charming. I'd practiced good behavior in my head; I'd imagined, step by step, being gracious: *What a lovely home you've made! It was good of you to invite me. I've always loved your Chicken Marbella.* But once I was there, the disorienting strangeness of familiar furniture in an unfamiliar place and my wife's breezy withdrawal of intimacy undid me. She was trying to force me to acquiesce genteelly to the role she had chosen for me, and I was frantic to fracture the façade of politesse.

I do not, and I am grateful for this, remember what snippy unpleasantness issued from my mouth, but Kathleen informed me that if I couldn't be civil, I'd have to go home. She was right of course, but I couldn't bear the stiffs we had become, unable to talk easily and intimately with each other. Not five minutes went by before I made another nasty crack, probably mocking her taut propriety.

"I'm afraid I'll have to ask you to leave," she said. I had become the boss who expected her to make coffee, the geology professor who had condescended to her, the law professor who expected her to participate in class.

I walked out her front door miserable, humiliated, and defeated, heading down the walkway to my blue Volkswagen parked at the curb, the one with the leaking shocks that she refused to ride in because the ride was rough and the engine deafening. It was also ugly. I'd hand-sanded the rust off the doors and brushed a can of DAP Derusto over the entire car. The Montgomery night was suffused with the scent of spring flowers, freesia and honeysuckle, and half-way to my car, in the middle of her front lawn, I began to laugh. If she were standing at the door, I imagine she heard my laughter as nasty pride at my crummy behavior. It wasn't. I was ashamed and laughing at my shame—but laughing even more at the soap opera portentousness of "I'm afraid I'll have to ask you to leave" and the way my own robotic anger, which possessed the limited virtue of honesty, made me act like a jerk. We had become the puppets of our own pretensions. The me that was walking out that door to his battered blue Volkswagen Beetle felt infinitely superior to the me I had been just moments ago, and I was relieved to have left him behind.

Standing in the middle of her rented lawn, I laughed and laughed, gut-deep and wholeheartedly. I had done exactly what I had vowed not to do and confirmed all of my wife's worst opinions of me. How could that not be funny? And I laughed at the loss of love, the loss of faith in that love, and the loss of my understanding of a life that had been shaped by that love. It was a laugh of freedom, and of terror at that unsought emancipation.

Denis Dutton in *The Art Instinct*, writing as a Darwinist, cites joke-telling as an extension of the use of language in the courting process:

> As a form of cognitive foreplay in courtship, language can give us, in Geoffrey Miller's words, "a panoramic view of someone's personality, plans, hopes, fears, and ideals." If Darwin himself was right in his own speculation about the origins of language, foreplay of a sort is indeed where it began: as a means for first arresting the interest of members of the opposite sex and then demonstrating something to them. . . . Language originated in grabbing attention and expressing something compelling. Miller argues that this aspect of language, verbal courtship, spreads

through cultures and has come to be associated with many social skills and capacities: "Language puts minds on public display, where sexual choice could see them clearly for the first time in evolutionary history."

But what began in the courtship context seeped into areas of human life far removed from sex. Art in the most general sense is also an extension of this capacity into imaginative realms of story-telling, picture-making, crafting artifacts, music, poetic language, joke-telling, dance, and ordinary banter.

Joke-telling, along with banter, music, and poetic language may have grown out of courtship, but in the process they have become integral to it. I can't imagine not laughing with someone I love.

Before I fell in love with Jill—truth to tell, this happened in the last month of my first marriage—I loved the way she laughed. She was younger than I was by seven years, a recent graduate of the branch college where I taught as a temporary instructor. When she told a joke, she waited eagerly, expectantly, hopefully, for the listeners to laugh, and then, whether we did or not, she laughed at her own joke, with a peal of pleasure that tapered off into a long appreciative cackle, her face lit with intelligent, flirty mischief.

Her favorite joke was the one about two good ole boys who are walking down the street, when they see a bulldog squatting on the sidewalk. One of the dog's rear legs is hiked up in the air and he is thoroughly and enthusiastically licking his balls.

"Oh, man—that looks *good!*" says one of the men. "I wish I could do that."

"Ooooh weee," the other says, "that dog *bite* you!"

I loved the way she threw herself into the joke, circling her head in an upward clockwise motion, mimicking the dog's licking, and she emphasized the first boy's lust and longing by elongating *good* into two lascivious syllables: *guh uhd!* She stretched out the second boy's astonished *ooooh wee* and *bite*. Her punch line intimated her pleasure in sex, words, and performance; it's much more playful than the trenchant and skeptical punch line I had heard before: "Well, it's your dog. . . ." And of course, I heard the earthy delight in mocking male sexual avidity.

"That dog *bite* you!" became our first and most treasured private joke, though it wasn't very private. She told the joke to everyone we knew, and then I pedantically stepped in and offered the alternate punch line, milking the joke for a couple of extra chuckles.

The last eighteen months of a foundering marriage do not overflow with mirth. I needed to laugh, and so did Jill, rebounding from a couple of bad relationships, so we laughed with a hysterical need that made it all the sweeter. We suspected our love, by its very intensity and timing, was bound to fail, but maybe we could beat the odds. Maybe we'd be the happy exceptions to the rule.

From time to time, I pull out the memories of our happy times, like sharpened candy canes, to pierce my heart. Once we parked near the Capitol building in Montgomery, and on cardboard sheets, slid down the green slopes of Goat Hill (as it's still called, from the time before the Capitol was built)—mostly just holding each other as we tumbled off the cardboard and down the dry lawn, laughing wildly in our dizziness.

The first of the two Christmases we were together I bought Jill a burgundy sweater. Twenty dollars from Lands' End, a stretch since I'd returned to graduate school. She loved the sweater because I'd given it to her and I loved her loving it. She'd pull her hands up into the sleeves, ask, "Where did George Washington keep his armies?" then she'd pop her hands out, wave them in front of her, and sing out, "In his sleevies!" cackling with delight at the childishness of the pun and doubly at her own delight in childishness. She adored the joke because she'd heard it from her little brother, seventeen years younger than she, whom she was crazy about. She loved another of his jokes too: Where does the Lone Ranger take his trash? To the dump, to the dump, to the dump dump dump—sung to the theme music for *The Lone Ranger*.

She scoured the tacky mall store Spencer's for gag gifts, and for months carried around a Popping Martian, a vaguely penis-shaped, rubbery tube with a face painted on it. She called it the Greenie Weenie, and when she squeezed it, its eyes, nose, and ears bulged; it looked like a sexually alert space alien.

As a man right out of a marriage, a man who had only ever had sex with his wife, I was thrilled to laugh with a woman who, often while wearing that burgundy sweater, clapped her hands over her breasts as if she were being grabbed from behind. "Move those hands!" she sharply ordered the imaginary masher. After a pause, she mock-caressed her own breasts, moving her hands but not removing them. Her laugh was lusty and long. I gleefully took to grabbing her from behind and responding the same way to the same command.

Oh, I felt like a different Little Moron now, a bit like the one in another of her favorite jokes. A policeman finds the Little Moron running along the road, naked, so he stops and asks him what he's doing. The Moron says, "I was in the car with my girlfriend and she pulled off down a dirt road and drove off under some trees. Then she pulled off all her clothes and said, 'Go to town,' and that's where I'm headed."

The joke captured my sexual fear as I began life again as a single man. It amused me because, like the Little Moron, I have never been able to sense when a woman is interested in me. But I knew Jill was. "Go to town"—another private joke.

Here's yet another: Three couples die and go to the pearly gates together. The first man goes forward, and St. Peter informs him, "You will not be permitted to enter heaven. You are a man given to gluttony. You have such a sweet tooth you even sought out and married a woman named Candy."

When the second man goes forward, St. Peter peers down at him from his high desk and pronounces, "You too will not be permitted to enter heaven. You are a man given to greed. You are so greedy you even sought out and married a woman named Penny."

The third man turns to his wife and says, "We might as well leave now, Fanny."

We might as well leave now, Fanny. Private joke.

A couple of Jill's favorites were misogynistic or racist jokes I'd known for a long time and never thought funny until she gave me new ways to understand them. Hearing them again, not from men, but from the lips of a woman I loved, someone who clearly enjoyed them without malice, I understood them differently, if not correctly.

"Morning, ladies!" as the blind man said as he passed the fish market was, as I've said, a joke that always embarrassed me, yet when Jill told it and hooted, unembarrassed by the idea that women might have a healthy sexual scent, I was at first disturbed and then exhilarated. If men told the joke with varying degrees of distaste, for Jill it was a joyous avowal of animal vitality. "Morning, ladies!" became another of our catchphrases, and one I take pleasure in still. When my wife comes back into the bedroom with our current dog, a Coonhound bitch, to wake me when I've slept late, I always say, "Morning, ladies," as the dog sticks her sharp snout into my face and, as Erin has taught her to do, ardently licks the top of my bald head. It's like being swabbed by an extremely affectionate slice of baloney, and I can't bear it too long before I have to get up.

Jill's other favorite joke, another I'd heard long before I met her, was a room clearer; at least twice, people stood up and walked away when she told it.

Willie gets up in the morning. The sun's shining. He's had a good eight hours of sleep. The first thing he says is "I feels goooood."

He goes down to the breakfast his wife has fixed for him, and she says, "Willie, is you okay? You looks bad."

Willie says, "I don't know why I looks bad, but I feels good."

I will spare you Willie's identical conversations with the bus driver and his boss. But when the boss insists that he go to the doctor immediately because he looks so *baaaaad*, Willie goes, though he insists again that he doesn't know why he looks bad because he feels *goooood!*

Willie is immediately issued into the doctor's office and the doctor says, "Willie, you looks terrible."

Willie replies, "That's the problem. Everybody say I looks *baaaad*, but I feels so *goooood*."

The doctor reaches behind himself, takes a book off the shelf, and flips through it, muttering:

"'Looks bad, feels bad.' No, that's not it.

"'Looks good, feels good.' No, that's not it either.

"'Feels bad, looks good.' Not it.

"Ah, here it is, 'Looks bad, feels good.'"

"What is it, doc? What do I have?"

"Willie, it say right here in this book—you's a vagina."

Sometimes when Jill told the joke, a listener or two would laugh out of shock. But mostly people waited a few civil minutes and then drifted into another room.

"I *wish* she wouldn't tell that joke," three different people said to me at different times.

Mostly the joke is misogynistic, but the racism plays an important supporting role; it does a lot of work for the joke teller, other than just distracting us with racism to surprise us with sexism. The caricatured, minstrel-show blackness of the characters provides a reason for Willie's ignorance as well as the doctor's comically exaggerated attempt at diagnostic logic and pretentious misuse of medical terminology, just as it prepares us for the down-and-dirty lubricious turn at the end of the joke. The racism has been stripped out of almost all the versions I've heard or read lately; the result is a somewhat less offensive but much more pallid joke. The characters' ignorance becomes incomprehensible, the doctor's behavior is disconnected from any understandable context (except for one intriguing variation in which the doctor plugs the research terms "looks bad, feels good" into a diagnostic medical computer program), and the transformation at the end becomes a half hearted stab at a dirty joke. The oldest version of the joke that I've found, in Legman's *Rationale of the Dirty Joke*, also eschews racism for a straightforward misogyny that's, if anything, even nastier: *"A man who says that he may look lousy but feel good is called 'Mr. Cunt,' on the grounds 'That's the only thing that looks so lousy and feels so good.'"*

Along the way, the older joke seems to have merged with elements of the minstrel show (I can find no evidence that it emerged from it). The doctor in Jill's joke takes on the role of the Zip Coon, the stock character in minstrel shows who pretends to knowledge and education mostly denied African-Americans at the time. Willie's doctor is a descendant of Dr. Squash in John W. Smith's 1851 blackface play *The Quack Doctor: A Negro Farce*. Dr. Squash has a high opinion of his medical expertise:

> *So com to me all you niggers what's ill,*
> *For I am a doctor ob wonderful skill.*

> *I can cure de cholera, cholic, or cramp,*
> *I can cure de worst fevers, coast, typhus, or camp:*
> *I am death on de diarreah, can physic off fits,*
> *And can drive off de small-pox widout leaving pits.*

Despite his burgeoning self-esteem, though, he is no more accomplished a diagnostician than Willie's physician. When Crow comes to him with a self-diagnosed toothache, Dr. Squash analyzes the evidence and arrives at a different conclusion:

> I wants you to substantiate on your understanding dat de occipital plugatorial bonum, vulgarly called a toof, am not in and within its own individual functuation liable to the fluctuations and sensations which you, nigger, am just now experiencing in a highly antagonistical degree, but on the contrary am entirely unperceptible to the warious contortions and laminations usually ascribed to it. Darfore, I hold dat it am not de toofache.

Instead, Crow is actually suffering from "de disagreeable ailimentary symptoms in medica phraseology denominated, achabus toothabus."

Even Willie's finding himself an embodied and ambulatory genital has an old and entertaining ancestry. Ann Marie Rasmussen's *Wandering Genitalia: Sexuality & the Body in German Culture between the Late Middle Ages & Early Modernity* recounts a couple of poems in which private parts, after tiffs with their owners, set out on their own. The fifteenth-century poem *Das Nonnentumier* (*The Tournament of Nuns*) stars a penis that persuades the knight to which he is attached to set him free. The penis has quite a list of grievances:

> It's on my account that you are warmly received, and you have acquired more honor and dignity because of me than because of the most precious treasure you ever possessed, and yet you have never let me benefit in the least. Oh no, you have forced me into a corner, into the nastiest nook you possess, one even the basest servant would refuse. I want you to know that I've had it. If you weren't such a base and lowborn coward, you would just cut me off right now so that women and men alike can see which of us fares better.

Not the first or the last man to be persuaded by what his penis tells him, the knight castrates himself, but instead of being celebrated, he is derided, mocked, and beaten by the women he thought would celebrate his new enforced chastity and he "spends the last thirty-five years of his life as a hermit in a cave."

The emancipated penis, not knowing what to do on its own, retreats to a convent and holes up under the stairs. After a year, despondent, suicidal, but unable to kill itself, it decides to stand in the cloister walk until the nuns discover it and kill it. The nuns, though, take turns chastising the penis alone in their rooms. Some sterner nuns chastise the penis so ardently and long that other impatient nuns, chafing to chastise it too, complain to the abbess, who declares the nuns will compete for the penis in a tournament: "The nuns assemble the next day on a meadow, riding in formation under the banner of a naked man and carrying the penis on a silken pillow, which is placed so that it can view the jousts. The tournament degenerates into a wild brawl, during which the penis is stolen."

The penis watched the jousting nuns! Despite Jill's love of the Greenie Weenie, I am uncomfortable imagining a penis with eyes.

Not only penises were discontent during the German Middle Ages. In *The Rose Thorn*, a magic root enters a young virgin's *fud*, miraculously enabling it to talk—and not just talk, but whine. The *fud*, it turns out, is nearly as annoying a kvetcher as its male counterpart: "I think it's too much that you are thriving and yet I am not allowed a share, especially considering that men everywhere adore you only because of me, and if you were to lose me, every single one of them would find you completely worthless."

The virgin and her *fud* exchange hot words and heated abuse before separating, and the young lady then accepts a suitor who, the moment he understands just how she is incapacitated, rejects her. Word of her condition gets out, and the townspeople respond with all the pity and commiseration you might expect. They point her out on the street and shout, "There goes the cuntless woman!"

Things don't go markedly better for the *fud*. It offers itself to a young man, who mistakes the talking vulva for a talking toad and kicks it. Chastened, the roving *fud* retraces its path back to the lady, and the narrator of the poem helps them out by "nailing the vulva back in place."

I had always hated the joke about Willie for its *Amos 'n' Andy*-style racism and its in-your-face disgust with women's bodies—a twofer if there ever were one—but hearing it from the lips of a woman I loved madly made me rethink its merits. Jill wasn't interested in the racism or misogyny in the joke. She relished drawling the Dionysian pronouncement "feels goooood," and her open delight in sexual pleasure was my relish and delight. Underneath the joke's ugliness she heard the sexual joy celebrated in the medieval folktales.

I was twenty-nine, and Jill was twenty-two. I fretted about the age difference; she didn't. So I told her about the old man in his nineties who was marrying a woman who was—oh, just to pick an age at random—twenty-two. The night before his marriage, his friends and family come to him and say that, though they didn't want to intrude, they were very concerned about the disparity in ages between him and his wife. They didn't know quite how to say it but they hoped that on the wedding night he'd take it easy because the exertions could—well, you know—prove fatal.

The old man tells them that he deeply appreciates their concern but life is sometimes a matter of chance and hard decisions, one has to take the good with the bad. As far as he's concerned, if she dies, she dies.

Whenever I worried about how much older I was, Jill simply laughed and said, "If I die, I die"—punning on the Elizabethan use of *die*, meaning to have an orgasm.

Once when we were making love, long and strenuously, I was

so lost in the act that, mouth open, I looked down and saw a long, looping strand of drool unfurl from my lips and hang connected between us for an eternally unfolding half second. Then it dropped. Oh my God, I was mortified. She howled with laughter at my distress and the reason for it, neither of us separating. I was beyond gratified that, instead of fussing at me, she preened. She was, she said, so sexually accomplished she'd reduced her man to a slack-jawed, drooling mouth-breather. It was true. When I told her I was going to fuck her brains out, she always grinned and said, "Duh!" What could I do now but look at her and say, "Duh!"?

Does every love have a moment that turns into a symbol when the love is over? Jill and I were still in the early stages of being in love, living together in the cheap first floor we rented in an old house in bad repair. It was a fraught and tender time. One evening as we sat down to dinner, the frosted glass fixture came off the light, hit the table between us, and exploded, flying apart in splinters. I both did and did not understand what was happening, as unmoving, I seemed to see every glass fragment as it flew around, over, and at us. Glass shards clung to our clothes and our hair. I was seized with guilt. When I last replaced the bulb, I hadn't tightened the retaining screws enough. I leapt up and quickstepped over crunching glass around the table to Jill, who had not moved. We were fine. I plucked white flakes from her black curls. We were not hurt at all until, in trying to tweak a splinter from her cheek, I pressed it into the flesh and blood trickled down her face.

If I hadn't touched her, she wouldn't even have been cut.

After nine months, the usual time it takes for the crazy expansion of self in new love to begin contracting, we shrank back toward our regular selves. She loved playing Scrabble with friends, and she didn't believe me when I told her that friendly competitions do not remain friendly when I'm involved. She insisted, I capitulated, and despite a genial beginning, I soon became an impatient, aggressive, and self-loathing player, berating myself for bad decisions and cursing unlucky dispositions of chance. Like me, she didn't like the person I hadn't wanted her to see.

For my part, I was annoyed and troubled by her casual, even amused, dismissal of the things I was wrestling with then—Freud, faith, and history. I was particularly irritated by her insistence that when she was fifteen and saw her father wheeled out the kitchen door, dead of a heart attack, she knew instantly there was no God. That's not good enough, I said. It's simplistic and emotional. Everybody dies. You can refuse to believe in God but that isn't a good enough reason. Didn't matter if it was logical or not, she said. She knew what she knew. Later, much too late, I came to understand she was of course right and reasonable—death is the test of God.

We knew the joke: What are the three stages of love? Kitchen sex, bedroom sex, and hall sex. In kitchen sex, you are so madly in love, so crazy for each other, you screw everywhere—living room, couch, floor, kitchen. In bedroom sex, passion simmers down and you make love exclusively in the bedroom. And in the final stage, hall sex, you pass each other in the hall and say, "Fuck you!"

We never reached that last stage, but as time passed we fussed and fought, arguing more and more sadly. Let one detail suffice for a hundred: Jill was an avid moviegoer, one who sat through every minute of the credits while I considered the damn movie over as soon as THE END appeared, and I wanted to go home. I hated being trapped in a theater, unable to leave when I was bored. During *Yentl*, the Barbra Streisand film of an Isaac Singer story I like, I repeatedly left the theater and stalked around the lobby, enraged by Streisand's self-adoration. In one scene, Streisand, the director, aims the camera reverently upward at her face while light shines down, beatifically. Her profile fills the screen, and at one moment, the camera is staring up her left nostril, which is lit like a stained-glass window. Big noses, as the comedians say, are always funny, and in over-loving her own visage, Streisand inadvertently created a moment of anti-Semitic caricature that made me bark out loud and slide down in my seat, giggling. Jill was steaming. She thought I was mocking the movie and her for liking it. She was half right. Maybe, I'm pained to admit, three-quarters right. But the middle of a movie is no place to hash out fine distinctions in mirth, artistic merit, and two lovers' widening divergence in taste. By the time we left the theater, we were both too angry and hurt to sort out our concerns. We had begun to think they didn't matter

For the last six weeks or two months of our life together, as we waited out the end of our lease, she slept in the bed and I slept on the floor beside her, holding hands until one of us rolled over, seeking sleep.

After we broke up, I relearned the truth behind "The Single Life," an epigram by my old teacher Henri Coulette; it's probably the most wince-eliciting couplet ever written: "Being a bachelor's not so hot. / I find I sleep on the wet spot." A world of pathos (and the simply pathetic too) hides, poorly, behind the bravado of these two lines and fourteen words. Along with whatever life experience he brought to it, Coulette almost certainly wrote his poem with another poem in mind, the famous Middle English lyric fragment that we call "Westron Wynde":

> Westron wynde, when wilt thou blow,
> The small raine down can raine.
> Cryst, if my love were in my armes
> And I in my bedde again!

Something like the same longing runs through both poems, but Coulette's couplet is both more refined in meter and rhyme and coarser in sentiment. The speaker of the "The Single Life" has clearly not always been single. Like the lonely lover in "Westron Wynde," our modern lover too imagines his woman—or *a* woman—back in bed with him, but it's a manual imagining. A bit of an awkward romantic himself, he eschews the tidiness of Kleenex and creates the love spot, which he sleeps on in a sort of perverse nostalgia. But since he's alone, the act lacks the practical gallantry it would have if the lover were actually there. He affects a jaunty tone to mock his own predicament, while pretending to be surprised ("I find") to discover himself seeking such uncomfortable comfort. Beneath the calculations of his rhyme and meter, the poem sounds like something blurted out late at night, the sort of joking maybe-I-mean-it, maybe-I-don't confession that makes us turn away in discomfiture, uncertain if our friend understands just how much he's revealed and wondering if he'll remember in the morning, sober, what he's said. What makes us embarrassed for him is the human longing he's inappropriately and graphically revealed.

When I recall my single life, the time between Jill and Erin, my wife, I prefer to remember the times I wasn't entirely single. Depleted by a divorce from a woman Erin calls my "evil, training wife" and an agonizing split with Jill, I spent a couple of months with Julia, a psychologist in training, who was wise, kind, my age, funny, and married. One of the first jokes she told me was similar to the medieval German ones. A man's penis and his feet get into an argument about who has it rougher. The feet say, "I've got it tougher than you. No question. Every morning, he straps me in a dead animal hide and walks on me all day long."

"I wish I had it that easy. Every night, he puts a bag over my head and makes me do push-ups till I puke."

In response I told her why being a dick is the worst job in the world. You hang out with two nuts, your best friend's a pussy, your nearest neighbor's an asshole, and when you get excited you throw up and then faint.

Early in our joke flirting, she told me the old racist joke that Jill had also loved. A black man goes to the doctor to get a vasectomy. When the doctor enters the examining room, he sees his patient is wearing a tuxedo. "Why in the world are you wearing a tuxedo?" the doctor asks.

The black man replies, "If I'm going to be impotent, I'm going to look impotent." Zip Coon returns to mispronounce a word for us in a parody of black dialect, and once more he is associated with sexuality. The joke was regrettably prophetic. Because I felt guilty dating a married woman, I was borderline impotent much of our time together. A curious additional guilt exacerbates the gnawing culpability of adultery when you're unable to give your lover the full benefit of her transgression. But Julia was, as I said, kind and wise. When, talking about my divorce and breakup, I said something about being depressed, she softly corrected me, saying, "No wonder you are sad." She was right. Calling sadness by its right name gave it the dignity it deserved and held out the hope that it was transitory. Her wisdom extends even to herself. Years later, reconciled with her husband, she told me over coffee horror story after horror story of counseling beaten, starved, prostituted, and incestuously raped children.

"My God," I said, "that must be depressing. I'd want to kill myself."

"Why should I be depressed?" she said calmly. "I'm *helping* them."

And she loved parrot jokes.

One involves a Jew who enters a pet shop and a parrot shouts "Awwwk! Moshe Dayan is a jerk-off! Awwwwk! Moshe Dayan is a jerk-off!"

Enraged by this slur on the Israeli minister of defense, the Jew confronts the pet shop owner, who says that he's embarrassed, but what can he do? He bought the parrot from the estate of an anti-Semite before he knew its quirks. Eyeing the Jew, the owner says, insinuatingly, "The parrot's for sale, you know."

After a moment's thought, the Jew buys the parrot and, all the way home, the parrot, in his cage on the front seat of the car, screams, "Awwwk, Moshe Dayan is a jerk-off! Awwwk, Moshe Dayan is a jerk-off!"

Once they get inside the front door, the new owner grabs the bird out of his cage and yanks its tongue out. Then he returns to the pet shop, hands the cage to the owner, and smirks, "Here, see if you can sell a parrot that doesn't talk."

Pleased with himself, he drops by the pet store a week later to see what's happened. As soon as the bird sees him, it flips one wing over his left eye, imitating Dayan's eye patch. He drops the other wing to his crotch and makes an exaggerated wanking motion.

The joke's only fairly amusing, and fewer and fewer of us can recall Moshe Dayan and his eye patch, but what's irresistible to me was seeing, and now remembering, a good-looking, thirty-year-old curly-headed doctoral student throwing an imitation wing over her eye with one hand and jerking the other hand up and down in front of her crotch, imitating a speechless parrot imitating Moshe Dayan masturbating.

Julia was also the first person to tell me one of the great jokes of the last fifty years. Man buys a parrot. Parrot curses all day and all night without ceasing, flaunting the most inventive invective and curdled filth imaginable. After a while, the man becomes worn out from being subjected to the relentless barrage of profanity, and he's embarrassed and lonely because the parrot has driven away all his friends and potential girlfriends. He tries to reason with the bird, asking it to temper its language, at least when people are around.

His request makes the bird even more profane. Cursing up

a storm, it mocks the man for being a friendless, unloved pansy. Infuriated, not knowing what to do, the man picks the parrot up by its feet, slams it into the freezer, slams the door, and stalks off. After a couple of hours, he begins to worry about the parrot freezing to death. Bracing for yet more swearing and insults, he opens the freezer door.

To his surprise the parrot immediately says, "Sir, I want to apologize profoundly for my terrible behavior, and I want to assure you, sir, that from this moment on I will be the model of good behavior and civility. You will have, sir, no further complaints about my vocabulary or behavior."

The man is dubious, but the parrot is as good as its word—polite, deferential, and even obsequious in its desire to please. After three weeks the parrot, though, clearly has something on its mind. "Sir," it begs, "do please forgive me if I'm being too inquisitive, and of course you don't have to answer. That's entirely up to you. But if you don't mind, would you please tell me what the chicken did?"

For me, the bird's voice is forever Julia's oleaginous creation of it, and the bird's last question is a triumph of her storytelling. I wonder if she didn't see me as a bit like the parrot. Over another cup of coffee a few years ago, she told me that, as a psychologist, she had long speculated that I might suffer from a mild form of Tourette's syndrome. I have a propensity for profanity and a delight in invective, like Caliban in *The Tempest*, who tells Prospero that he is grateful for the darker resources of the language: "You taught me language, and my profit on't / Is I know how to curse." And of course Jill had taken a professional interest in my twitchy legs and my susceptibility to muscular and vocal tics, some of them nearly involuntary.

Did my compulsive joke telling, especially of offensive and vulgar jokes, give me a marginally acceptable way to use profanity in public? she wondered. At times I think she was right, given my powerful impulse toward crude joking. At other times I think she is wrong. I get no pleasure, merely relief, from jerking my head to the side, as I used to do, or by popping air against the roof of my mouth with my tongue, as I now find myself doing, sometimes startling even myself with the sharp clicking noise. Occasionally the joking is compulsive, and I'm startled by what I hear coming out of my mouth. More often, though, I simply take immense, deliberate plea-sure in laughing, making others laugh, and thinking about laughter.

There were other girlfriends, other jokes. I must also celebrate the girlfriend with the marvelous dark throaty chuckle who asked me a question that has haunted me for twenty years: Why do cheerlead-ers wear such short skirts? She wasn't telling a joke. She'd heard only that much and assumed that I would know. Though I have searched high and mostly low for an answer, I've never found one. I'm afraid the punch line might be something as insipid as "so the losers will have something to cheer for." Did she perhaps mishear the homophobic riddle that asks, "Why do cheerleaders in San Francisco *not* wear short skirts?" "So that when they sit down their balls won't show?" Or is the mystery of the joke still a mystery, wait-ing to be appreciated? (Mystery solved: A copy editor of this book just told me the punch line is "To make the fans' root harder.") The classic joke on ladies' garments is probably, "Why do widows wear black garters?" "In memory of those who have passed beyond." It is a joke so close to benign I believe I first heard it from one of my godly minister uncles.

Because we lived thousands of miles apart and rarely saw each other, our relationship wasn't destined for the long haul, but every week when I called her I fell in love again with her laugh. You are "so silly" she told me over and over again, laughing, because I'd say almost anything to provoke her great dark-chocolate chuckle. I rev-eled in it the way an otter revels in water.

Silly, my girlfriends called me, knowing I made myself silly for their delight, knowing too that sharing jokes with someone is a way of saying to them that you trust them enough not to think you are stupid but deliberately aping stupidity and that you trust them to trust your good intentions. *Cill Lee*, they said, playing with the pronunciation, pulling it out, making *silly* silly.

Sometimes jokes make it clear when a relationship is bound to founder short of love.

In the early days of getting to know each other, a girlfriend and I drove the tedious length of Illinois together. I liked her very much. I wanted to love her. I was taking her home to meet my father in Montgomery. As the cornfields of southern Illinois went on for mile after unvarying hot green mile, I ran through every bit of conversation I could think of and then started telling jokes. The one that caused the problem might have been one of the racist jokes I've written about earlier. Or it could have been a joke I'd heard just recently from Henri Coulette, who lived almost his entire life in Los Angeles.

"What are the first three words a Mexican baby hears?" Henri asked as I was driving him from his room in the student union at the University of Iowa to the Kmart so he could buy toiletries. My mind raced to the famous three words "I love you," then tried to figure out what they would be in Spanish. Before I could go any further, Henri answered, "Attention, Kmart shoppers." I laughed so hard I almost drove into a telephone pole, and Henri laughed too, enjoying his own joke and my response. I had to pull over to the side of the road while Henri and I composed ourselves.

"Why do you think that would be funny?" my girlfriend asked, wanting me to justify my apparent racism.

Though I bristled, I tried to explain my complex attraction to the joke. First, I laughed simply because the joke had taken a turn I hadn't expected. It also amused me because I knew that Henri had only thought of the joke because we were driving to Kmart. And it opened a world I hadn't thought about. The jokes I'd heard about Latinos were few, rote, and mostly served to support the familiar homegrown racism: Why do Mexicans refuse to let their kids marry blacks? They are afraid the kids will be too lazy to steal. But Henri's joke went in an entirely new direction. It mocked Latinos for being poor and for shopping at the déclassé Kmart—the very store we were driving to and a chain I had patronized without irony since high school, my mother and I chasing the blue light around the store to see what was on sale. The prejudice against Kmart startled me almost as much as the one against Mexican-Americans because it was also a joke on me.

"Are you sure there isn't really another reason you are laughing at the joke?" she asked. Her eyes were bright and encouraging, the eyes of a parent trying to elicit a confession from a pigheaded adolescent.

"What would that be?" I asked. I'm sure I must have snarled.

"It's a very unpleasant joke."

"Yes, it is."

"Then why did you tell it?"

"I just explained that."

"Do you think what you said really explains why you laughed?"

"It's the best I can do. Look, it was just a joke," I told her. "It failed. I'm sorry. Let's let it go, okay?"

"Do you know people who'd think that joke was funny?"

"Yeah, rather a lot of them in fact."

With each of us silently reassessing the other, the next hundred miles or so of green cornfields, silos, and the occasional red-winged blackbird plucking at something dead alongside the road were less agreeable than the identical hundred miles that had preceded them. Alert to the joke's disparagement of Latinos as impoverished but inveterate shoppers, she was disturbed at being in the car and maybe in love with a possible hate-monger who apparently swapped jokes with many other hate-mongers. For my part, I was exasperated to be interrogated like a xenophobic bigot unaware of the offense inherent in the joke. I felt I had earned the benefit of the doubt for good intentions with wicked jokes. In something as short as a joke, context is so thin that sometimes it's impossible to tell if there is a nasty intention in the heart of the teller. The joke was morally indefensible, but I thought it was funny anyway. I foresaw a future of justifying every laugh that passed my lips. Amazingly we didn't break up before crossing the Kentucky state line, but stayed warily together for a few more months before drifting apart.

If there is a joke that encapsulates the joy and mistakes, anxiety and missteps I felt for these failed lovers, it's this. A composer writes the most beautiful love song ever created, but despite having sent out tapes and CDs, he's never been able to get the song published. Finally, in desperation, he sneaks into the largest music publishing company, forces his way into the president's office, and begins to play the song on his violin. The song is so beautiful that secretaries and janitors, accountants and lawyers find themselves drawn into the president's office to listen, rapt, as the music immerses them in memories of loves old and new, good love and sorrowful love, failed love and sustaining love. They are radiant with joy while weeping with sorrow. When the composer finishes, the president of the music company says, through tears, "That truly is the most beautiful love song. I can't believe it hasn't been published. What do you call it?"

"I Love You So Fucking Much I Could Shit."

Thirteen

You Two Just Crack Each Other Up

I always felt like Jack, the Jack of giant-killer fame, who in a lesser-known tale, "Lazy Jack," is forced out of the house by his mother to find work. The first day, Jack hires out to a cattle farmer, who pays him with a jar of milk. Jack puts the jar in his jacket pocket, and of course on the way home he spills it.

His mother shrieks, "You stupid boy. You should have carried it on your head."

Jack says, "Next time I'll do that."

The following day, he works for a cheese maker. Wages: a block of cream cheese. As he promised his mother, he carries it home on his head, where it melts in the heat and becomes matted in his hair.

Mother once more pronounces Jack a stupid boy and tells him he should have carried it in his hands; he promises to do so. The next day: a baker. Wages: a cat. When Jack holds it in his hands, it scratches the daylights out of him and runs off.

"Stupid boy, you should have tied it on a string and dragged it home behind you."

"Next time I'll do that."

The following day: butcher. Wages: a lovely shoulder of mutton. Jack ties a piece of string to the mutton and drags it home with results predictable to everyone but Jack. This time Jack's mother calls him a "ninny-hammer" (a charming disparagement dating to at least 1592) and tells him he should have carried it on his shoulder.

"Next time I'll do that," promises our slow study.

The next day, Jack goes back to the cattle farmer and at the end of the workday he is given a donkey. It's a job to hoist the donkey on his shoulders, but Jack does it and slowly staggers home, bent under the weight of his wages. Jack's path home takes him by the house of a rich man with no wife and only one child, a beautiful daughter who is deaf and dumb. We will call her Erin. And while we're at it, let's change Jack's name to Andrew.

Our folktale Erin had never laughed, and the doctors, being folktale doctors, had prognosticated that she would never speak until someone made her laugh. Now Erin just happened to be looking out her window when Andrew stumbled past, the donkey on his shoulders, the donkey's legs sticking up in the air, kicking wildly. Erin burst out laughing at the silly man, and, laughter being the best medicine, she immediately regained her speech and hearing. Her overjoyed father married Erin to Andrew, who felt richly rewarded for his silliness all the rest of his life.

Moral: You're just an idiot with an ass on your shoulders until someone laughs.

I first saw my future wife drinking a beer on the porch at Yaddo, the artists' colony in Saratoga Springs. A common friend had told me Erin would be there and she'd gently nudged us toward each other, though she'd warned me Erin was a California-style Catholic handwringer, one who anguished over the plight of the downtrodden. Sometimes she had a good sense of humor, the friend said, and sometimes she was earnest and touchy, so I should watch my mouth until I figured out whether my, uh, particular sense of humor meshed with hers. What I saw, looking at the woman I was to marry, was a tall, open-faced, attractive woman with a jolt of curly hair off her forehead. Unlike the folktale Erin, she looked eager to laugh. In fact, hers was the face of someone who gravitated to laughter the way other people gravitate toward good looks or the palpably powerful. I decided to go with my instinct, rather than our friend's warnings, which I'll admit were more catnip than red flag.

She had a name. Erin McGraw—a name so Irish it might as well be Ireland McIrish, and when she told me who she was, I immediately asked if she'd heard about the Irishman who drowned in the vat at the brewery.

"No," she said.

"They knew he was Irish because, before he died, he crawled out twice to take a leak."

I held my breath for half a second, fearing a pointed rebuff, but she laughed and didn't feel a need to inform me that not all Irish were drunks, thank you very much. *Good sign*, I thought. I didn't know how good. I soon found out her brother was in AA and her father had been addicted to prescription meds for years. But I dialed back anyway and asked a cutesy riddle: What's Irish and stays out all night? Paddy O'Furniture. She groaned with a smile and said, *Bah dum bump, Czh!*, tapping out a rimshot on her thighs. Not much of one for puns, apparently, but happy to play.

After confirming that she, as her name suggested, was Roman Catholic (or *cat lick*, as my Uncle Buddy invariably, derisively pronounced it), I told her about the three Irishmen sitting in a pub opposite a whorehouse in Dublin. Looking out the window, they see the local rabbi walk down the street and, after a quick look around, slip into the whorehouse.

"Och, and it's sad to observe the depravity of the Jews," says Paddy to Seamus and Murphy, and all three shake their heads knowingly.

(I love this part of the joke because it lodges in the listener's mind as an uneasy anticipation of anti-Semitism. It goes nowhere, but does raise the tension level.)

The three Irishmen order a second stout, and as they are drinking, the Presbyterian minister walks quickly down the street and scuttles into the whorehouse.

"Well, and if that doesn't demonstrate what we've always known about the morals of the Protestants," says Murphy to Seamus and Paddy, who nod in sage agreement.

As they are all relaxing into their third stout, the parish priest, Father Quinn, strolls down the street, hesitates a moment, and steps over the threshold into the whorehouse. The three Irishmen say nothing for a moment until Paddy says, "It's good of the Father to visit them, it is. One of the poor misguided girls must have fallen ill."

"Sounds about right," Erin said, laughing.

A lot of RCs would resent hearing these jokes from a southerner and a Protestant. Erin, though, has a fond but jeweler's eye for the foibles and venalities of her Church and its priests, as well as a wariness of the self-exculpating sentimentality of the Irish—and this joke indulged both misgivings.

Thinking back, I am almost certain that, over the course of the evening and dinner, I told her the joke about Dewey the leprechaun, the joke that ruined my injudicious play for Condi Rice—and she got a kick out of it. Her sense of humor revealed her flexible-mindedness and intelligence, her instinctive desire to sympathize with both sides of an issue but still able to take a firm moral stand.

We were just getting to know each other as lovers and as

people—I think we'd made love twice—when I invited her to listen to a comedy tape I'd just bought, by Sam Kinison. I had heard Kinison on TV, I told her, and he did a bit that always put me in stitches. Looking out at the audience, he yelled, "You can't scare me." Then he'd bend forward and bellow as loud as he could, "I'VE BEEN MARRIED!" The first syllable of *married* was a sustained low note, which then rose to the high piercing long *e* in the second syllable, which he held like a crazed soprano unwilling to end her aria, all the muscles in his neck taut as the wires stabilizing an electric transmission tower.

Even in my tame imitation, Erin, who had also been married, liked the joke. "That's funny," she said, charmed. "That's very good."

As she settled into a chair on the other side of the room, I snapped the cassette into my screaming-yellow boom box and punched PLAY. Almost immediately Kinison began screaming at the entirety of sub-Saharan Africa, telling the starving masses that they live in a fucking desert and they are always going to be starving if they don't move. "Move, you fucking morons! Move to where the food is!"

"See this?" he bellowed. "It's sand. A hundred years from now, it's still going to be sand! We have deserts in America—we just don't live in them, assholes!" The sheer audacity of the line about sand jerked a choked snort out of me—choked off, because I was wondering nervously how I looked to Erin. Maybe this crude rant would conjure up the bleeding-heart California Catholic I'd been warned about and I'd have to hear for the rest of the night about how crass and cruel Kinison was and, by logical extension, how cruel I was to laugh, though I myself was hearing the tape for the first time, and so certainly couldn't be advocating—could I?—the moral contents of it, which I didn't in fact find terribly funny except for the one laugh he'd forced out of me, which really was, in its own awful way, funny, wasn't it—a little bit, maybe?

"I've, uh, only heard him on TV," I said. "I had no idea he was this, uh, vulgar."

"That's okay," she said. "I see what he's doing."

But what exactly was he doing? Kinison was a shock comedian, but Kinison was also an ex-evangelical preacher whose rage at the world's shortcomings frequently broke into long frustrated screams. It was hard sometimes to hear past the anger to the perverse glee of a man who has shed the illusions of his faith and was now performing his balked idealism in front of an audience. Reading *Brother Sam*, Bill Kinison's account of his younger brother's life, I discovered my assumptions were mostly right. But there is another devastatingly simple reason why Kinison often seemed deranged. According to his brother, Sam had been "a mild little boy" until the age of three, when he ran into the street after a rubber ball and "a semitruck struck him flush on the side of his head." The doctor diagnosed him as having suffered "thirty percent brain damage."

Erin and I were relieved when Kinison finished the bit about Ethiopia, but we weren't relieved for long. The next rant was about cunnilingus, which Kinison did not call cunnilingus. He bellowed at women in the abstract because of how freaking long they take to climax and how unbelievably tired his tongue got in the laborious process of gratifying them. With a muffled sort of speech impediment, he mimicked the act while yelling at his imagined recipient to please hurry the fuck up and come because he's dying down here. His tongue is falling off, for Christ's sake.

Then he described how he both satisfied his lover and relieved his boredom by spelling out the alphabet on her clitoris with his tongue. Again with the muffled speech impediment: *Ah! Bah! Sah! Dah!*

Though Kinison's rant about oral sex deliberately overlooked the pleasure of giving pleasure, he said something that most men think but know not to say. With a new lover sitting on the other side of the room, one whom I hoped would continue as a lover, I felt no particular desire to say, "You know, he kinda has a point," though now, after twenty years of marriage, I probably would say it, if for no other reason than to provoke a look of amused forbearance. We sat silently, listening to Kinision scream, unable to bring ourselves to look at each other. Was she offended or would I offend her more by turning off the tape and seeming like a chivalrous dolt, determined to protect fair maiden from foul taint? I shifted uncomfortably in my chair and swept quick glances in her direction, trying to gauge her mood. Her studiously neutral face was poised above her carefully open, but very still, posture.

"Well, that's enough of that," I said, and hit the EJECT button.

Immediately she was on her feet, ready to go. We smiled brief, forced, uneasy smiles at each other and then decided it'd be a good idea to walk into town for an ice cream cone. Walking, we talked about suffering and humor. The gap between our concern for the hungry, unhoused, and afflicted, and what we actually do to help them—our self-preserving hypocrisy—is the sort of cognitive dissonance that is the stuff of humor. And our acknowledgment of our hypocrisy while still doing nothing or little is the source for more and different laughter. As Kinison himself said in an interview, "You can't just cry."

A joker, but seldom a joke teller, Erin loves to laugh as much as anyone I've ever met. From the beginning I loved the way our voices joined in laughter, as singers delight in their voices uniting in song. Everyone knows music is sensual, but the free jazz of laughter— soloing and asking for a response, like a clarinet calling to a saxophone, the sax replying with its solo, and the two then combining in harmony—is sensual and even openly erotic. Erin rarely finds puns funny, which is a relief; while I enjoy puns myself, I don't like being caught in a barrage of them. She doesn't laugh at racist or violent jokes unless they really catch her off guard, and she laughs briefly before the ugliness catches up with her, but she's interested in the forces behind them. She wants to understand the psychology of the racist joke and joke teller *because* they are alien to her.

I wooed her and her pealing musical laughter with the jokes Jill loved: "That dog bite you!" And as we got to know each other better: "We might as well leave now, Fanny." And "Morning, ladies!"— which to my amazement she both knew and thought funny. Not until much later did I tell her about Willie going to the doctor because he looked good but felt bad, and when I did tell it, as a specimen of the racist jokes I heard in high school, she took a moment to work through revulsion to puzzlement at the intricate conflicting ugliness of the joke.

I felt a bit like an adulterer, delighting one lover with the pleasures learned from another. Between Jill and me, the jokes were an open intimacy, the hilarity sparked by our delight in each other and flaring to a frantic flame by the romantic disappointments that had brought us together. Each of us then became another one of those disappointments to the other. But the things that made us laugh still seemed to me so intimate that I felt, irrationally, as if I were sharing pillow talk or the details of our sex life if I repeated them. But jokes are not wholly owned by the context in which we first enjoy them or enjoy them the most; they have a life of their own. I got over my sentimental attachments and discovered that not every joke of Jill's was a hit with Erin.

Sure, she loves and still urges me to ask people, "Where did George Washington keep his armies?" so she can laugh happily when I shoot my hands out of my cuffs and crow, "In his sleevies!" And she laughs though she knows that every single time I tell it, I think of Jill, who first told it to me.

She's not so fond of another one of Jill's, which I like simply because it's silly, a pun so dumb it's pure idiot music.

"Where does the Lone Ranger take his garbage?"

"To the dump, to the dump, to the dump, dump, dump! To the dump, to the dump, dump, dump!"

"When'd you learn that one, third grade?"

"And what do you have against third grade, Miss Big Shot College Professor?"

But I had learned a few new ones. After making love one afternoon, I asked her what a man could do in bed to ensure that his woman enjoys a massive, life-affirming, even life-changing orgasm every single time they make love.

"Okay, what?"

"Who cares?"—delivered with a dismissive shrug. Oh, she howled at that one.

It's a guy joke. And it's an ugly joke if one takes the speaker seriously. But most guys telling the joke are, I think, acknowledging that while there are guys who think that way, the ones telling the joke are not like them, or else the orgasm wouldn't be so lovingly described. Some men certainly have no interest in anyone's pleasure but their own, but it's also true that there are times when one partner is going to climax and the other, for whatever reason, isn't, and then one either tends to one's own pleasure or is left unsatisfied. Would I have told this joke to my wife before we made love? Probably not. But afterward the implicit message is different: It says not only am I not one of those guys, I hope I've shown you I'm not. And as Erin and I age, that nasty punch line takes on a compassionate, even a deeply loving, note. If one of us doesn't finish, who cares? The act of love is still love, dammit, if not as entirely satisfactory as sex.

Obligatory large penis joke: My wife has never had an orgasm. She passes out first from the pain.

Erin and I laugh at most of the same things for most of the same reasons, but with different slants. Her laugh seems to me more compassionate, imbued with a generous Catholic sense that people, by revealing their flawed nature, are somehow reaffirming an ordered universe with God at the top and humans below. To her, the self-serving gratification of the "Who cares?" is, in its own small-minded way, life-affirming because, as St. Augustine says, "To blame the fault of a creature is to praise its essential nature." There is some of that acceptance in my laughter. I wish there were more. But the Calvinism of my childhood makes me expect the worst from people. I see and celebrate the occasionally necessary selfishness behind "Who cares?" but I also deplore it. Erin disapproves of it too, but finds the cheerful lack of hypocrisy charming, just as she laughs with pleasure when she sees a dog unabashedly being a dog, even if it's protecting its food bowl from a passing shadow, trying to steal another dog's toy, or running to the basement to hide from thunder.

In the first weeks that I knew her, I told Erin the joke that became her favorite—another joke I first heard from Jill—and it's no surprise that it's about sex and levels of sexual avidity. A man has been on a desert island for twenty years, utterly alone, and one day, as he is walking along the beach, scavenging, he finds a woman washed up on the shore. He goes to attend to her and sees that it's Sharon Stone. She must have fallen off a passing yacht. (Which means she fared better than another famously beautiful actress who stars in another joke. "What kind of wood doesn't float?" "Natalie." Erin does not care for that one.)

The castaway carries Sharon Stone up to his hut, cleans her up, feeds her warmed-up coconut milk, and slowly, tenderly nurses her back to health. After three months, when she is completely well, he says, "Sharon, I'm nervous about bringing this up because I don't want to offend you and this is a little embarrassing to say, but, you know, I've been here alone on this island for twenty years and I've never seen a ship. I've never been close to being rescued. The chances of our being saved are virtually nil, and I hope you won't think I'm being forward if I suggest we might want to think about, you know, maybe having sex."

Sharon isn't so wild about having sex with a scroungy beach-comber, but the prospect of spending the rest of her life on an island with no sexual companionship is a pretty convincing argument; he has saved her life and taken care of her. With a little reluctance, she agrees. For the next two months they have almost nonstop, frantic, insane, passionate sex—the best sex either of them has ever had.

After three months, though, Sharon notices that her lover's ardor has begun to decrease, and she thinks she ought to raise this issue with him.

"Yes, Sharon, you're right," he says. "I guess I haven't been as fully engaged with you, as fully besotted with you, as I was in the beginning."

"You know we're likely to spend the rest of our lives here on this island," she says. "Is there anything I can do, anything at all, that will get you excited again—that will make our love complete for you?"

"Well, yes, there is. Do you mind if I call you Bob?"

Sharon is taken aback. Nothing in the castaway's demeanor had prepared her for this. But twenty years alone on an island . . . no real hope of rescue . . .

She shrugs, and says, "Yeah, sure, you can call me Bob."

"Hey, that's great. Thanks. Why don't you come here and sit down beside me, Bob?" he says, and pats a spot on the log he's sitting on in front of the fire.

With a sigh Sharon sits down, not sure what's going on.

The castaway looks at her, smiles, and says, "Hey, Bob! Guess who I've been fucking?"

How lovely to tell this joke to a woman with whom you are in the wild, first stages of a love affair! We were both besotted with each other and yet wondering whether the passion would turn to enduring love or, as it were, peter out, and this joke let us acknowledge that fear and laugh about it while reveling in what we had at the moment. But being a joker—carrying a donkey on your back—exacts a toll on one's dignity. When Erin and I decided we were serious, she called her mother and told her she was seeing a new man. "Oh," her mother said. "What's he like?"

"Uh, uh, well, he's southern." Erin knew her father, a lifelong Californian, had gone to medical school at Louisiana State University, where he'd joined a fraternity. To the last year of his life, he kept his initiation pledge to stand whenever he heard the song "Dixie," even if he were alone in his house watching football on TV and the band struck up the tune. He'd love having a southerner in the family.

"Oh, southern!" said her mom. "Is he courtly?"

Long pause, interspersed with giggling.

"What's so funny? Are you laughing at me?" Her mom was imagining Ashley Wilkes, not a man carrying a donkey on his shoulders.

After we married, the second marriage for both of us, Erin and I spent a lot of evenings and weekends watching music videos and stand-up comedy on TV—talking and joking as we watched. We were tuning our sensibilities, learning in greater detail which music the other loved and what we both laughed at. We were trying to understand and embrace the other's pleasures.

We also watched home-decorating shows, trying to coordinate our tastes. We wanted to furnish our new house with something other than the graduate-student furniture we'd dragged around into middle age—bookshelves made of concrete blocks and two-by-sixes, sofas cast off by friends and family, and twenty-year-old, swaybacked mattresses. We were fond of a short-lived show called *The Furniture Guys* on PBS. Ed Feldman and Joe L'Erario stripped, refinished, and reupholstered furniture while keeping up a farrago of sub-Grouchoesque puns and insults. On one episode, they brought in a woman who specialized in stenciling, and while she earnestly stippled flowers around the edge of a refinished cabinet, Ed and Joe mocked her, laughing and egging each other on. The more they joked, the stiffer her neck grew, until finally, upper lip curled back on her incisors, she snarled, "You two just crack each other up, doncha?"

It was the first catchphrase of our marriage, one we still use, burnishing and cherishing it. When one of us amuses the other in a way too silly for others to bear, one of us sneers, "You two just crack each other up, doncha?" The joke is a warning about making our private jokes in public, a caution against being so into each other we're rude. But it's true that we have become dedicated to making each other laugh or smile. I will mention only the lifelike plastic lizard that appears regularly in coffee mugs, in the silverware drawer, pressed into the bottom of a bar of soap, or poised to fall off a cabinet door. Taking the time to polish a pun or fine-tune a practical joke is a way of saying, *I'm thinking about you and I want to please you.* It is the opposite of "Who cares?"

The catchphrase I'm most fond of is one I stumbled on at the biennial meeting of the Fellowship of Southern Writers a few months after we were married. In the hospitality suite of the hotel, I loved listening to the banter of luminaries like Louis Rubin, Wendell Berry, Ernest Gaines, Shelby Foote, Elizabeth Spencer, and Fred Chappell—writers whose works I have admired for decades. I'd never dreamed of meeting them, much less hanging out with them as they gossiped, played guitars, and sang.

Among the stars was Andrew Lytle, a novelist and one of the authors of the famous southern agrarian manifesto *I'll Take My Stand: The South and the Agrarian Tradition.* A bit overawed by the folks in the hospitality suite, I'd been talking to John Jeremiah Sullivan, then an undergraduate at Sewanee: The University of the South. John, who lived in a downstairs apartment in Mr. Lytle's house, was at the meeting to tend to the elderly writer. But I had failed to get John's name, and when he left the group, I asked someone what his name was.

"Who?"

"The kid who was just here," I said. "Mr. Lytle's boy."

From across the circle, a man who'd heard only the last part of the conversation looked up from his guitar and snapped at me, "He has a name! It's John!"

I was abashed. Bourbon and sloppy camaraderie had led me to a patronizing characterization of a young man I'd just met. When I repeated the story to John a decade later, he laughed: "But I *was* Mr. Lytle's boy!"

That night, though, when I called Erin, I was still embarrassed by my gaffe. Erin consoled me. The stranger, she said, perhaps feeling the bourbon himself, had seized a harmless blunder and chastised me in public to make himself look good in front of the famous writers—a true egalitarian who nobly rebuked the snob who did not trouble himself to learn the names of the little people. And so our most enduring catchphrase was born.

At breakfast last week, I asked Erin, "Do you want me to clean it?"

"What?"

"The thing there," I said, nodding across the kitchen counter. I'd gone blank.

"It has a name!" she said. "It's TOASTER!"

Being married also meant integrating myself into a new family, and telling jokes was how I worked out a relaxed relationship with my father-in-law, both in person and on the phone. Tom wasn't much of a joke teller but he loved hearing jokes. Like his daughter, he loved to laugh. One of his favorite stories, one that still made him chuckle seventy years after it happened, was about being aboard the SS *President Hayes* as a marine in World War II. Tom bunked in the extreme forward area of the ship, two decks down in the narrow part where the prow comes to a point. Because of bad weather, the ship pitched up and down dramatically at both ends like a teeter-totter, and he was surrounded by the vomiting and moaning of the men inclined to seasickness. Once he stumbled to the crowded head and saw that the pipes had backed up and troops were slipping on the vomit.

The SS *President Hayes* was headed to Guadalcanal, and the old hands on the ship's crew amused themselves by telling the young marines frightening tales about the dangers of amphibious landings and the horrors of island combat. The night before the assault on Guadalcanal, the marines were lying in their bunks, nervous, unable to sleep, wondering how a landing that had been so chaotic in practice would unfold under enemy fire. In the hot, anxious darkness, someone ripped an enormous, reverberating fart.

Embarrassed silence. Then one marine sang out, "Sing again, sweet lips, that I may find thee."

The men exploded in laughter. According to Tom, they laughed till they wept. He knew that the men's fear, perhaps the greatest fear they would ever feel, fueled their laughter, and, after the catharsis of that giddy, anxious hilarity, he relaxed enough to fall asleep.

Fear fueled the laughter, but what makes the wisecrack crackle? The lofty and archaic poetic language connected to the earthy business of ripping a big one is part of it. The sweet lips and the antique *thee* suggest chivalry, romance, and female companionship—now a world away for men anticipating some of the most savage fighting of World War II. But the sweet lips are not the cherry-red lips of an idealized woman in song and poetry, but the anus of another man. The combination of bleak conditions, men alone, and the hint of homophobia must have fired the nervous laughter for a group of young men concerned with manhood and how those around them measured it. Men and fart jokes—we are a marriage that will last until the last puts out the light.

Obviously the line was not ad-libbed. But where's it from? At first I thought it was a line of highfalutin romantic poetry called up from memory and applied to a note played on the butt flute. Who'd have thought a poetic line about seeking sweet lips to kiss had actually come from a 450-year-old poem and had been about farting to begin with? I should have. A little rooting around took me right to the source: Chaucer's "The Miller's Tale," probably the greatest bawdy story in all literature. I'd spent an entire summer at the University of Alabama studying *The Canterbury Tales* under the tutelage of Dr. Woodrow Boyett. In the tale, two young men are courting a young woman behind her husband's back, and while Alisoun, one of the sexiest minxes in all literature, is lolling in the sack with Nicholas, Absalom, the town clerk, comes by, whispers to her through the window, and refuses to leave till she grants him a kiss. To give Nicholas a laugh, Alisoun sticks her butt out the window and that is what Absalom kisses. He becomes aware of his error immediately:

> Aback he leapt—it seemed somehow amiss,
> For well he knew a woman has no beard;
> He'd felt a thing all rough and longish haired,
> And said, "Oh fie, alas! What did I do?"

Absalom hightails it to the blacksmith, borrows a red-hot coulter, which is the cutting blade on the front of a plow, and returns to Alisoun's window to beg another kiss. This time, Nicholas sticks his ass out to receive the suitor's kiss. In the dark, Absalom calls out, "Speak, sweet bird, I don't know where you are." Nicholas "let loose a fart / As strong as a thunderclap, / So that Absalom was almost blind with its force." But he still possesses the stamina to wield the hot iron effectively: "He struck Nicholas in the middle of his arse: / Off went the skin a hand's breadth on each side." Ouch.

The red-hot chunk of iron my father-in-law met the next day was Guadalcanal. He didn't talk about the war, and I imagine a medic on Guadalcanal had more to forget than most World War II vets, a famously reticent cohort, but he loved to tell the story about meeting the love of his life on that island. He was walking by a group of Quonset huts one day when he saw something he'd never seen before, something beautiful. In a cage was a dog, a Doberman, and Tom, a dog lover, climbed into the cage without a second thought and within seconds, as he told the story, he had the dog on his back, legs in the air, tongue lolling ecstatically to the side as he scratched its belly and talked loving nonsense to it.

From the distance, the dog handler came racing down the beach, yelling, "Get away from that dog! He's a trained killer." Yeah, well, not to Tom McGraw he wasn't. Tom loved to tell his cherished stories, and I liked laughing and listening to them. The shared humor helped us understand and take pleasure in each other, and the stories helped me understand Erin.

Like her dad, Erin is a dog lover. She was the sort of toddler who terrified her parents by crawling into strange doghouses and throwing herself across any canine she could reach. Even now she bolts through traffic on downtown streets when she sees a dog. As I cringe in embarrassment, she looks hulking, beleathered drug dealers and ferrety, deranged loners in the eyes and inquires, "May I pet your dog?" Sometimes they are amused and say yes. Few say no, though some gruffly mumble that their Rottweiler or pit bull is not that friendly with strangers, but if she really wants to, yeah, she can pet Spike. "Oh, you," she warbles to the dog, stroking its head, "you are happy to see me, aren't you? Yes, you are. You are happy to see me. That's Andrew back there. Don't mind him. He's happy to see you too. He's just shy." One such encounter with a Bernese

Mountain Dog ended with my stalking nervously around the emergency room on a Sunday morning, while Erin, with a bite on her neck and her T-shirt soaked in blood, sat and read magazines for a couple of hours while waiting to see a doctor.

One of the first stories I ever told to amuse her is a wonderful anecdote from Eileen Simpson's *Poets in Their Youth* about Caroline Gordon and her dachshund. Gordon and her husband, Allen Tate, spent the winter of 1925 in rural New York State, living outside of New York City to save money, and they took in Hart Crane, who was even poorer than they were. As the long and very cold winter ground down the financially stressed writers, civility between Crane and the Tates wore so thin that they slipped notes under each other's doors to complain about perceived transgressions. Once, when they were actually speaking to each other, though, Gordon reproached Crane for "being inconsiderate" and he "made the mistake of defending himself by saying he was 'nervous and sensitive,' and shouldn't be held to the standards of behavior demanded of others." Crane must have quickly come to regret indulging in that particular moment of haughty self-pity. Both in Crane's presence and for friends over the next several decades, Gordon often held her dachshund in the air and, speaking for it, said, "I'm nervous and sensitive, aren't I, Mama? Like my uncle Hart Crane."

Through the twenty years and four dogs of our marriage, Erin has perched Rosie, Buddy, Max, and Sister on her lap, wagged their paws at me, and made them say, "I'm sensitive and nervous, like my uncle Hart Crane." I like to think Caroline Gordon is looking down on us from heaven, a besotted dog-mama beaming with happy malice.

The most loquacious of all our dogs was Buddy, whom we met at a cocktail party on the veranda of Rebel's Rest at the Sewanee Writers' Conference. A polite and handsome yellow dog with a fine black muzzle, he stood by the hors d'oeuvre table and waited for shrimp to fall from the plates of drinkers.

I held a shrimp out to him. He gravely nosed it and then with delicate reverence lifted it from my fingers. I next saw him two days later, nosing a dog biscuit held by the long fingers of the fiction writer Amy Hempel, with that same odd mix of gratitude and wariness. Amy travels with her purse and pockets stuffed with dog biscuits and pigs' ears in plastic Baggies. During the course of the writers' conference, she had already placed another stray with someone, and she was quick to notice Erin's and my interest in the cheerful yellow dog with the black snout.

"He'd be a great dog for you guys," she assured us.

"He seems more obsequious than I'm comfortable with," I said.

"That's how he's made his living for the last couple of years, sucking up to people for food. He'll adapt to however you want to do things."

"I'm worried about that green puss oozing out of his penis. That could be something expensive."

"Oh, that!" Amy said, laughing easily. "Don't worry about that It's completely normal. All my dogs do that."

I gaped in admiration at the lie. It was hard to come up with another objection in the face of Amy's determination.

Amy could tell I was weakening. If I were to adopt the dog, she said, she'd pick up half his first vet bill.

"I'll pay for my own dog," I said stiffly, and then laughed at how deftly she had set the hook.

Erin and I took Buddy to the vet, and when we picked him up—flea-dipped, neutered, and checked over—Erin asked if he'd had worms.

"That dog had every kind of worm there is to have, except earthworms," the vet said.

The neutering incision became infected, and for a couple of weeks, Erin had to hold, three times a day, a warm washcloth over the wound and, by proximity, over his penis to draw out the pus.

The dog mistook her intentions and insists that they now share an erotic bond stronger than the one between Erin and me, and frankly I think the dog's got a point. Though I've asked—and asked repeatedly—I have never been granted that special treatment.

Despite the minor incarnational inconvenience of being four years dead, Buddy is a talking dog, with a bit of a formal bent. Buddy perceives me as a romantic rival. He constantly informs Erin that she deserves better than the Sir and that he's the dog for the job. In Buddy's voice I can say the kind of love words that, as a guy, I find it hard to say. Buddy's a flirt. He has none of my romantic reticence, but as he fills Erin's ears with elaborate courtly compliments, I get some of the credit.

A talking dog, it turns out, is an invaluable asset to a successful marriage. If I speak harshly to Erin, either from carelessness or moral failing, Buddy might say, loud enough for her to hear, "Sir, I don't think I'd have used that tone of voice to address the lady, but maybe that's just me." Or "I'd never use that tone of voice to address you, ma'am. Because I'm better than the sir." Or he might just whisper to me, "Iks-nay on the nger-aay, etard-ray." (Lately he's been into pig Latin.) And the sweet part is that Erin immediately takes my side.

"Buddy, we don't use that kind of language in this house, and your sir is not a retard. He just made a mistake, that's all."

"Keep using that tone of voice while talking to my lady, sir. It'll just drive her into my arms."

"You don't have arms, Buddy," Erin says. "You have legs."

"Into my legs then, ma'am. I've dreamed of the moment you'd say such a thing."

Buddy's a blowhard, if a charming one, much like the dog a man encounters when, driving down a country road, he sees a sign saying, TALKING DOG FOR SALE. An old, grizzled yellow dog is tied to the sign. The man pulls over and yells out his window, "You the talking dog?"

"Yes, sir, I am indeed," says the dog.

Surprised that the dog really can talk, the man gets out of his car and walks up to the dog.

"So, what's your story?" he asks.

The dog says, "I'm the result of secret CIA experiments to genetically modify dogs so we could talk, and I'm the only one who mastered the lingo. I went undercover as a fake Seeing Eye dog to a diplomat, who left me in the room while foreign diplomats and world leaders talked. Later I'd brief the CIA on what I heard. Soon the agency was jetting me all over the world, and the intelligence I gathered was so important that I was given over twelve secret medals for clandestine services to my country. But all the travel began to wear me down as I aged, so I moved back here and got a job in Homeland Security. I just wandered around the airport, sidled up to suspicious characters, and listened in on their conversations. In four years, working part-time, I made five major drug busts and broke up two terrorist plots. Then I figured it was time to settle down, get married, and raise a passel of puppies, so that's just what I did."

The man is so astonished he walks across the lawn, knocks on the farmhouse door, and asks the owner how much he wants for the dog.

"Ten bucks."

"Ten bucks? That's all? Why you selling him so cheap?"

"Because he's a liar. That dog ain't never done none of that shit."

After the vet had to express Buddy's anal glands twice, I asked the vet techs to instruct me in the procedure because I suspected, rightly, that impacted anal glands were going to be a persistent problem. I didn't want to pay thirty-five bucks every few months for the rest of Buddy's life to have someone squeeze them empty. The techs were surprised but amenable. Two months later, I caught the tell tale smell coming from under his tail, and a tentative and very self-conscious touch revealed that the glands were swollen and tender.

After talking it over, Erin and I decided she'd hold Buddy's head between her knees, while I, wearing a surgical glove on my right hand, would do the job. As I was pulling myself together to insert my index finger into the dog's rectum, Erin looked the trembling and unhappy dog in the eye, and said, her voice solemn with theatrical empathy, "I want you to tell me if Daddy ever touches you in a way that makes you feel funny." Then we fell apart.

Erin and I rolled back and forth on the kitchen floor, slapping the linoleum in our hilarity, unable to stop. When we tried to stand, pulling ourselves up on kitchen cabinets, we got to laughing again and collapsed, and once I was down for the second time, Buddy, who'd been staring at us anxiously, raced away, picked up the first toy he came to—a heavy length of sawed-off cow's shinbone—and flipped it at me. It smacked my forehead with a painful clunk that drove Erin to even wilder laughter, and her laughter reignited mine. How do couples without dogs survive?

Sometimes when Erin's traveling and can't find anything else to buy me for a remembrance, she'll pick up a joke book. I'll crack it open on the kitchen counter and every evening as we make supper, I'll read a joke or two out loud. Every now and then we'll find a new one, like this great joke about marriage. A traveling salesman has been on the road for three months straight, and one night at the bar in the Ramada Inn, he falls into an utterly delightful conversation with a beautiful young woman. After an hour, she mentions that she needs to move along; she's not just chatting, she's working.

"Wow, you're a prostitute?"

"Yes," she says with a hint of exasperation.

"That's great. Hey, listen, if I gave you five hundred bucks, would you give me a mediocre blow job?"

"I do this for a living. For five hundred dollars I'll give you the best blow job of your life."

The salesman is horrified. "Oh, no, no, no! This isn't about sex! I'm homesick."

Erin isn't fond of this joke, though I have repeatedly explained to her why she should be. Like every woman I've told it to, she hears a put-down of wives' sexual prowess. Compared with those of a professional, their blow jobs are only mediocre. And they are right to hear that. They might also be right to suspect the man is deluding himself into thinking his garden-variety philandering is something more complicated, even nobler. But something oddly sweet lies underneath that obvious meaning. The salesman doesn't desire meaningless sex with a stranger; he wants the beautiful prostitute to eschew her professional skills and simulate the less exciting, but loving, sex he has with his wife. In intention, his five-hundred-dollar blow job is an act of fidelity, but probably not one he'd care to explain to his wife.

Erin knows my fidelity is almost comically complete. I'm the guy who wakes up from a party with a huge hangover, no memory of how he got home, and vague memories of getting thrown out of the office Christmas party. *God,* I think, *I'm going to get reamed by my wife. I'll never hear the end of it.* I open my eyes cautiously, and see a glass of water and two aspirin placed on the bedside table. At the foot of the bed, my clothes are laid out for me—cleaned and pressed—and on the floor sit my dress shoes, newly shined.

When I swallow the aspirin, I happen to glance in the mirror and see that I'm sporting two enormous black eyes and a fairly deep cut in my forehead.

But as I look at the mirror, I see Erin has written in lipstick on the glass, "Honey, breakfast is on the stove. I've gone to the store to buy steaks for dinner. I love you."

As I'm sitting at the kitchen table, eating the enormous pile of pancakes, eggs, and sausages Erin has fried up for me, my son walks in. Well, in the original joke it's the narrator's son, but since I don't have a son, it's Buddy the talking dog who walks in. "What happened last night?" I ask him.

"You got home about four this morning, babbling about being fired, tripped over the coffee table, and broke the glass top. That's when you cut your head. Then you staggered off down the hall, tripped again, and smacked your face on the door handle to the bathroom. That's when you blackened both eyes. Then when the lady tried to pick you up, you puked on her bedroom slippers."

"Then why is she being so nice?"

"Well, she dragged you upstairs to the bedroom, and when she tried to take your pants off, you kept yelling, 'Leave me alone, lady. I'm a married man.'"

For the twenty years we've been married, I've been so happy I can barely conceive of happiness without marriage. A good-humored wife who appreciates most if not all of my humor—her price is far above rubies, as the book of Proverbs doesn't quite say. How good is this marriage? The day before trash day, we *compete* to sneak the trash can and recycle bins to the curb before the other notices. We alternate making dinner and have an iron clad rule that the one who didn't cook cannot criticize the meal. Usually the cook is the tougher critic anyway. Most of my joking now is centered on making Erin laugh, and one of my great pleasures is e-mailing her a joke and then hearing from her office, which is on the second floor directly above me, a guffaw reverberate down through my ceiling. As Erin and I grow old together, I hope Mikhail Bakhtin, the literary theorist, was right when he wrote, "Death is inseparable from laughter." He must be, judging from the jokes about aging, decrepitude, dementia, and death e-mailed to me by friends my age. Of all the logical impasses, unknowings, paradoxes, and terrors that provoke laughter, death by its finality and unsolvable mystery is paramount. I am older than Erin by seven years, and we both know she is likely to outlive me. Her grief and the life she'll live will be a blank to me. (Andrew: My wife's an angel. Some other guy: You're lucky, mine's still alive.)

When someone dies, people say life goes on. Or we think it. Life goes on, until of course it doesn't. First I'll go, then Erin, and later still, you and those who come after you. As a child, I gnawed at this leapfrogging chain of obliterations night after night, as I lay awake unconvinced by my parents' vague, easy assurances of a happy afterlife, my longing for it stymied by my inability to believe in it or convincingly imagine it. Angels? Wings? Harps, for God's sake! It was all just too stupid even as a parody of a hope of paradise.

One Sunday, a preacher declared from the pulpit that in heaven the saved sang God's greatness eternally and without cease, and if we didn't like praising the Lord now on earth, we weren't going to have the opportunity to do it in paradise. His definition of eternal bliss was unintentionally helpful. Though I knew he was either wrong or heaven was eternally, mind-wrenchingly boring, I saw that he, though a supposed expert on the subject, was as inadequate to the task of imagining paradise as I was. The door between life and death has only ever opened in one direction. We have not even the first scant fact to begin working from and our imaginations are too poor to construct a feasible alternative to oblivion, except by conceiving of one that looks pretty much like the lives we live. Life, in that way too, goes on. But some people recover from grief more quickly than others, and if your husband comes home one evening and tells you that he's going to die in twelve hours, you will understand that, whether his soul is in heaven or nonexistent, in the morning you will still have a life to live.

A man returns from a visit to the doctor and tells his wife, I've got twelve hours to live. I'll be dead by sunrise. At first they are stunned, grief-stricken, unable to comprehend the news. But soon the wife fixes the husband a good meal, and they open the expensive bottle of wine they'd been saving since their vacation in France twenty years ago, because if this isn't the special occasion they'd been saving it for, what is? They reminisce fondly, if elegiacally, about their life together before they go to bed, make long, slow, and deeply meaningful love, and then drift off to sleep. An hour later the husband, unable to sleep and still yearning for the love he is leaving behind, wakes his wife and again they make love. She falls back asleep, but he is still unable to sleep, fretting about dying, and, Eros defeating Thanatos however briefly, he nudges her yet again for more love, and she says, "That's fine for you, but I've got to get up in the morning." As she knows, life goes on, and it's better to face the first day alone after a good night's sleep.

Or to die laughing.

Until I started keeping a short list of people who died laughing, I thought I'd outgrown role models. Theirs is a death to which I aspire. In 1975, Alex Mitchell, a bricklayer in Norfolk, England, started laughing at a TV show called *The Goodies* and did not stop until he died twenty-five minutes later. In the fatal skit, a master of the esoteric and imaginary Lancastrian martial art of "Ecky Thump" is challenged, successively, by a karate master; a blackfaced minstrel parody of Muhammad Ali; a baguette-wielding French mime; and an Australian in outback garb who flings a boomerang at him. The boomerang misses. The Ecky Thump master pulls a blood pudding from his waistband and in turn thumps each on the head. Finally, he is challenged by a Scotsman in full Highlands regalia. The Scot prances about, quickstepping in place, emitting guttural "Scottish" vocalizations, and jabbing at the Ecky Thumper with the drone tubes of his bagpipe. Just as he is about to dispatch the Ecky Thump master with a final swipe of his bagpipes, the Australian's boomerang circles back out of the sky and lays him out. The ridiculous, prancing Scot always makes me laugh, but not for as long or as wholeheartedly as he did Alex Mitchell. *Slapstick!: The Illustrated History of Knockabout Comedy* quotes Mitchell's wife about her husband's final twenty-five minutes:

> Alex just couldn't stop laughing. He was a Scot, you see, so he was especially tickled to see a Scotsman wrestling with his bagpipes! And he kept laughing, right through the programme. Well I think he just laughed too heartily and too long, because just before the closing titles he gave a tremendous belly-laugh, slumped on the sofa, and died.

The BBC apologized, and Mrs. Mitchell wrote *The Goodies* and thanked them for making her husband's last twenty-five minutes of life happy ones.

As impressive as Mitchell's death is, the most famous hilarity-induced final exit in history belongs to Chrysippus, the Stoic philosopher, who committed the faux pas of laughing himself to death *at his own joke.* When he saw his donkey eat figs that had been prepared for his meal, he told his servant to give the donkey unmixed wine to drink too—and he laughed so violently that he died. Apparently the joke is that the ass was eating not just Chrysippus's own food, but food exclusively for humans, and that by ordering the servant to serve the beast wine he was treating it even more like a privileged human guest. I like to think the notoriously arrogant philosopher glimpsed himself in the ass and collapsed in appreciative laughter. There is no evidence of his wife writing a thank-you note to the donkey—or of Chrysippus ever having carried it about town on his shoulders.

With the whole of human history to survey, my list of people dead of hilarity has stalled at a paltry ten. So I have to confront the sad fact that I am unlikely to be number eleven and that Erin will never be afforded the pleasure of thanking someone for making my last minutes mirthful. I will have to do that bit of work myself.

Last year, when my father was in the hospital dying, he tried to say something as I stood by his hospital bed. His throat was raw and his voice whispery from dehydrating medicine, and I asked him twice to repeat himself before I leaned down, ear to lips, and asked for a third time. Suddenly, clearly, he said, "What's the matter? You losing your hearing?"

Was it a joke? Mike, standing at the foot of the bed, laughed.

"Yes," I said. "I've been diagnosed with hearing loss."

"What caused it?"

"You." He looked confused. "Genetically, I mean," I added, and forced a smile. Like a couple of my brothers, I've inherited his hearing loss.

I do think he was trying to joke, and so was I. But the old, sad father-son aggression was hard to miss. He was angry at not being understood, and I, annoyed at being snapped at, instinctively reacted in kind. Still, Mike laughed. Dad was three months short of his ninetieth birthday, in pain, dying, and Mike admired his spunk—and Dad and I had both tried to make the moment funny. Better to go out with a misunderstood joke on your lips than no joke at all. And it was better, I hope, to joke with the dying man than moon over him.

At noon, Dad didn't want us to leave him alone, so Mike went to Subway and brought back sandwiches. After we'd eaten, Mike, Roger, and I balled our sandwich wrappers around the uneaten pickles and shot them like basketballs at the trash can by the head of Dad's bed. As each shot missed, we taunted the shooter, laughing. I gathered the wadded paper off the floor, and we each shot again. One errant shot bounced off Dad's pillow, but he was asleep by then and didn't stir as we giggled sheepishly. Mike's wife, Gina, and Erin, though they'd been laughing too, told us it was time to stop acting like children and let Dad sleep.

A few days later, just after ten PM on June 30, Dad died, exactly three months shy of his ninetieth birthday, all of us—sons and daughters-in-law—plus Tim and his wife, who'd driven in from Atlanta, gathered in a small room in the hospital to discuss the funeral. Mike mentioned with a truncated laugh that if Dad had lived two hours longer we'd have his July pension check to split among us. I chuckled briefly, reassuringly. Mike didn't care about the money for himself, but his mind, in the autonomous way of minds, was both grieving and already moving on to the practical business of arranging and paying for Dad's funeral. Mike told us there was some confusion in the cemetery office about where Dad's plot was. He'd double-check to make sure the grave was dug in the right place.

Before I could stop myself I said, "If we let them bury Dad in the wrong plot, we can probably sneak out without paying." In the silence that followed, all three of my brothers looking at me quizzically, Erin put her hand on my knee and said firmly, "Not now."

At the funeral on a hilltop in Griffin, Georgia, while my cousin Julie led the funeral service, a solemn service with an air force honor guard, I looked down at the highway and thought of the joke in which a preacher new to town is rushing out into the country to conduct a funeral for a homeless man. Because he's driven down the wrong road a couple of times, he's running very late when he sees two men standing in a field with shovels in their hands. He races toward them, and glancing into the grave, he sees that the concrete grave liner is already in place. Determined to give the poor homeless man, with no family or friends to mourn him, as fine a farewell as any rich man could wish for, he launches into an impassioned sermon. When he finishes the eulogy, he leads the two diggers in a mournful chorus of "Amazing Grace" that leaves the three of them in tears. He shakes their hands, and as he walks back to his car, proud of his efforts, he hears one man say to the other, "I ain't never seen nothing like that before—and I been puttin' in septic tanks for almost forty years."

I waited until Erin and I were back in the car before I told her what I'd been thinking.

"I'm glad you waited," she said.

I too am glad I waited, but I cherish the skewed pleasure of finding something funny, and thus life affirming, in sorrow: the reminder that not every hole in the ground is a grave and that our rituals are both deeply meaningful and deeply meaningless at the same time; they are both consoling and ineffectual. The mind recognizes the simultaneously opposing truths, and the mind's having a mind of its own is one of the great delights of human intelligence. Humor is thus a way of being serious in a serious world. Laughter seems to me the only viable response to having a speeding mind in a slowing body, logic in the skull of an animal. We love a life we cannot keep, and so I want to go out cracking wise—even if my idea of cracked wisdom is a fart joke.

A good ending for Erin and me might be the two of us lying in adjoining beds in a nursing home forty years from now, and we overhear the head nurse (that's the one with the dirty knees, you know) tell her supervisor, "I think we are losing that old couple in Room 5C. They talk to each other in the voice of a dog that's been dead for fifty years, and then they laugh till I think they are going to die."

I'll look at Erin and say, "You two just crack each other up, doncha?"

In heaven we will be joined by that dead yellow dog, and he'll greet us by saying, "Hi, ma'am. Hi, sir. Glad to see you. Hey, sir, pull my dewclaw."

"No, I know what you are going to do. You're going to fart."

"Oh, no, Sir. I'd never do that to you."

"Yeah, you would."

"Oh, honey, go ahead and pull his dewclaw. You know how much he loves that joke," Erin will say.

So, yeah, I'll pull the damn dead dog's dewclaw—and then look into heaven or the void and listen hopefully for laughter.

Postscript

So maybe I die in a car wreck along with my good friend Tom Doherty and my brother Mike. As we line up at the pearly gates, St. Peter says to Tom, "Thomas Patrick Doherty, you old reprobate, I never thought I'd see you here. But let me ask you this: When you are in your casket and your friends and family are standing around mourning your passing, what would you like to hear them say about you?"

Tom says, "I want to hear them say I was a great film scholar, a demanding teacher, and a loving husband."

"How about you, Mike?" St. Peter asks.

Mike says, "I'd like them to say I was a wonderful husband and father—and a businessman who always kept his word."

"And you, Andrew, what would you like to hear the people gathered at your casket say about you?"

"I'd like them to say, 'Andrew loved Erin with his whole heart—and hey, look, he's moving!'"

Acknowledgments

Except for my immediate family, I have changed the names of just about everyone in the book whom I know personally. I am grateful to the editors who published sections of this book in *Image: A Journal of Religion and the Arts*, *The Kenyon Review*, *Oxford American*, and *Shenandoah*. My wife, Erin, read countless drafts of this book over almost a decade and her encouragement and sharp editorial eye were crucial. Rich Kelly's close editing and advice were extremely valuable. My agent, Marianne Merola of Brandt & Hochman, was a strong advocate for the book, and Jon Karp has been a wonderful reader and editor. Thanks to John Ernst and Ann Marie Rasmussen for their generosity when I approached them out of the blue with what must have seemed very peculiar questions.

About the Author

ANDREW HUDGINS was born into the US Air Force in Fort Hood, Texas, in 1951. As a military brat, he lived in Texas, New Mexico, Ohio, and England before elementary school in North Carolina and California. His family lived for one year outside Paris before his father was transferred to Montgomery, Alabama, in 1966, the year after the Selma-to-Montgomery march. He has attended Huntingdon College, the University of Alabama, the Iowa Writers' Workshop, and Stanford University. His poetry, published by Houghton Mifflin Harcourt, has been a finalist for the Pulitzer Prize and National Book Award. His family lives in Columbus, Ohio, where Hudgins teaches at The Ohio State University, and in Sewanee, Tennessee.